RELIGIOUS RHETORIC AND AMERICAN POLITICS

RELIGIOUS RHETORIC AND AMERICAN POLITICS

The Endurance of Civil Religion in Electoral Campaigns

CHRISTOPHER B. CHAPP

CORNELL UNIVERSITY PRESS
Ithaca & London

First published 2012 by Cornell University Press
Printed in the United States of America

Library of Congress Cataloging-in-Publication Data

Chapp, Christopher B., 1979–
    Religious rhetoric and American politics : the endurance of civil religion in electoral campaigns / Christopher B. Chapp.
        p. cm.
    Includes bibliographical references and index.
    ISBN 978-0-8014-5126-3 (cloth : alk. paper)
    1. Religion and politics—United States. 2. Rhetoric—Religious aspects—Christianity. 3. Rhetoric—Political aspects—United States. 4. Identity politics—United States. 5. Civil religion—United States. 6. Political campaigns—United States. I. Title.
    BL2525.C443 2013
    324.7—dc23
                                                    2012016338

Cornell University Press strives to use environmentally responsible suppliers and materials to the fullest extent possible in the publishing of its books. Such materials include vegetable-based, low-VOC inks and acid-free papers that are recycled, totally chlorine-free, or partly composed of nonwood fibers. For further information, visit our website at www.cornellpress.cornell.edu.

Cloth printing   10 9 8 7 6 5 4 3 2 1

For Jolene and Cecilia

CONTENTS

ILLUSTRATIONS

PREFACE

In spring 2011, I attended a speech by Representative Keith Ellison (D-Minn.) at an interfaith dialogue at St. Olaf College in Northfield, Minnesota. Ellison's talk occurred just a few weeks after he had taken part in controversial congressional subcommittee hearings that had been called to investigate "The Extent of Radicalization in the American Muslim Community and that Community's Response." As the first Muslim American elected to Congress, Ellison expressed regret over the "premise of the hearings." His comments at the interfaith event, however, carried a tenor far different from the sectarian pitch that had surrounded much of the hearings. Reflecting on the founding of the nation, Ellison remarked, "We the people, create our nation to establish Justice, insure domestic Tranquility, promote the general Welfare, and secure the Blessings of Liberty. People make a mistake when they say that when these words were written they were not true. I say they weren't true *yet*. I say they were our aspiration. An America to be hoped for and to be worked for. An America that has to be built and is being built by all of us. I look at these words, and I reflect upon them, and I think about them as *America's prayer*."

Ellison's remarks go further than simply calling for religious tolerance and putting aside religious differences by suggesting that there is something sacred within American political institutions. The Constitution is to be interpreted not just as a blueprint for democracy but as a prayer for the American people. This prayer, as Ellison characterized it, does not favor any particular denomination or sect. Rather, Ellison's speech promoted a spiritualized understanding of American political institutions and culture—an understanding that could resonate across denominational divides. In short, Ellison's reading conceived of the Constitution as a religious document by invoking prayer in a universalistic manner.

As I listened to Ellison's remarks, it was clear that this characterization of American politics struck a chord with the vast majority of the audience at a Lutheran-affiliated liberal arts college. Ellison found, in this civil religion understanding of the U.S. Constitution, a point of commonality that appeared to be both deeply heartfelt by the audience and inclusive enough to be met with near-universal approval from a religiously diverse crowd. But, even though most of the audience was moved, the response was not entirely uniform. Illustrating the complex array of emotions engendered by religious language, several comments by audience members during the question-and-answer period revealed a degree of discomfort with the melding of American national identity and faith, no matter how inclusive that faith might be.

The phrase "America's prayer" provides a good introduction to the topic of religious rhetoric. Displays of faith have long been intertwined with political commitments, and they are almost always met with a complex and varied reaction from the American public. Ellison's remarks, which downplay denominational divides to assert a shared American faith, represent an important trajectory in American political culture—one that is comfortable with religious pluralism and seeks to find points of shared spirituality between faiths. Indeed, seeking religious common ground is not just undertaken in the name of cooperation but is ultimately part of what it means to be an American. Of course, not all religious rhetoric casts aside differences. Like much of the commentary surrounding the Muslim community hearings, religious rhetoric is often used to call attention to differences, not find points of agreement. Each of these modes of public religious discourse has important precedents in American politics, and each carries the potential to shape American democracy in important ways.

My goal in writing this book is to better understand the dynamics of religious political rhetoric. The regular melding of religious displays and political speech led me to seek a framework to better understand how religious language is invoked in the public square and how it influences American public opinion and culture. Even though religious rhetoric has long been a source of scholarly interest, we actually know very little about the effects this rhetoric has on the mass public. Do religious appeals work? Do they help candidates garner favor with the American public? Moreover, how do these appeals influence the political culture at large? Is religious rhetoric consistent with a political culture that welcomes religious difference and encourages pluralism, or is religion more often used to divide and marginalize?

Adequately addressing these questions requires both an appreciation of the rich tapestry of ways in which religious rhetoric is used and a nuanced understanding of how citizens process information about the political world. To this end, I have marshaled a range of qualitative evidence on religious political rhetoric to develop an analytic framework and then used this framework to quantitatively test a series of predictions about the impact of religious rhetoric on voters in contemporary campaign environments. In *Religious Rhetoric and American Politics*, I begin by looking at the use of religious rhetoric in American political history, concluding that the genre can best be understood in terms of how it evokes *identity*, as well as its *emotive* force. Using this framework for guidance, I then use a quantitative content analysis to address the implications of religious identity and emotive religious rhetoric in American presidential campaigns. Finally, building on the findings from the content analysis, I use surveys and experiments to uncover the effects of identity and emotive rhetoric on the American public mind.

Although this degree of methodological pluralism is unusual, the underlying logic of this approach should allow readers to both appreciate the complexity of religious rhetoric in American politics and make sense of its nuanced effects on a religiously diverse public. For the ease of presentation, I rely on relatively simple figures and graphs to illustrate the main characteristics of religious rhetoric and how these appeals impact the mass public. Interested readers can find more comprehensive statistical analyses and methodological details in the online appendix, available at http://facstaff.uww.edu/chappc/. The result, I hope, is an approachable and informative window onto how candidates use religious language and how it influences American politics and political culture. The effect of religious rhetoric depends largely on how it activates emotions and a sense of shared identity in the public. Nevertheless, religious political rhetoric is received in varied ways depending on individuals' religious predispositions—what sounds like a unifying message to some is often marginalizing for others. As this book will make clear, religious rhetoric thus contains the germs of both political unity and religious fragmentation.

This book owes much to the assistance, patience, and goodwill of countless friends and colleagues. From start to finish, no one has been more of a source of scholarly wisdom and genuine inspiration than James Druckman. It is not at all an exaggeration to say that without Jamie's generosity, encouragement, and razor-sharp insight, this project would have never happened. Likewise, conversations with John Sullivan, Wendy Rahn, and Chris Federico all helped give rise to this book, and they continued to lend their valuable judgment and expertise as the project developed. Moreover, it is hard for me to imagine writing this book without the broad network of support I found at the University of Minnesota. In particular, Paul Goren provided tremendous feedback on countless aspects of this project, encouraging me to think about how the present research speaks to our understanding of political behavior more broadly, greatly improving the book as a result. James Farr helped me think about how the use of religious rhetoric throughout history connects to present-day patterns and trends. John Freeman, Ben Ansell, Mark Snyder, Joanne Miller, Logan Dancey, Steve Hanson, and Paul Soper all helped me work through important methodological and substantive issues. Countless other faculty and graduate students at the University of Minnesota provided insights and assistance far too vast to enumerate in full.

My gratitude extends to many beyond the University of Minnesota. I am grateful to faculty in the political science department at St. Olaf College, who offered valuable feedback on the book-in-progress at every turn. In particular, Dan Hofrenning and Douglas Casson provided valuable insights into the nature of American civil religion. I also thank faculty in the political science department at the University of Wisconsin–Whitewater, who have provided regular constructive feedback. Samantha Luks at Polimetrix provided considerable assistance in implementing the survey used in chapter 6. I am also grateful to many others who have taken the time to read and offer valuable comments on this work at different stages, especially Booth Fowler, Laura Stoker, Paul Djupe, Lydia Pfotenhauer, Elaine Atcheson, Katie Chapp, and Greg Vonnahme. Alex Fietzer, Caleb Eboch, and Patrick Reinikainen all provided substantial content analysis assistance. David Bierly, Ryan Sommers, Steve Chappell, and Amanda Persak all assisted with data collection efforts. At every stage, the generosity of others has enabled this project to go forward, and I thank you all.

This research would not have been possible without support from a wide range of institutions. I received a Doctoral Dissertation Fellowship from the University of Minnesota Graduate School (2007–2008) and research grants from University of Minnesota Minor in Political Psychology in 2005 and 2006. A generous Faculty Development grant from St. Olaf College allowed me to conduct much of the original survey research presented in chapter 6. I am also grateful to the College of Letters and Sciences and Office of Research and Sponsored Programs at the University of Wisconsin–Whitewater for their publication support. In addition to data I compiled myself, the research presented herein relies heavily on American National Election Study data, Pew Research Center data, the Annenberg/Pew Archive of Presidential Campaign Discourse, and the Stanford Political Communication Laboratory. I am indebted to the efforts of others in gathering and compiling these data and making them publicly available.

I feel very privileged to have this book published with Cornell University Press, and I am grateful to all those who have had a hand in helping this book take shape. In particular, Michael McGandy has been a tremendous source of constructive feedback, encouragement, and collegiality from start to finish. I am also grateful for the efforts of the anonymous reviewers Michael identified. Their careful reading and insights have helped produce a much better book.

Above all else, I thank my family. My parents, Katie and Terry, and brother, TJ, have always encouraged me, and they have always been a source of inspiration. This book is dedicated to my wife, Jolene, and my daughter, Cecilia. Before writing, I would not have guessed that the greatest challenges to producing a book are often the emotional ones: coping with frustrations, setbacks, and long hours in front of a computer. Jolene and Ceci are always there for me, and I feel truly blessed.

RELIGIOUS RHETORIC AND AMERICAN POLITICS

1

A THEORY OF RELIGIOUS RHETORIC IN AMERICAN CAMPAIGNS

Beyond all differences of race or creed, we are one country, mourning together and facing danger together. Deep in the American character, there is honor, and it is stronger than cynicism. And many have discovered again that even in tragedy—especially in tragedy—God is near. In a single instant, we realized that this will be a decisive decade in the history of liberty, that we've been called to a unique role in human events.

— President George W. Bush, 2002 State of the Union Address

During the 2004 presidential election, voters chose between candidates advocating starkly different approaches to a myriad of issues of national consequence. The United States was entangled in two costly wars and was still feeling the effects of the September 11, 2001, terrorist attacks. Domestically, President George W. Bush and the Congress had just passed major prescription drug reform, enacted controversial tax cuts, and legislated dramatic changes to American education. Yet in the aftermath of the 2004 presidential election, many political observers roundly concluded that Bush's reelection was not due to any of these factors but was largely the product of Americans' concern with *moral values*.

In the months before the election, political observers were already predicting that existing religious and moral cleavages might decide the day. One *New York Times* headline read "Battle Cry of Faithful Pits Believers against the Rest" (Kirkpatrick, October 31, 2004, 24). The *Chicago Tribune* reported that "this presidential campaign had become one of the most spiritually saturated in memory with people of faith bombarded with entreaties from Republicans and Democrats" (Anderson, November 4, 2004, C1). The significant role of religion in the election gained considerable support from the Election Day exit polling, illustrating a substantial "God gap" between religious and secular voters. George W. Bush received 64 percent of the vote among those attending religious services more than once a week, whereas Kerry received 62 percent support among those never attending services. Moreover, fully 22 percent of the voting public responded that "moral values" were the most important issue facing the nation, a group of voters that swung decidedly toward the Republican Party (however, see Hillygus and Shields 2005). Asked to interpret this statistic in a *Meet the Press* interview shortly following the election, Karl Rove characterized these voters as a group of Americans most concerned about a certain "coarseness of our culture." Voters, Rove argued, saw in President Bush the "vision and values and ideas that they supported" (*Meet the Press* 2004).

This was not the story of the 2008 election, however. In that election, voters gave comparatively little weight to religious or moral considerations. The day before the election, Stephen Prothero, a religion scholar at Boston University, editorialized that "much of the energy that Democrats and Republicans alike have pumped into the religion question seems to have dissipated. Voters tomorrow will be thinking more about the economy, health care and war than about the social and sexual issues that preoccupied 'values voters' in the 2004 election" (Prothero, November 3, 2008, 15A). Exit polls were consistent with this assertion. The Republican support among those attending church more than once a week had been reduced from 64 percent in 2004 to 55 percent.[1] The Democratic candidate, Barack Obama, actually won the vote among those attending church "monthly," a demographic group that John Kerry had failed to capture four years earlier. A Pew study published immediately after the election concluded that, although sizable religion gaps persisted, "Among nearly every religious group, the Democratic candidate received equal or higher levels of support compared with the 2004 Democratic nominee, John Kerry" (Pew Research Center for the People and the Press 2008). And, whereas *religion* and *values* were the hot topics on *Meet the Press* following the 2004 election, these words were not even mentioned on the 2008 post-election roundtable of the program.

Why was religion the story of the 2004 election but not in 2008? The difference in electoral dynamics is puzzling for two reasons. First, in both elections there were other, deeply salient, competing issues that may have distracted voters. Whereas the economy and the first viable African

American candidacy may have diverted attention away from religion in 2008, the economy was also highly salient in 2004, along with terrorism, two major wars, and tax cuts.[2] But despite these strong similarities in salient secular issues, religious cleavages decided the day in 2004 but not in 2008. Second, there are plenty of reasons to suspect that religion should have been even *more* important in the 2008 election. For example, 2008 had Sarah Palin, a vice presidential candidate who was in part selected to bring moral and cultural issues to the forefront. Moreover, 2008 was witness to one of the most intense religious campaign issues in recent memory when Obama's former pastor, Reverend Jeremiah Wright, made controversial remarks at the intersection of religion, race, and politics, arguing that "The government gives [African Americans] the drugs, builds bigger prisons, passes a three-strike law and then wants us to sing 'God Bless America.' No, no, no, God damn America, that's in the Bible for killing innocent people" (quoted in Murphy 2008). Given all this, it is surprising that religion factored more prominently in the public consciousness in 2004 than in 2008.[3]

We know relatively little about why the influence of religion waxes and wanes from one election to the next, raising ambiguities that operate at multiple levels. At one level, the intermingling of religion and electoral politics raises important normative questions about the nature of political representation in a country characterized as having a "wall of separation" between church and state. When religion is a factor in an election, how should leaders deliver representation to their constituents? Moreover, given the tremendous religious diversity of Americans, is a genuinely inclusive religious representational style even possible?

At another level, religion plays an ambiguous role in U.S. elections because of the varied forms that public religious expression can take. Historically, religious political rhetoric can be roughly classified into two genres. *Culture war* religious expression generally focuses on deep-seated religious differences in American society and the intractable political conflicts produced by these divisions (Hunter 1991; Evans and Nunn 2005).[4] *Civil religion* appeals, on the other hand, are nondenominational declarations of spiritualized American national identity. Civil religion appeals generally stress points of spiritual commonality among all Americans and posit a transcendent religious ethos that permeates American institutions and culture (Bellah 1967, 1975). Despite volumes of research on these rhetorical genres, we know relatively little about how civil religion and culture war messages are actually received by the public at large. When candidates deploy religious messages, do divisions emerge, or are religious appeals a cultural glue uniting Americans across diverse backgrounds?

In this book, I am principally concerned with the ambiguous role of religious expression and how it comes to shape the American politics. Grappling with this issue will not only explain the role of religion in the 2004 and 2008 presidential elections—it will also help make sense of the meaning of religious and cultural divisions in a country premised on church-state separation. The way in which political elites use religious rhetoric in the public sphere determines the exact role that religion plays in American elections, political culture, and the representative dynamics of the country. At the heart of the argument is the observation that nearly all forms of religious rhetoric can be understood in terms of how they express themselves along two key dimensions: *emotion* and *identity*. Religious rhetoric gains its unique political command because it is well equipped to resonate with individuals' emotions and identities—two factors that, not coincidentally, are central to political persuasion.

The extent to which an election takes on a religious character depends on how successfully elites use religious language to activate emotions and identities. This analysis is not limited to 2004 and 2008. Indeed, I contend that religious rhetoric is an evolving genre that has its emotive and identity-laden roots in early Puritan sermonizing and Revolutionary pamphleteering. The success of the genre is due to its use having been so congruent with basic psychological persuasive properties and its being flexible enough to fit with the religious sensibilities of an incredibly varied religious constituency. The religious character of American politics—both now and throughout history—depends on how well religious political rhetoric activates the emotions and identities of a diverse and deeply religious public. Moreover, the activation of religious considerations has consequences that extend far beyond electoral outcomes. The religious nature of political debate and discussion ultimately shapes the nature of political representation and the contours of the political community. As we will see, American civil religion has a special place in this story. Civil religion rhetoric can simultaneously be an electorally powerful persuasive tool and point of shared religious identification, and also a source of alienation from the political process.

In this chapter, I elaborate a theoretic framework for how religious rhetoric intensifies the emotions and identities of the American public and what the consequences of these rhetorical choices are. Doing so requires knitting together several diverse strands of scholarship, encompassing research on religion, voting behavior, political communication, and social psychology. The basic argument, illustrated in figure 1.1, has several moving parts. The religious character of American politics is shaped by a confluence of three factors: the religious makeup of the U.S. electorate, the psychological basis of persuasion, and the political demands imposed by competitive winner-take-all elections. Religious rhetoric (particularly the civil religion genre) is uniquely adept at satisfying the demands imposed by each of the factors, enabling candidates to form deep connections with voters in competitive electoral environments. Moreover, when specific forms of religious rhetoric are strategically deployed by candidates, the consequences extend far beyond the realm of any single electoral contest. Precisely *how* candidates locate themselves at the intersection of these factors not only determines their electoral success but also has implications for defining the boundaries of

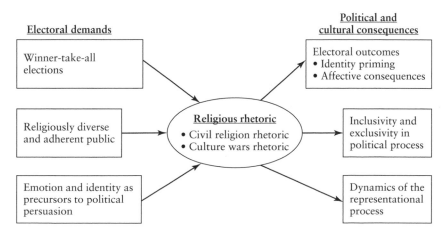

FIGURE 1.1 Causes and consequences of religious political rhetoric

How religious rhetoric connects electoral demands to political and cultural consequences. The dominant forms of religious political expression are the results of a confluence of political, religious, and psychological factors. In turn, these forms of expression have consequences on electoral behavior and American political culture.

the American political community and for shaping the dynamics of the representative process.

Psychological, Religious, and Political Factors in American Elections

As figure 1.1 illustrates, candidates making their case before the American public must deal with multiple crosscutting pressures, the first of which is political. Most U.S. races are winner-take-all, meaning that to hold office a candidate must win a plurality of the votes (or a majority of electoral votes at the presidential level). Unlike many other electoral systems, seats are not allocated for second place. Accordingly, candidate rhetoric must appeal to an audience that holds a diverse array of religious beliefs. The United States is unique among world democracies in this regard, having both high levels of religious adherence and no single dominant sect (Greeley 1972; Pew Research Center for the People and the Press 2007; Putnam and Campbell 2010). Thus, candidates cannot afford to ignore religion, nor can they afford to privilege a particular faith tradition.

These political and religious pressures have an interesting point of intersection with what is known about the psychological basis of political persuasion. As previously noted, political psychologists have identified two factors—identity and emotion—that play a central role in how voters think about political candidates. While many factors can awaken emotions and identities in the public, religious appeals are particularly well suited to this task and are at the same time capable of effectively satisfying the competing political and religious pressures incumbent on candidates.

By *identity*, I refer here to "social identities," or individuals' awareness of objective group membership and the sense of attachment they get from belonging (Tajfel 1981; Conover 1984, 1988). Although "being religious" need not imply social identity as a matter of definition, scholars have recognized that religion does play important identity-relevant functions (Emmons and Paloutzian 2003).[5] Social identities have been found to have numerous political implications, the most consequential and widely replicated being ingroup favoritism, even when group attachment is fairly minimal (Huddy 2001). That is to say, even when group boundaries are arbitrarily assigned, individuals still tend to demonstrate a persistent bias toward their own group. And, because religious group attachment is far from arbitrary, religious social identities should engender substantial favoritism toward those with whom the individual shares group membership.

Candidates commonly use political rhetoric to prime identities. *Priming* refers to "provok[ing] opinion or behavior change not because individuals alter their beliefs or evaluations of objects, but because they alter the relative weight they give to various considerations that make up the ultimate evaluation" (Mendelsohn 1996, 113). In any given election, voters have numerous competing considerations, from issues to images to social group memberships (Valentino 1999; Druckman and Holmes 2004; Druckman, Jacobs, and Ostermeier 2004; Jackson 2005). By rhetorically emphasizing social identities (or any number of other considerations), candidates make these group attachments a salient basis of political evaluation. In this way, expressions of religious identity can create deep feelings of group favoritism between candidates and the public.

Of course, candidates can make direct appeals to denominational subgroups (such as Catholics and Baptists) even though, with no single dominant religious denomination in the United States, subgroup appeals have a somewhat limited audience. What is more likely is that religious identity priming operates by engendering a sense of *civil religion identity*. The concept of American civil religion asserts that a broad religious identity unites virtually the entire nation. In this way, civil religion appeals should theoretically serve as a solution to the challenge of appealing to a religious constituency that is both committed and diverse. With the possible exception of appeals to national identity, no other group-based appeal (e.g., to race, gender, or class) has the potential to codify political support around such a broad (yet salient) group. Thus, when Bush said (see quotation at the outset of this chapter) that "God is near. In a single instant, we realized that this will be a decisive decade in the history of liberty, that we've been called to a unique role in human events," he was asserting a leadership role in an overarching spiritual community.

Scholars emphasize different points regarding precisely how public expressions of civil religion should be characterized and where it gains its cultural and political significance. For example, Martin Marty (1987) identifies both "priestly" civil religion, which is primarily concerned with legitimizing state practices, and "prophetic" civil religion, which seeks to guide the nation to meet certain ethical benchmarks (see also Wald and Calhoun-Brown 2006). Whereas Marty ascribes an ongoing sociological significance to both forms of civil religion in American politics, others have suggested that the cultural force of civil religion has declined since a peak in the 1950s (Ahlstrom 1972; Marty 1987). Other scholarly debates revolve around whether civil religion sits in tension or in harmony with religious pluralism. Some argue that civil religion can unite common elements of different religious traditions; others contend that it carries with it an implicitly sectarian impulse (Lambert 2008, 26–27; see also Mead 1974). Taking up this latter point, Herbert Richardson concludes that, in the end, "civil religion always tends to generate the very situation it seeks to prevent" (1974, 165).

I address these debates in this book. The theory of identity priming, however, suggests a somewhat different starting point for grappling with language of civil religion and its consequences for American politics and culture. Specifically, understanding religious identity priming requires that we draw a clear connection between rhetoric in the public square and its influence on the attitudes and opinions of the electorate. What considerations are primed by these nondenominational appeals? Moreover, how do these appeals shape political behavior and political life? Civil religion appeals are quite common in political rhetoric, and evidence suggests that they should have broad appeal to religiously diverse constituencies. Indeed, the perseverance of the genre throughout American political history is a testament to the degree to which it has mass appeal (Bellah 1967). If civil religion references tended to fall flat, it is unlikely that candidates would still be making references to America as a "City on a Hill" and asserting a shared spiritual bond (Wimberley 1980). It should be noted that just because the genre does not appeal to a readily definable group (such as Methodists) does not mean that it cannot activate group identity. Michael Billig (2003) argues that adept rhetoricians often attempt to foster a sense of shared identity with the members of their target audience by linking them with cherished national values. Even the "banal use of political clichés" and strategic deployment of pronouns like "we" can cement ingroup allegiances and commitments to group values (Billig 2003, 238). Because these values (in the American case) are often religious or quasi-religious, it makes sense that civil religion appeals are amenable to the activation of group identity. Empirical evidence has documented the political significance of these broad identity appeals (Gaertner and Dovidio 2000). John Transue (2007), for example, has found that national identity can supersede the effects of subgroup attachment. In short, public figures' use of language that yokes together religion and country has a dramatic impact on the "self-image" of the public and ultimately "what it means to be an American" (Domke and Coe 2010).

In stark contrast, culture wars appeals drive a wedge into the American public, asserting that there are exactly two religious groups in American politics and that they are locked in an intractable political conflict over the moral standing of the nation.[6] The potential target membership of culture wars appeals is smaller than civil religion appeals, making it unlikely that this rhetorical style will be deployed with the same regularity as civil religion rhetoric, despite fears by many scholars that a culture war is on the rise (Hunter 1991). Nevertheless, the stakes are always high in culture wars rhetoric, suggesting that, although they might not mobilize support in a pluralistic state as effectively as civil religion rhetoric, self-identification with orthodox or progressive camps will still be deeply felt and politically salient.

Culture wars and civil religion appeals thus implicate different understandings of religious identity. Each also carries a specific emotional tenor, ranging from enthusiasm to anxiety to anger. Understanding the tenor of religious rhetoric is important because emotions are known to have significant consequences on political judgment (Marcus, Neuman, and MacKuen 2000) and because political messages are, at least in part, responsible for bringing about these emotions in message recipients (Brader 2006).

Emotions work in two principle ways. They can work directly, by transferring the emotive content of a stimulus onto a message recipient. Simply put, if a candidate puts you in a positive mood, you will like her more, and the opposite is also true (Ladd and Lenz 2008). Emotions can also work indirectly by altering the decision-making process (Marcus, Neuman, and MacKuen 2000; see also Schwarz, Bless, and Bohner 1991). Psychologists argue that emotions play an evolutionarily adaptive role, and accordingly, different discrete affective states have arisen to meet specific situational demands (Bodenhausen, Sheppard, and Kramer 1994; Nabi 1999; Lerner and Keltner 2000; Marcus, Neuman, and MacKuen 2000; DeSteno, Petty, et al. 2004; Brader, 2006). For example, enthusiasm cues tend to be consistent with heuristic processing or with reliance on stable preexisting political affiliations (Brader 2006). Negative emotions often do the opposite. Norbert Schwarz concludes that, "In a nutshell, we usually feel bad when things go wrong and feel good when we face no particular problems. Hence, negative affective states may signal that the current situation is problematic and may hence elicit a processing style that pays close attention to the specifics of the apparently problematic situation" (2000, 434). Not all negative moods lead to systematic processing, however. For example, Galen Bodenhausen, Lori Sheppard, and Geoffrey Kramer (1994) find evidence that, whereas sad individuals tend to engage in effortful processing as a means to alleviate the sad situation, angry individuals tend to engage in heuristic processing due to reduced cognitive capacity and reduced motivation for thoughtful analysis.

Likewise, David DeSteno, Nilanjana Dasgupta, and colleagues find that "anger, because of its basic association with intergroup competition and conflict, evok[es] a psychological readiness to evaluate outgroups negatively vis-à-vis ingroups, thus creating an automatic prejudice against the outgroup from thin air" (2004, 323).

Anxiety has also been theorized as a distinct emotional state associated with a distinct processing style.[7] Ted Brader argues that "fear ads" used in political campaigns elicit anxiety in individuals, causing them to "place less weight on prior convictions and more weight on contemporary evaluations" (2006, 182), a conclusion that is consistent with the Affective Intelligence model of George Marcus, W. Russell Neuman, and Michael MacKuen (2000). For example, enthusiastic individuals tend to rely on heuristic judgments in their reasoning about candidates, whereas anxious individuals tend to engage in a deeper, more effortful information search (Brader 2006). In short, by making voters anxious, angry, enthusiastic, sad, or calm, candidates may be activating a number of psychological processes that are important to how voters think about candidates.

More important, the civil religion and culture wars genres are each closely identified with a highly emotive communication style. Culture wars rhetoric, for example, regularly uses anxiety and fear to characterize competing worldviews. The civil religion tradition, in contrast, is characterized by its hopefulness and optimism about the future of America, as well as a lament about U.S. moral shortcomings (Murphy 2009). Thus, given this close association between the dominant forms of religious political communication and emotion, on the one hand, and the importance of emotion in political persuasion, on the other, it is important to investigate how religious rhetoric influences the public mood of the electorate (Rahn, Kroeger, and Kite 1996).

The Consequences of Religious Rhetoric

It is clear that political, religious, and psychological factors combine to make religious rhetoric an optimal strategy for ambitious public elites, but in this book I am not concerned just with why various modes of religious communication are employed but also with the consequences of religious rhetoric in the public sphere. As figure 1.1 illustrates, three consequences of religious rhetoric are of particular interest: its impact on electoral outcomes, the contours of political community, and the dynamics of political representation.

First and foremost, religious appeals are common because they work. In this book, I provide evidence that religious rhetoric is used to activate religious identities as a basis of candidate evaluation and to elevate the emotive tone of campaigns. But the connection between rhetoric and voting behavior is complex and sometimes counterintuitive. For example, although it is often suggested that Bush garnered favor among religious constituencies because of his stance on issues such as same-sex marriage, in chapters 5 and 6 I provide evidence that, instead, Bush's success in 2004 had to do with his effective use of civil religion appeals, causing much of the electorate to evaluate him on his ability to provide moral leadership for the nation. These patterns of voting behavior were ultimately lodged in a sense of shared religious identity with Bush—not any particular affinity with his stance on the so-called cultural issues. In this way, scholars and pundits bemoaning the rise of a culture war have missed a critical component of religious rhetoric. What made Bush effective with religious audiences (at least through the 2004 campaign) was his ability to solidify the support of a rather diverse group of believers rather than the use of religious rhetoric calling attention to cultural differences.

If citizens are voting for candidates based on a shared religious identity and emotional arousal, this raises a corresponding set of questions about how religious rhetoric influences American political culture. That is, if religious identity is part and parcel of political identity, then religion may be playing a role in who is and who is not included in particular visions of the American political community. Religious rhetoric sets the tone for political debate and discussion, and whether it is conducted in a spirit of cohesion or competition, optimism or anger. Thus, candidates' religious discourse is at the heart of questions of inclusion and exclusion in the political community.

Perhaps even more critically, insofar as religious communication influences the voting behavior of the mass public, it is also influencing the representational activities of leaders, guiding how they govern based on the substantive and symbolic demands of various religious constituencies. In a country premised on an ostensible wall of separation between church and state, it is important to explore what consequences free religious expression has on promoting a religious mandate for officeholders, once elected. If religious identities are able to sway elections, how are officeholders to govern a constituency that is religiously diverse?

Understanding the dynamics between would-be representatives and the governed ultimately requires a deeper theoretical elaboration of the recipients of religious messages—the voters. Rather than treating the religious vote as monolithic and static, it is more appropriate to think of the numerous and varied religious identities that could potentially be activated by candidate rhetoric. Although it is common to think about direct appeals to different denominations or to the religiously progressive and orthodox, we need to take stock of an additional politically salient religious identity, informed by the importance of civil religion rhetoric in American politics. Specifically, I articulate the concept of a civil religion identity, arguing that identification with this nondenominational American spiritual community is key to understanding the dynamics of political representation in America. Civil religion identifiers hold a deep sense of attachment to an explicitly spiritualized understanding of America. For civil religion identifiers, the United States—vested with a sacred sense of purpose in the world order—is as much a religious community as a political entity. As the psychological analog to civil religion rhetoric, civil religion identity provides the key to understanding how commonplace religious rhetoric can turn the attention of voters to religious evaluative criteria. Many Americans strongly identify with the basic tenets of American civil religion, and in fact for many a latent attachment to this quasi-religious identity is a foundational component of their political DNA. The evidence indicates that civil religion voters are not motivated by cultural issues such as abortion and same-sex marriage, issues which often dominate political debate.[8] Instead, civil religion voters are looking for a prototypical leader who offers a representational style consistent with the tenets of American civil religion. In this sense, religious representation may not be a mandate for policy change but, rather, an endorsement of leadership offering a nondenominational spiritualized sense of the place of America in the world order.

This model of religious rhetoric has consequences, not just for our understanding of religion but for how we think about political campaigns and political behavior more generally. Scholars have long questioned whether campaigns can substantively change Americans' attitudes, especially when the factors that often influence electoral decision making (such as party identification) tend to be stable from election to election. The model I present here suggests that stability and change are not mutually exclusive. Stable predispositions such as religiosity might not fluctuate much in the American public, but campaign rhetoric can certainly play a role in activating these predispositions and making them germane to the task of evaluating candidates. Moreover, campaigns do not merely mobilize fixed constituencies. Instead, who is and is not a member of a particular constituency is itself the product of rhetorical forces. Instead of speaking just about mobilizing constituencies, we also need to think of campaigns as activating different parts of the individual, changing the American consciousness about group membership and group values, and making different identities politically salient. Even though there is no formal membership in the civil religion community, civil religion is something that is very real to many Americans. Civil religion exists as an identity that is itself actively reified through political rhetoric and made salient to the electoral process.

Overview of the Chapters

In this book, I establish a number of conclusions about the impact of religious rhetoric on American politics, ranging from broad historical judgments about the place of civil religion in American culture to narrowly tailored arguments about the psychology of religiosity and vote choice. The key premise is that these macro and micro approaches are mutually reinforcing. It is impossible to understand the success of religious appeals across history without thinking critically about the psychological processes that undergirded the persuasive efforts of historical figures, and it is impossible to understand present-day patterns of religious voting without placing the campaign rhetoric in its proper historic context.

Accordingly, the evidence presented in this book unfolds at several levels of analysis, moving from a historical examination of religious rhetoric, to a content analysis of religious rhetoric in contemporary campaigns, and finally to an examination of individuals' voting behavior using surveys and experiments. Although the scope of the book changes, the evidence consistently indicates that religious rhetoric is effective primarily because of its ability to induce a sense of *shared identity* and *emotions* in message recipients. In chapters 2 to 4, I focus on identity-laden and emotive cues in rhetoric, addressing exactly how public figures craft religious expression and what this rhetorical nuance says about American political culture. In chapters 5 and 6, I shift the scope of the argument from identity cues in rhetoric to religious identity as experienced by individuals and from emotive language to emotions in the mass public. Ultimately, the argument is consistent across levels of analysis. Emotion and identity are both important components of the terms and tenor of political debate, and they are important parts of how individuals understand the political world.

Chapter 2 begins by addressing emotion and identity from a historical vantage, examining the use of religious rhetoric in American politics from early Puritan political communities through the twentieth century. By examining the evolution of religious rhetoric over time, I provide insight into how religious rhetoric is constitutive of American political culture and how it is used politically across contexts. My principal argument here is that emotion and identity have been central elements in religious rhetoric throughout American history (although how they have been invoked has evolved over time). They are neither fleeting elements nor elements emerging only in contemporary politics, and they have consistently played a prominent role in shaping American political discourse. This finding has important consequences for the book as a whole, suggesting that, even amid substantial contextual variation, identity and emotion provide considerable insight into American political culture and political preference formation. Religious rhetoric is not joined at the hip to any one political issue or ideological outlook. It is a flexible genre that has been appropriated to fit numerous political causes.

Chapter 3 builds on this historical analysis by exploring the invocation of religious identities in modern campaigns. In this chapter, I present evidence that religious rhetoric is rarely concerned with taking stances on issues or rationalizing a complex policy agenda. Rather, religious rhetoric is principally in the business of building a sense of shared identity between citizens and candidates. Three types of identity references are common: *subgroup* references to specific denominations and faith traditions; *civil religion* appeals, aimed at engendering a spiritualized sense of national identity; and *culture wars* identities, which seek to make cultural fault lines salient. These identities have important consequences for how the boundaries of the American political community are characterized. A content analysis of over 1,300 speeches by Republican and Democratic presidential hopefuls from 1980 to 2008 indicates that candidates make frequent reference to a nondenominational spiritual identity that permeates the American experience. As we will see, the language of civil religion identity is far more common than the language of culture wars, indicating that American religious identity—at least in the realm of political discourse—is more a source of unity than a source of division. But even though these civil religion appeals typically downplay religious pluralism in the interest of emphasizing what faiths and peoples have in common, they also often marginalize and alienate key segments of the American electorate. Ultimately, then, the rhetoric of religious identity—although central to understanding American politics—neither sows the seeds of a large-scale cultural battle nor constitutes a panacea for social cohesion.

In addition to identity, emotion is a key element of American religious political rhetoric. Chapter 4 begins by developing a strategy for identifying emotive elements in speeches. Using the same rhetoric database as in chapter 3, I conclude that candidates adopt specific emotive frames to make identity-based appeals. Religious rhetoric tends to be exceptionally optimistic—far more positive and hopeful than secular campaign speech. I also present evidence that is generally inconsistent with claims that there is a growing divisiveness in religious rhetoric; there is little evidence to suggest that presidential campaign religious rhetoric is being used as a tool to leverage large-scale cultural rifts. I do find, however, that there are significant partisan dimensions in the emotive characteristics of religious rhetoric, a conclusion that follows from the nature of existing religious divisions in the electorate.

Chapter 5 argues that religious rhetoric is one significant cause of the relationship between religion and politics in the mass public and that this process can be understood by examining both the specific qualities of religious messages and how varied message types interact with different religious predispositions. I use statistical tools to merge the religious rhetoric variables from chapters 3 and 4 with survey data collected in presidential elections from 1980 to 2004. The results indicate that how candidates craft the identity and emotive elements of religious rhetoric influences how they are viewed by the electorate. Specifically, different rhetorical nuances tend to activate different dimensions of individuals' religious orientations. For example, when a candidate speaks in the language of American civil religion, the religiously committed become more favorably predisposed toward that candidate, but the religiously orthodox actually tend to lower their opinion of the candidate. These findings are consistent with the hypothesis that identity priming and emotion are a basis for political persuasion and provide strong evidence that candidates' religious rhetoric is, in part, responsible for the relationship between voters' religious and political attitudes.

Chapter 6 uses experiments to add a layer of confirmatory evidence to the findings from chapter 5, and using the concept of civil religion identity, it extends the conclusions drawn in chapter 5 to provide a deeper understanding of political representation. Civil religion identity has broad adherence in the American public, and political rhetoric often primes civil religion identity as a basis of candidate evaluation. Voters who strongly identify with the American civil religion are attracted to candidates who invoke this genre and see them as prototypical group leaders who share their moral outlook (although not necessarily their substantive policy outlook). The representational consequences of this identity, however, are crosscutting. Although theoretically civil religion identity is nondenominational, in practice its membership is essentially limited to Christians. Non-Christians find themselves unrepresented by candidates who embrace the tenets of American civil religion. The consequences of civil religion rhetoric are thus mixed—although it provides a form of meaningful leadership for many Americans, it leaves others feeling excluded from the political system.

Using corroborating evidence from multiple methodological approaches, I conclude that religious rhetoric is a central force responsible shaping the contours of American political culture. Religious rhetoric is also electorally consequential and culturally significant, with important implications for how we interpret American political representation. Even though its use has changed over time, it has been remarkably consistent in its ability to stir the emotions of the mass public and to engender a sense of shared spiritualized identity.

2

RELIGIOUS RHETORIC IN AMERICAN POLITICAL HISTORY

*Let us resolve tonight that young Americans will always see those
Potomac lights; that they will always find there a city of hope in a
country that is free. And let us resolve they will say of our day and
of our generation that we did keep faith with our God, that we did
act "worthy of ourselves;" that we did protect and pass on lovingly
that shining city on a hill.*

　　　　　　　　　　　　　　　　—President Ronald Reagan, 1980

Religious political rhetoric can overwhelm citizens with an array of different emotions, leading individuals to identify with a broad and varied
range of groups and interests. We know very little, however, about exactly which group identities and emotions religious rhetoric is bringing to
the surface. Although it seems likely that many voters will have some sort
of emotional response to a passage such as the Reagan statement quoted
here, it is unclear precisely what kind of affective punch this statement
will have on a religiously diverse public. Moreover, it is unclear exactly
which religious identity Reagan is calling forth as a standard of political
evaluation. Phrases such as "our God" implies an appeal to a religious
group; however, the boundaries of this group are not easily identifiable.
Thus, although there are strong theoretical (and intuitive) reasons to suspect that Reagan's city on a hill speech mattered politically, there is little
research documenting how religious communication translates into political opinion.

　　Part of the reason this connection is so elusive is that religious identity is
so complex. If candidates were only making simple appeals to denominational subgroups, connecting candidate rhetoric to voter attitudes would
be a straightforward task. But there is nothing straightforward about
religious appeals in American politics. Indeed, it is virtually impossible
to make sense of the substance and the tenor of an appeal such as Reagan's without first understanding how nuanced rhetorical constructions

have evolved in American political discourse to become powerful markers of belonging in the political community.

To understand the effects of religious rhetoric, we first need to examine the question: How is the religious appeal crafted in the first place? Most scholars addressing this question have adopted a historical lens, examining the nuanced use of religious appeals throughout American political history. This approach makes sense. Religious rhetoric in contemporary campaigns does not occur in a vacuum but is, instead, the product of historical forces and discursive norms. Carefully examining this body of research is an important first step in understanding the effects of religious rhetoric in contemporary politics. In providing a descriptive account of the emotive and identity-laden elements of religious rhetoric, we learn exactly to whom religious appeals are directed, as well as the tone and tenor with which successful appeals are made.

The scope of this undertaking is vast; however, two distinct consistencies emerge across American political history. First, American religious political rhetoric almost always tends to construct religious identities as a *superordinate* concept—blurring the boundaries of sects and subgroups to assert a politics of religious commonality. Of particular interest is the rhetorical construction of an American civil religion identity, stressing a transcendent religious ethos that unites Americans. Second, religious rhetoric has a distinctly emotive tone, blending a lament about American sin with a sense of optimism about the future. In analyzing the character of these identity-laden and emotive elements, this chapter provides a framework for assessing religious language in contemporary campaigns.

Rhetoric and Identity

From the early Puritan communities forward, religious identity was a concept closely intertwined with the fate of the entire political community. Puritans employed biblical concepts such as a covenant with God to construct an intense political identity lodged in a sense of a shared fate. The idea of a covenant with God was the Puritans' *raison d'être*, and upholding their end of the agreement necessarily implicated political cohesiveness. Colonial political rhetoric thus asserted a highly robust form of spiritualized collective identity, positing the existence of both a collective mission and a collective fate.

The most well-known example of this is probably the *Mayflower Compact*, undertaken by Pilgrim settlers in 1620. In this document, the signers agreed that "Having undertaken for the Glory of God, and Advancement of the Christian Faith, and the Honour of our King and Country, a voyage to plant the first colony in the northern parts of Virginia; do by these presents, solemnly and mutually in the Presence of God and one of another, covenant and combine ourselves together into a civil Body Politick, for our better Ordering and Preservation, and Furtherance of the Ends aforesaid" (*Mayflower Compact* 1620). The *Mayflower Compact* brings a sanctified sense of collective identity to the forefront. It was not enough to simply reform the individual soul—if this were the case, the flight from England would not have been necessary. England as a nation had failed to uphold its end of the agreement (Morgan 1958, 18–21, 69–70), and so the Puritans undertook the formation of a new political body—subsuming the individual in the collective covenant (Morgan 1965, xxii). As Jerald Brauer summarizes, "Though the relationship between God and the soul is highly individual and subjective, it occurs only in the context of a community, the church" (1976, 8). The Puritan errand was, thus, nothing if not undertaken with a shared communal vision.

As this example suggests, from very early on American political identity was rhetorically conjoined with a special place in God's divine plan. Puritans regularly drew on the example of Israel, according the New Englanders an "elect" status before God.[1] On this point, Sacvan Bercovitch (1978) cites Richard Mather, the influential Puritan minister, extolling the special status of the American colonists: "For as some passages in this Scripture were never fully accomplished, so many things that literally concerned the Jewes were types and figures, signifying the like things concerning the people of God in these latter days. And this place seemes not onely to be meant of personall coversion, but also further, of the open and joint calling of a company, so noting the joyning of a company together in holy Covenant with God" (quoted in Bercovitch 1978, 45–46). Mather is suggesting that, despite the lack of direct mention of America in the Bible, the experience of Israel nevertheless signifies the elect status of the colonies. This applies to the collective and not just "personal conversion," a rhetorical move that Bercovitch calls an "implicit yoking together of social identity and the claim to election" (1978, 46).

The notion that the colonists were God's chosen people—with God's covenant with Israel as a model—is prevalent throughout early Puritan political rhetoric. For example, in a 1690 Massachusetts election sermon, Richard Mather's grandson Cotton Mather preached that "you may see Israel in America, by looking upon this Plantation; may peace be upon this Israel of God! It is notorious, That a settlement in this part of America, was first endeavored by some that had no designs but those of a Secular interest: but the God of Heaven blasted all those designs, and broke up one Plantation after another by very terrible frowns of His Holy Providence" (1690, 241). As was Richard Mather in the earlier passage, Cotton Mather is engaged in building a sense of shared social identity both by identifying an opposition ("secular interests") and suggesting that the intervention of God had played a role in the creation of a people.

Covenant theology also lent itself to the rhetorical construction of a common identity by creating a sense of shared fate, in that breaking a covenant with God would have severe consequences for the entire community. John Winthrop's "Christian Charitie: A Modell Hereof" is one well-known example. Winthrop characterizes the community as a body, whereby the constituent parts are bound together in Christian love. To break this body apart, Winthrop explains, would mean a breach of covenant and ultimately the ruin of the community: "The Lord will surely breake out in wrathe against us be revenged such a perjured people and make us knowe the price of the breache of such a Covenant. Now the only way to avoid this shipwracke and to provide for our posterity is to follow the Counsell of Micah,[2] to doe Justly, to love mercy, to walke humbly with our God, for this end, wee must be knitt together in this worke as one man, wee must entertain each other in brotherly Affeccion" (1630, 92). Winthrop's appeal to brotherhood is not merely a polite request. Breaking the covenant would mean facing God's wrath, as Micah (6:9–16) foretold, and the colonists could not uphold the covenant without being knit together as one. Thus, a common identity as a people was absolutely necessary to avoid complete ruin and to stand, as Winthrop concludes, "as a Citty upon a Hill, the eies of all people . . . upon us" (1630, 93).

Although the concept of covenant remained an important part of religious rhetoric into the American Revolution, over time the "we" in this identity broadened considerably, moving from the strict boundaries of the Massachusetts Puritan "elect" to an inclusive pan-colonial identity. Scholars often attribute this rhetorical shift to the Great Awakening—specifically citing the preaching of Jonathan Edwards (Brauer 1976; Bercovitch 1978). In Edwards' formulation, America was at the center of the unfolding of God's plan and enjoyed a special status in God's eyes (Brauer 1976, 21).[3] For Edwards, the key to this formulation centered on a *postmillennial* eschatology. Earlier Puritans had typically been *premillennial* in their outlook; that is, they believed a long period of tribulation would precede Christ's Second Coming. Edwards' postmillennialism offered a more optimistic outlook, interpreting scripture to indicate that Christ would return after a period of Christian rule and dominance on earth (Brauer 1976, 22). America, in Edwards' view, was the realization of this period of Christian glory.[4] The rhetorical construction of a distinctly American identity is thus inseparable from religious developments of the time, whereby a nondenominational sense of common religious purpose served to bridge other colonial differences.[5] In Eugene White's words, "as the first mass movement which tended to draw the colonies together in a common bond, the Awakening offered a new emotional identification, a democratic unification, and an inclination toward intercolonial unity transcending sectionalism and denominationalism" (1972, 58).[6]

Following the American Revolution, religious political rhetoric continued to articulate this vision of an American religious identity that self-consciously transcended sectarian divisions. Moreover, the evolving genre began to characterize even ostensibly secular national symbols in religious terms. As Berkovitch writes:

> Washington . . . enshrined as savior, his mighty deeds expounded, his apostles ranked, the Judas in their midst identified, the Declaration of Independence adequately compared to the Sermon on the Mount, the sacred places and objects (Bunker Hill, Valley Forge, the Liberty Bell) properly labeled, the Constitution duly ordained (in Emerson's words) as "the best book in the world" next to the New Testament, and the Revolution, summarily, "indissolubly linked" (as John Quincy Adams put it) with "the birthday . . . of the Savior," as being the social, moral, and political correlative of "the Redeemer's mission on earth" and thus "the first irrevocable pledge of the fulfillment of the prophesies, announced directly from Heaven." (1978, 129)

Examples of these rhetorical developments abounded during the ratification debate. For example, Elizur Goodrich's "The Principles of Civil Union and Happiness," preached just days before the Constitutional

Convention convened, drew parallels between the American states and the tribes of Israel (1787, 929), comparing the blessings of America to Jerusalem (913). Goodrich explicitly stresses the commonalities between denominations: "What is more necessary, than union among the ministers of CHRIST?" (1787, 935).[7] Goodrich also consecrates the founding of the nation, arguing that the Revolutionary War was won through the "interposition of a wonder-working Providence" (1787, 938).[8]

During the ratification debate, this rhetorical style was imported from sermons to popular editorializing and speechifying.[9] Consider the case of an anonymous editorial (actually authored by Benjamin Franklin) published in the *Federal Gazette* in April 1788. The editorial is essentially an ad hominum, comparing Antifederalists to the Israelites who had rebelled against Moses. The majority of Franklin's editorial consists of an emotive retelling of Numbers, contending that discontented members of the "thirteen tribes" had rejected the Constitution implemented by Moses. This retelling is a thinly veiled attack on the Antifederalists, overdrawing parallels between Constitutional ratification and biblical events.[10] Franklin concludes by arguing, "I beg I may not be understood to infer, that our General Convention was divinely inspired, when form'd the new federal Constitution . . . yet I must own I have so much Faith in the general Government of the world by *Providence*, that I can hardly conceive a Transaction of such momentous Importance to the Welfare of Millions, and to exist in the Posterity of a great Nation, should be suffered to pass without being in some degree influence'd, guided, and governed by that omnipresent, omniscient, and beneficent Ruler" (1788, 404–5). This is an argument by paralipsis. In begging the audience not to infer divine intervention, Franklin is drawing precisely that conclusion. Given the parallels between the Israelites in Numbers and the religious identity of the American people, to reject the Constitution would amount to disobedience to God.

As Berkovitch argues, the case for ratifying the Constitution gained its strength by constructing American religious identity and fate in religious terms—contrasting "apocalyptic disaster," on the one hand, with the promise of the Constitution—"millennial glory"—on the other (1978, 136). According to Bercovitch, the Federalist jeremiad "gave the nation a past and future in sacred history, rendered its political and legal outlook a fulfillment of prophesy, elevated its 'true inhabitants,' the enterprising European Protestants who had immigrated within the past century or so, to the status of God's chosen, and declared the vast territories around them to be their chosen country" (1978, 140). For God's chosen people, crisis could be overcome through divine intervention. Just as God favored the American cause in the Revolutionary War, so too was the Constitution of divine design.

This is even the case in the Federalist Papers, which on the balance avoided explicitly religious justifications for the Constitution.[11] For example, in *Federalist 37* James Madison writes, "The real wonder is, that so many difficulties [in framing the constitution] should have been surmounted; and surmounted with a unanimity almost as unprecedented as it must have been unexpected. . . . It is impossible for the man of pious reflection not to perceive in it, a finger of that Almighty hand which has been so frequently and signally extended to our relief in the critical stages of the revolution" (1788a, 179). Madison's rhetorical move here is consequential. He uses inclusive language ("our relief") and national history (the Revolution) to invoke a sense of spiritual cohesion and common national identity. The framing of the Constitution is, then, built into this sacred history. To resist the Constitution would be to resist God's intentions. Madison's use of religious language thus folds a spiritualized sense of national identity and divine intervention in national affairs into the crafting of the Constitution, a document that would itself, in time, be raised up to near-biblical significance.

As these examples illustrate, American political rhetoric has been saturated with claims of collective religious identity that in time would be termed an American civil religion (Bellah 1967). This religious identity is almost always multidenominational and aims to infuse the founding of America with collective religious purpose, and no single candidate, party, or interest group has had a monopoly on the rhetorical use of collective religious identity to build movement solidarity and assert a sense of divine purpose.

And nowhere is the rhetorical contestation over the rightful inheritance of the American collective religious identity more evident than during the Civil War.[12] Both North and South made claims to divine providence, and both sought to sanctify national symbols to build common identity. In the South, American identity was reconstituted to make the Confederate secession consistent with biblical necessity, with writings routinely equating the Southern cause with God's divine blessing. For example, James Henley Thornwell, the well-known Presbyterian minister and author, characterized secession as the necessary consequence of the Northern rebuke of God's wishes:

They have put their Constitution under their feet; they have an-
nulled its most sacred provisions. . . . On the other hand, we are
struggling for constitutional freedom. We are upholding the great
principles which our fathers bequeathed us, and if we should succeed, and become, as we shall, the dominant nation of this continent,
we shall perpetuate and diffuse the very liberty for which Washington bled, and which the heroes of the Revolution achieved. . . .
We shall have a Government that acknowledges God, that rever-
ences right, and that makes law supreme. We are, therefore, fighting
not for ourselves alone, but, when the struggle is rightly understood, for the salvation of this whole continent. (1862)

This is not an outright rejection of the Constitution as a "higher" document. Rather, Thornwell is rejecting what the Constitution had become
and claiming the sacred character of American identity as the property of
the Confederacy. Moreover, Thornwell's claim that the Confederacy
acknowledged God was not, in the mind of Southerners, empty rhetoric.
Unlike the preamble to the federal Constitution, the preamble to the Confederate Constitution stated as its purpose to "secure the blessings of liberty
to ourselves and our posterity invoking the favor and guidance of Almighty
God," a move aimed at claiming providential blessing on the Confederacy
and infusing the *new* Constitution with an element of the sacred.

Assertions of shared spiritual identity—coupled with labeling the
North as an outgroup—were common in secessionist rhetoric. For example, the 1863 Address of the Virginia Baptist Association was both a
lamentation for the sins of the South and a claim on its holding a privileged religious position: "Though God in scourging us has used the hand
of a wicked nation as His avenging instrument, we are daily more con-
vinced of the righteousness of our cause, and have abiding faith, through
His favor, of ultimate, and we trust not distant deliverance from our
ruthless enemy." Even though Southerners were being punished for
transgressions—transgressions that did not include slavery—they nevertheless remained the chosen people of God. The Virginia Baptist Association address takes pains both to divorce the North from its spiritual
Puritan ancestry and to declare the righteousness of the Southern cause.
As Harry Stout and Christopher Grasso summarize, "With secession . . .
previously patriotic [Southern] American men of God put aside their past
and reinvented themselves as divine spokesmen for a new Christian nation" (1998, 318).

Northern abolitionist and unionist rhetoric also asserted a spiritualized national identity, although to very different ends. Daniel Webster's Plymouth Rock address (1820) serves as one illustrative example. The purpose of the speech was to commemorate the Pilgrim's settlement in North America. The site is described as the place "where Christianity, and civilization, and letters made their first lodgement" and the "Pilgrim Fathers" are venerated as national heroes for their commitment to piety and liberty. Webster uses the occasion to denounce the slave trade, characterizing it as a national sin, out of step with the American spiritual charter: "It is not fit that the land of the Pilgrims should bear the shame longer" (1820). Webster concludes on a note of hope, arguing that on the day slavery ends, "the voice of acclamation and gratitude, commencing on the Rock of Plymouth, shall be transmitted through millions of the sons of the Pilgrims, till it lose itself in the murmurs of the Pacific seas" (1820). In this densely packed sentence, Webster epitomizes every aspect of the American religious identity, building a sense of common identity through the consecration of a national symbol, the creation of a sense of shared ancestry, and a shared manifest destiny in the westward expansion. This is a promise to be fulfilled once America pleases God by casting off its sinful nature. Craig Smith's interpretation of Webster concurs with this assessment, arguing that Webster's rhetoric was successful in part because of his ability to create a "psychological identification between the speaker and the audience" to advance the cause of the Union, aiding in the "development of a civil religion [that] resonated with the evangelism of the times" (2005, 2).

Northern rhetoric regularly infused American founding documents with religious purpose to advocate for Union (and abolitionism). For example, in discerning the proper scope of constitutional authority to regulate slavery, William H. Seward argued on the Senate floor that a "higher law" directed and guided the Constitution (1850). In this speech, Seward invokes religious language in a plea to uphold the Union, "for then it will be seen how calmly, how firmly, how nobly, a great people can act in preserving their Constitution; whom 'love of country moveth, example teacheth, company comforteth, emulation quickeneth, and glory exalteth'" (1850). Lincoln similarly sanctified the Declaration of Independence. In a speech on the Kansas-Nebraska Act, Lincoln held up the Declaration of Independence as "our ancient faith" (1854, 32) and urged Americans to "re-adopt" the Declaration as a necessary precondition for moral righteousness—to both save the Union and make it "worthy of saving" (1854, 34). Lincoln's rhetoric is significant, both characterizing the Declaration as a sacred document and urging all Americans to adopt this document as the reference point for a shared political culture.

For both North and South, collective identity became increasingly intertwined with a spiritualized sense of national purpose. Like previous rhetorical instantiations of American civil religion, this identity cut across denominational and sectarian lines. Nevertheless, it is also possible to see in the religious rhetoric of the Civil War elements of a culture war in an earlier time. National sin was framed in terms of "they" and "them," not "we" and "our." The causes of the war and all the strife that came with it were rooted in the identification of an outgroup that was making similar claims on religious grounds. Given this, Reconstruction era religious rhetoric demonstrates the flexibility of the genre, broadening the boundaries of American national identity to reinvent a spiritualized sense of purpose.[13]

In the face of this trial, Lincoln's rhetoric emerges as codifying the basic tenets of an American civil religion, identifying a point of shared spiritual identity for North and South. Robert Bellah's well-known paper on American civil religion sees in Lincoln's rhetoric the affirmation of a "universal and transcendent religious reality as seen in or, one could almost say, as revealed through the experience of the American people" (1967, 49).

Consider, for example, Lincoln's Second Inaugural Address: "Both [North and South] read the same Bible and pray to the same God, and each invokes His aid against the other. It may seem strange that any men should dare to ask a just God's assistance in wringing their bread from the sweat of other men's faces, but let us judge not, that we be not judged" (1865). When saying this, it would have been possible, within the bounds of the religious rhetoric genre, for Lincoln to claim that God had looked more favorably on the victorious North. Instead, Lincoln takes the opportunity to assert that both the North and South share a similar vantage to providence: "The prayers of both could not be answered. That of neither has been answered fully. The Almighty has His own purposes" (1865). Essentially, Lincoln argues that God did not "take sides" in the war and that divine providence is ultimately unknowable. This is an important rhetorical move, because it allows Lincoln to address his audience within the framework of the established genre (the United States is a blessed nation) without indicting the South or praising the North. Lincoln urges Americans to proceed as God would want them to, "With malice toward none" to "bind up the nation's wounds" (1865).

Just as civil religion can be seen as a rhetorical devise that advanced reunification, the genre has also been appropriated by numerous social and political movements to promote movement cohesion. For example, during the Populist movement the rhetorical construction of a spiritual identity became a defining feature of the movement identity, characterizing members of the diverse Populist constituency as a distinct and unified embodiment of the American ideal (Williams and Alexander 1994). Perhaps the most well-known populist speech, famous specifically for its use of religious rhetoric, is William Jennings Bryan's "Cross of Gold" speech at the 1896 Democratic National Convention. Bryan's address contains the by-now familiar appeal to a common American identity, with the added element that laborers are being unfairly excluded from the fulfillment of the American way of life. Bryan invokes identity by making reference to the shared (and storied) American ancestry: "It is the issue of 1776 over again. Our ancestors, when but 3 million, had the courage to declare their political independence of every other nation upon earth. Shall we, their descendants, when we have grown to 70 million, declare that we are less independent than our forefathers?" (1896). Bryan then argues that the gold standard is standing in the way of achieving the same level of independence achieved by the venerable forefathers of America: "Having behind us the commercial interests and the laboring interests and all the toiling masses, we shall answer their demands for a gold standard by saying to them, you shall not press down upon the brow of labor this crown of thorns. You shall not crucify mankind upon a cross of gold" (1896). Labor, in this passage, is given a Christ-like status by being forced to wear a crown of thorns. In this way, Bryan invigorates the identity of laborers hurt by the gold standard, characterizing them not as the poor but as Christ-figures suffering for the sins of America.

This rhetorical strategy was employed specifically to align the emerging partisan identity with a spiritualized sense of Americanism. For example, Henry Demarest Lloyd argued that "The People's Party represents the mightiest hope that has ever stirred in the hearts of the masses—the hope of realizing and incarnating in the lives of the common people the fullness of the divinity of humanity" (1894, 70). The People's Party, it is suggested, was capable of realizing the divine status of America. James H. Davis, a Texas Populist, made a similar appeal to partisan identity, suggesting that the "National Demands of the Populist or People's party" was on a par with the Declaration of Independence and the Constitution as documents consistent with the realization of "the grandest and most perfect civilization" (1894, 204). Davis's treatise—suggestively titled "A Political Revelation"—is largely an attempt to codify the spiritual status of these documents and align them with Populist identity. Mary Elizabeth Lease also constructed party identity in religious terms, invoking a post-millennial eschatology reminiscent of Jonathan Edwards: "The old parties have set up statute laws against the natural rights of man, and thus, though his image, they strike at God. All true reforms, says Mazzini, are religious. So the populists of today represent a demand for enactment into law of the truths taught by Jesus; the truths which must prevail before Christ's kingdom can be established, and the earth made a fit abode for man" (quoted in Williams and Alexander 1994, 8). Here Lease is arguing that, to prepare America for Christ's coming, it is necessary to enact Populist Party goals. Populist identity is contrasted against the alternative parties, which are in direct defiance of God.

Identity-laden religious rhetoric used to foster coherent movement identity extended far beyond Populism. Indeed, given the tendency of the genre to assert a politics of shared identity, it is not surprising that the same rhetorical constructions show up across a variety of political movements. Red Scare anticommunism is an illustrative case. In the 1950s, anticommunism linked with American spirituality asserted a reified cross-denominational unity to assert a point of contrast with an irreligious outgroup (see especially Aiello 2005; Bates 2004).[14] Joseph McCarthy posited one famous formulation of this identity in a well-known address in Wheeling, West Virginia, in which he alleged that the U.S. State Department had been infiltrated by communist sympathizers, arguing that "we are engaged in a final, all-out battle between communistic atheism and Christianity" (1950). McCarthy painted identity in Manichean terms, as a struggle between good and evil in which a distinctly American Christianity was responsible for world salvation. Writing in 1954, the Reverend Billy Graham put it in equally stark terms: communism was "Satan's religion," and "either communism must die, or Christianity must die" (1954, 42). The weapons to defeat communism included "Old fashioned Americanism," which meant a "faith in God" and an "adherence to the Bible" (Graham 1954, 45). J. Edgar Hoover developed a similar contrast between American spirituality and the evils of communism in a 1957 *American Mercury* article titled "God and Country—or Communism?" In it, Hoover contends that the evils of communism could only be bested by "the American ideal," which was "woven of unfaltering faith in God, faith in the destiny of this nation, of battles and of Valley Forge and Gettysburg" (1957, 100).[15]

The Red Scare, and in particular the drive to develop meaningful contrasts between the United States and the Soviet Union, led to a particularly explicit campaign to sanctify American symbols. McCarthy's Wheeling speech included a somewhat contrived reference to Abraham Lincoln, immortalizing the president but also probably attributing him a deeper sense of religious attachment than is historically appropriate.[16] Likewise, Billy Graham took pains to draw parallels between the U.S. Constitution and the Bible. In "Our Bible," Graham argues that "As the Constitution is the highest law of man, so the Bible is the highest law of God" (1955b, 123). Graham's implication is that the American Constitution has a special status before God and ought to be treated with divine reverence. Graham was adept at arguing the spiritual nature of American legal documents to denounce communism. In "A Christian America" (1955a), Graham developed an account of America's sacred history, citing the *Mayflower Compact*, the original state constitutions, the Declaration of Independence, the federal Constitution, and even the words "In God We Trust" on American currency. As Graham contends, "Our place of leadership in the world is far higher than the average American can possibly comprehend" (1955a, 68; see also Aiello 2005).

Perhaps the most significant (and still reverberating) attempt to sanctify an American symbol was legislation *mandating* a rhetorical linkage between God and country in the insertion of the phrase "under God" into the Pledge of Allegiance. The movement to insert the phrase "under God" into the Pledge formally began with the Knights of Columbus, a Catholic fraternal organization, in 1951. Following a letter-writing campaign by the Knights, Catholic Congressman Louis Rabaut (D-Mich.) introduced a bill to alter the Pledge to mark a contrast with the "philosophical roots of communism, atheism, and materialism," codifying the status of America as a nation "born under God" (quoted in Ellis 2005, 130; see also Domke and Coe 2010).

Although the movement struggled initially, it received the necessary shot in the arm in the form of a sermon delivered by the Reverend George Docherty at the New York Avenue Presbyterian Church in February 1954, for which President Dwight Eisenhower was in attendance. Docherty framed the "under God" revision as a necessary way to preserve "the American way of life" from the threat of "militantly atheistic communism" (1954). Docherty's sermon is a case study in building a spiritualized sense of superordinate identity, invoking the Puritan origins of America, Lincoln's sense of God and country, and America as the fulfillment of God's providence. Given this, Docherty argued, something appeared to be missing from the Pledge of Allegiance: "and that which was missing was the characteristic and definitive factor in the 'American Way of Life.' Indeed, apart from the mention of the phrase, the United States of America, this could be the pledge of any Republic. In fact, I could hear little Muscovites repeat a similar pledge to their hammer and sickle flag in Moscow with equal solemnity, for Russia is also a Republic that claims to have overthrown the tyranny of kingship" (1954). Docherty's sermon is thus a self-conscious reflection on exactly how to differentiate American identity from that of the Soviet Union. His conclusion is that the only answer to the Soviet Union is the American claim of divine grace: "To omit the words 'under God' in the Pledge of Allegiance is to omit the definitive character of the American Way of Life'" (Docherty 1954).

Although American civil religion is self-consciously multidenominational, the relative inclusiveness of the identity has changed substantially over time. In particular, for much of American history, nonsectarian appeals generally applied just to Protestant denominations (Prothero 2007). Religious rhetoric during the 1950s morphed these boundaries considerably, softening restrictions against Catholics, Jews, and other marginalized groups in an effort to develop a united spiritual front against the Soviet Union.[17] Thus, the exclusion of an outgroup necessitated the inclusion of other religious traditions.

This rhetorical shift is explicit in the Docherty speech. Docherty notes that America is rightfully one nation "under God," not under a particular church or under Jesus Christ, "to include the great Jewish Community, and the people of the Moslem faith, and the myriad of denominations of Christians in the land" (1954).[18] Eisenhower famously confirmed this sentiment, arguing that that "our government makes no sense unless it is founded on a deeply held religious belief—and I don't care what it is." (Quoted in Herberg, 1955, 84). In Eisenhower's estimation, denominational membership was secondary to religious faith more generally because the latter was the particular point of contrast with the Soviet Union.[19]

The move toward greater religious inclusiveness in the American identity may have been particularly consequential for Catholics. Several prominent Catholic leaders took rhetorical advantage of the communist menace to further integrate Catholics into the American religious narrative. One excellent example is Fulton J. Sheen, a Catholic bishop and star of the popular *Life Is Worth Living* television program. Sheen was a tremendously influential figure—winner of an Emmy for "Most Outstanding Television Personality" in 1952 and having a viewership of 5.5 million households by 1955—and also the American Catholic Church figurehead for anticommunism (Reeves 2001). Sheen embraced the main elements of the genre as an opportunity to develop an inclusive view of American spiritual identity. In contrast to the evils of communism, he declared on his television program that "the true battle against Communism begins in the heart of every single American. . . . If God is with us, then who can be against us?" (Sheen 1953, 62). For Catholics, a strong anticommunist stance thus provided a path to inclusion as Americans. As Donald Crosby writes, for Catholics, demonstrating patriotism through anticommunism was "an impenetrable cloak. . . . At last their critics would be unable to question their Americanism. They would be above suspicion, for they had become the most fully American of the Americans" (1978, 245; see also Ellis 2005, 130; Bates 2004).

From the Puritans to the Red Scare, American religious political rhetoric has undergone important transformations, from an expanding membership in American civil religion to a consecration of political symbols. And, of course, the aforementioned examples are not the end of the story. The role of religious identity rhetoric has been widely documented across numerous American political epochs, from the civil rights movement to the twentieth-century Christian social movements to the 9/11 response (Gutterman 2005; Lambert 2008; Murphy 2009). What is critical is that religious identity has been intertwined with the political in a remarkably consistent manner, constructing identity to build a superordinate sense of identity with a diverse American public.

THE EMOTIVE TENOR OF AMERICAN CIVIL RELIGION

Just as religious rhetoric is regularly coupled with a spiritualized (and nonsectarian) sense of American national identity, it is also delivered in a tone that adds a recognizable emotive punch to identity-laden appeals. And, just as appeals to the collective have their roots in covenant theology, the origins of emotive religious rhetoric can be found in the Puritan jeremiad,[20] a rhetorical style that contrasts a sense of fear and uncertainty with unyielding optimism about the future.[21] The jeremiad is inseparable from the concept of the covenant, lamenting the community's breach of contract and moral derangement but also suggesting an optimistic "sense of purpose" about the future (Miller 1953, 29; Bercovitch 1978, 9; Murphy 2009). This "joined lament and celebration in reaffirming America's mission" resulted in a mixture of positive and negative emotive impulses, contributing to a distinctive and rhetorically consequential tone (Bercovitch 1978, 11; Murphy 2009).

Perry Miller's (1956) analysis emphasizes jeremiads as grim and self-condemning, lamenting the downfall of society. This negativity is a logical extension of how the Puritans understood their initial mission—as time passed and the colony failed to become a "city upon a hill," the colonists blamed their own depravity. As Miller's summarizes, "I suppose that in the whole literature of the world, including the satirists of imperial Rome, there is hardly such another uninhibited and unrelenting documentation of a people's descent into corruption" (1956, 8) Examples of these negative lamentations abound in early Puritan rhetoric. In a quintessential example of the genre, Samuel Danforth lamented "*Iniquity aboundeth, and the love of many waxeth cold, Mat. 24. 12.* Pride, Contention, Worldliness, Covetousness, Luxury, Drunkenness and Uncleanness break in like a flood upon us, and good men grow cold in their love to God and to one another" (1670). These words take on an extremely negative emotive character, conveying both blame and anger. Danforth cites "unbelief" as the principal cause of these vices and blames hardships on an abandonment of the covenant: "Why hath the Lord smitten us with Blasting and Mildew now seven years together, superadding sometimes severe Drought, sometimes great Tempests, Floods, and sweeping Rains, that leave no food behinde them? Is it not because the Lords House lyeth waste?" (1670).

In contrast, Bercovitch argues that the distinguishing mark of "America's first distinctive literary genre" is not woe but, instead, "its unshakable optimism. . . . it inverts the doctrine of vengeance into a promise of ultimate success, affirming to the world, and despite the world, the inviolability of the colonial cause" (1978, 6–7). For example, in the same sermon, Danforth concludes with scripturally based optimism, asking and answering: "*But alas, our Bruise is incurable and our Wound grievous, there is none to repair the Breach, there is no healing Medicine.* The Lord Jesus, the great Physician of *Israel*, hath undertaken the Cure" (1670). In other words, New England has sinned just as Israel sinned, although the colonists have reason to be optimistic because they continue to enjoy special blessings as God's chosen people.

These dual characteristics—lament and optimism—are joined in Puritan religious rhetoric, and they continued to be a defining feature of religious rhetoric as it was incorporated into political discourse. As Andrew Murphy writes, "The jeremiad's political and rhetorical power, its ability to move Americans to social and political action, lies in its ability to evoke a dynamic tension between despair and hope" (2009, 12) The jeremiad is also inexorably connected to the American civil religion tradition. The narrative of decline often involves a fall from America's "chosen" status, and the logic of renewal makes sense only in the context of "God's providential oversight" (Murphy 2009, 11).

Over time, the emotive character of sermons shifted from being a by-product of biblical interpretation to the essential feature of religious discourse.[22] White describes this rhetorical shift as a transition from "proving a rationale for reasonable decision-making" to "persuading in the Ciceronian sense, that is, combining . . . the functions of teaching, winning over the listeners, and exciting the emotions" (1972, 29). No Great Awakening preacher had greater command of emotive rhetoric than Jonathan Edwards, who connected the rational faculty of the mind with the emotions, such that individuals comprehend both intellectually and emotionally (Miller 1956, 179). The "Affections," Edwards writes, "are not essentially distinct from the Will, nor do they differ from the meer Actings of the Will and Inclinations of the Soul, but only by the Liveliness and Sensibleness of Exercise" (1746, 124).[23]

The move to a self-consciously emotive style is important because this made civil religion amenable to mass consumption, similar to how contemporary political observers characterize emotive messaging strategies in contemporary campaigns (Lakoff 2008; Westen 2007). In other words, this shift in style is significant because it helped win converts (Finke and Stark 1989, 37–39). In justifying "the Affections" as superior to "the Understanding," Edwards rationalized a communicative style that could be mastered by untrained rhetoricians and that had tremendous appeal to unschooled audiences.

This emotive turn in discourse became politically consequential during the American Revolution. Whereas the intellectual grist of the Revolution came from liberal and republican traditions, the *mode* of communication relied heavily on revivalist traditions (Stout 1977). For example, Henry Cummings, a Harvard-educated Congregationalist heavily influenced by the Great Awakening argued on the anniversary of the Battle of Lexington that God had restrained the "wrath" of the British by giving Americans the courage to fight (Sandoz 1998, 658): "God restrains the wrath of man . . . by rousing those who suffer, or are likely to suffer by it, to stand in their own defense; and inspiring them with courage and resolution, to oppose and resist, to the utmost, all the mischievous efforts of the ambition, wrath, and anger of those proud aspiring mortals, who would, if possible, rob them of their natural rights, and plunge them into a state of servility" (Cummings 1781, 669). According to this, God intervenes directly in human affairs, "inspiring" the emotions necessary to fight off those attempting to vanquish natural rights (melding liberal "rights" discourse with emotive preaching). Even the secularly inclined Thomas Paine adapted emotive stylistic elements from revivalist preaching (Stout 1977, 537). For example, paying homage to the view of America as a "new Israel," Paine used emotionally evocative imagery and Biblical passages to argue that Israel's ultimate downfall was desiring a king: "And when a man seriously reflects on the idolatrous homage which is paid to the persons of Kings, he need not wonder, that the Almighty, ever jealous of his honor, should disapprove a form of government which so impiously invades the prerogatives of heaven. Monarchy is ranked in scripture as one of the sins of the Jews, for which a curse in reverse is denounced against them" (1776, 53).

In short, revivalist rhetoric provided an alternative to erudite religious rhetoric, affecting a style of rhetoric that was easily transmissible to mass audiences and influencing the spread of a democratic sentiment in the colonies (White 1972, 57). As Stout summarizes, "Despite the differences in intellectual substance between revivals and the rebellion, those movements exhibited a close rhetorical affinity that infused religious and political ideas with powerful social significance and ideological urgency" (1977, 521).

Given the accessibility and appeal of emotionally evocative religious rhetoric, it is not surprising that it has regularly been an important feature in social and political movements. Moreover, across a variety of movements, the emotive tone regularly combines lamentation with optimism about the future. For example, William Lloyd Garrison's *The Liberator* embodied key changes in the tenor of abolitionist discourse, from a legalistic and gradualist approach to an emotive argument urging immediate emancipation (Mayer 1998; Arkin 2001; Newman 2002). Stylistically, Garrison melded abolitionism with the emotive jeremiad, suggesting that the sin of slavery had corrupted the nation: "The Lord sees [slavery], and is displeased that there is no judgment; and he hath put on the garments of vengeance for clothing, and is clad with zeal as a cloak—and, unless we repent by immediately undoing the heavy burdens and letting the oppressed go free, according to our deeds, accordingly he will repay, fury to his adversaries, recompense to his enemies" (1838). The use of emotive religious language was a self-conscious move by abolitionist leaders to appeal to individuals' most fundamental moral fiber, a necessary move to shift the opinions of those for whom slavery was a righteous way of life. As Theodore Weld, a revivalist minister and abolitionist, reflected, "If it is not FELT in the *vital tissues of the spirit*, all the reasoning in the world is a feather thrown against the wind" (Weld, quoted in Young 2001, 103). Likewise, in reflecting on the use of language in the inaugural issue of *The Liberator*, Garrison remarked, "Tell a man whose house is on fire to give a moderate alarm; tell him to moderately rescue his wife from the hands of the ravisher; tell the mother to gradually extricate her babe from the fire into which it has fallen;—but urge me not to use moderation in a cause like the present. . . . I WILL BE HEARD. The apathy of the people is enough to make every statue leap from its pedestal, and to hasten the resurrection of the dead" (1831).

A similar emotive style was important to the Populist movement. A lamenting tone was adopted to describe the current moral and economic state of America, but enthusiasm was also generated about future prospects. Populist politics were, of course, a response to late-nineteenth-century social conditions, and these social conditions provided the grist for jeremiad-like lamentations that argued that economic disaster was the result of American moral shortcomings. For example, James Baird Weaver's 1892 populist book *A Call to Action* adopts the emotive tone of a jeremiad, asking "Does the young but great Republic hold out any hope for mankind? Are we still a beacon of light, or has our lamp soon grown dim?" (1892, 153). Protesting the American economic system while invoking the language of the Declaration of Independence, Weaver argues that depriving individuals of their "natural and inalienable safeguards, is an organized rebellion against the providence of God" (1892, 156). Weaver concludes what is largely a lament against the immoral state of the American economy with a hopeful call to action: "Throughout all history we have had ample evidence that the new world is a theater upon which the righteous movement now in progress should again forcibly remind us of our inevitable mission, under Providence, among the nations of the earth" (1892, 169).

Ignatius Donnelly's 1892 preamble to "The Omaha Platform"[24] follows a similar pattern, first invoking both the Declaration of Independence and asking for God's blessing and then lamenting that "The conditions which surround us best justify our co-operation; we meet in the midst of a nation brought to the verge of moral, political, and material ruin." In a rhetorical move offering hope through identity, Donnelly suggests that the party could ultimately transcend all that divided America, even the emotional baggage left by the Civil War: "We declare that this Republic can only endure as a free government while built upon the love of the whole people for each other and for the nation; that it cannot be pinned together by bayonets; that the civil war is over, and that every passion and resentment which grew out of it must die with it, and that we must be in fact, as we are in name, one united brotherhood of free men" (1892).

Evidence suggests that the emotive language of religious identity may have been a significant part of Populism's success. While Populism has largely been characterized as an economic movement—with the role of religion relegated to the periphery—Rhys Williams and Susan Alexander argue that "Populism's religious rhetoric was not superfluous; it became part and parcel of the movement's explaining itself to itself as well as to potential adherents and opponents. Religious themes were integral to the attempts to explain Populism's economic and political platforms, and they cannot be ignored if one is to understand Populism as a movement" (1994, 1–2). Building group identity through the language of civil religion is one key component of this argument. Populists were confronted with the need to build a diverse coalition across geographical regions. This consideration, coupled with the fact that solely class-based arguments have typically been unsuccessful in American politics, made the language of civil religion an ideal solution (Williams and Alexander 1994, 5).

Similarly, cold war identity construction made use of highly emotive religious language. This was often accomplished through the use of a jeremiad-like lament combined with a sense of the providential mission of America. McCarthy, for example, attributed communist infiltration to "an emotional hang-over and a temporary moral lapse" (1950). Likewise, James Fitfield, a Congregationalist minister, bemoaned the abandonment of the morals laws of the founding fathers and Pilgrims. Only "By bringing our individual lives into moral rectitude," he wrote in a 1954 *American Mercury* article, "[can] we eliminate anxieties and fears and experience within ourselves the peace and strength of God despite the A-bomb" (Fitfield 1954, 48). Fitfield thus employs a mixture of anxiety-inducing language—in particular the threat of nuclear war—and a glimmer of hope in suggesting that Americans might yet purify their morality. Bishop Fulton Sheen also adopted an emotive jeremiad tone, probing both why God had subjected Americans to their current plight and also how Americans might right the course to fulfill God's divine plan. In "The Role of Communism and the Role of America," Fulton Sheen argues that the world (including America) had become "sick" through a sort of moral lapse and that communism was one symptom of this. Nevertheless, "We are destined, under Providence, to be the secondary cause for the restoration of freedom and liberties of the peoples of the world" (Sheen 1953, 268). God, Sheen explains, is the primary cause, suggesting that America is God's instrument on earth. Sheen uses an emotive Christian metaphor to drive this point home for his listeners: "the world is being crucified by communism. The long arm of Providence is reaching out to America, saying, 'Take up thy Cross'" (1953, 270).

FROM AMERICAN POLITICAL HISTORY TO CONTEMPORARY CAMPAIGNS

The evidence reviewed in this chapter adds an important layer of context to Reagan's "city on a hill" passage quoted at the outset. Reagan was not inventing something new but was, rather, invoking a genre of American political speech, the principal elements of which have remained remarkably consistent over time. Religious rhetoric has persisted as a highly emotive genre, blending sorrowful lamentations with enthusiastic calls to action. Moreover, religious rhetoric has been consistently used to build a common spiritualized identity, transcending sectarian or denominational division. The ease with which Winthrop's core message was adapted by Reagan to fit into a contemporary campaign is a testament to the power of religious identity and emotion in American politics.[25]

Although it is clear that emotive and identity-laden cues are the defining features of religious rhetoric, it is less clear precisely how and why they impact American politics and culture. For example, we know that Populist rhetoric invoked a common spiritual identity, but we can only speculate as to how these messages were received by their target audience. Similarly, although the evidence points toward expanding "enfranchisement" in the civil religion tradition, we have little systematic knowledge about where religious rhetoric locates the boundaries of the religious community. The next chapters take up this charge, examining the consequences of identity and emotion in religious political rhetoric.

3

RELIGIOUS RHETORIC AND THE POLITICS OF IDENTITY

Family and God, honor, duty and country: now, let's face it, some
ridicule these principles as relics of the past. But when our problems
are at their worst, when our hope is strained, when drugs and crime
and the abandonment of children challenge the very character of our
country, we know where to turn. Our tested values provide the only
answers that work, the only answers that count.

—Senator Bob Dole, 1996

Speaking at an American Legion convention in Salt Lake City, Bob Dole
(R-Kans.) is characterizing drugs, crime, and child abandonment not just
as public policy problems but as threats to the moral fiber of America—
the "character" of the country. These challenges can be bested only by
yoking together the time-tested values of God and country. Real answers
to the most pressing problems of America must come through a reifica-
tion of an American spiritualized identity. Dole also indicates that an
outgroup is "ridiculing" this fundamental understanding. Although this
group is not explicitly identified, there is a clear contrast between a secu-
larized approach to politics and an approach reinforced by values and
faith. This approach will not only "work" as a practical response to a
policy problem but will "count" in a much more fundamental sense.

Understanding the content of appeals such as this is important. Whether
candidates are referencing a common religious ingroup or are identifying
"others" who threaten a specific worldview, the manner in which religious
appeals are crafted speaks to questions of how religion is invoked as a
matter of campaign strategy and, more fundamentally, to whether U.S.
politics is characterized in cohesive or divisive terms. Along these lines,
we ask in this chapter both which religious identities are being cued and
how they are being constructed. Like Dole's nondenominational call to
return to a spiritualized understanding of American political culture, religious rhetoric is generally used in the spirit of a cohesive civil religion, not

singling out particular traditions for benefit or blame as long as America is vested with some sense of the sacred. But religious rhetoric also contains an element of exclusivity. Even though candidates explicitly welcome members of all faiths into the American civil religion community, the civil religion has specific requirements and a particular creed that runs counter to many other religious traditions. Paradoxically, then, the language of American civil religion identity often contains an undercurrent of exclusivity in the name of political cohesion.

A CLOSER LOOK AT THE LANGUAGE OF RELIGIOUS IDENTITY

It is important to begin by making a distinction between religious identity as it is evoked in political rhetoric and identity as it exists in minds of Americans. A politician might be more apt to use the word *Christian* around a group of self-professed Christians; nevertheless, political rhetoric and an individual's propensity to identify as a Christian are ultimately two different things. The language of identity—the terms of campaign debate and discussion—should be studied as a distinct phenomenon in its own right. Rhetorical expressions of identity lend insight into how the American political community is being rhetorically constructed. If religious rhetoric constructs American identity in a manner that is too exclusive or too sectarian, it runs the risk of alienating large portions of a religiously diverse public. But if identity rhetoric is not explicit or exclusive enough, it could lose its potency altogether. In a country premised on the separation of church and state, it is important to understand what role religious identities play in the "national conversation" (Hart 2000, 139).

Three distinct rhetorical expressions of identity are important topics of inquiry. First, political speech invoking an American civil religion has profound implications for our understanding of the political community. It is important to understand how frequently candidates use these broad nondenominational appeals to engender a sense of religious cohesion in the American mass public. In other words, does the language of civil religion evoke a sense of religious community with many of the same features as more commonly recognized religious groups (such as specific denominations)? Evidence suggests that this may be the case. For example, Ronald Wimberley and James Christenson (1981) find evidence that the basic belief structure of civil religion exists alongside other types of religious group membership. Thus, civil religion rhetoric may itself be constitutive of a broad social group to which many Americans feel a strong attachment and from which many define their social selves.

It is also important to understand the place of religious subgroup appeals in political rhetoric. By subgroup I mean distinct religious groups such as denominations and interest groups. Subgroups provide an obvious point of religious identification for many Americans; however, the extent to which religious subgroups play an important role in political rhetoric is unclear. If candidates spend a good deal of time referring to denominational affiliations, voters could theoretically begin to view politics through a sectarian lens. At the same time, we know very little about how these subgroups are characterized—are specific denominations and traditions rhetorically privileged, or are they referenced only in the spirit of religious pluralism?

Finally, the culture wars genre is remarkable insofar as it finds a point of common identification with religious traditionalism or orthodoxy, gaining strength through the definition of religious outgroups. In other words, culture wars rhetoric seeks to generate ingroup favoritism through the definition of social others (Miller and Hoffmann 1999). Culture wars rhetoric is of interest not only in terms of which groups are favored but also in terms of how other groups might be characterized as a threat to religious identity.

These three types of religious identity rhetoric are theorized to have distinctly different consequences in the American public mind. As a point of illustration, consider the following statements, both made by Bill Clinton during his 1992 presidential campaign:

I was then, and I remain today, deeply drawn to the Catholic social mission, to the idea that, as President Kennedy said, here on earth God's work must truly be our own. (September 11, 1992, University of Notre Dame, Annenberg/Pew Archive of Presidential Campaign Discourse)

Let it be our cause to see that child reach the fullest of her God-given abilities. Let it be our cause that she grow up strong and secure, braced by her challenges, but never, never struggling alone; with family and friends and a faith that in America, no one is left out; no one is left behind. (July 16, 1992, Democratic National

Convention, Annenberg/Pew Archive of Presidential Campaign Discourse)

These passages bear certain similarities. Both passages, for example, use a personal story (Clinton's time at Georgetown and the birth of his daughter, respectively) to connect with the audience. In addition, both passages make a reference to God in support of a particular social agenda. Nevertheless, these passages are quite distinct in terms of the religious identities Clinton is evoking.

In the first passage, Clinton uses a religious reference to illustrate his connections with a particular religious group—Catholics—in a speech at the Catholic University of Notre Dame. Indeed, later in this same speech Clinton takes the time to illustrate the commonalities between the Baptist (his own religious affiliation) and Catholic outlook. This passage is indicative of religious *subgroup identity rhetoric*, or appeals to distinct religious subsets within the population, such as Catholics, Jews, specific Protestant denominations, and religious interest groups such as Focus on the Family.

There are several reasons to suspect that subgroup identity cues may be important in contemporary politics. First, subgroup references are uniquely equipped to resonate with specific segments of the electorate. The United States is characterized by tremendous denominational pluralism (Putnam and Campbell 2010), and the degree to which politicians make reference to these diverse groups is significant. Insofar as individuals' religious group affiliations are an important determinant of their voting behavior, politicians have an incentive to align themselves with religious groups through their rhetoric. In addition, even though subgroup appeals are distinct from culture wars rhetoric, they may have a similar impact. By reminding people of their denominational affiliations, the appeals may make voters inclined to more readily think about religious outgroups. We know very little about whether subgroup rhetoric is typically used in the spirit of religious favoritism, or, as in the Clinton example, in the spirit of inclusivity.

Of course, there are potential costs associated with subgroups appeals. Although it is unlikely that Clinton's single speech at Notre Dame alienated non-Catholic voters, sustained appeals to religious subgroups could have precisely this effect. For example, because about 20 percent of Americans are non-Christian, we can imagine that regularly invoking Christianity would seriously alienate these voters, accentuate tensions between religious subgroups, and suggest that the candidate might deliver representation with an explicitly Christian outlook.[1] Thus, although subgroup appeals have the potential to create a close bond between a candidate and a narrow constituency, these appeals are also potentially problematic, defining the political community in an exclusive manner.

In contrast, the second Clinton passage contains no reference to a particular religious subgroup. Rather, the passage uses religious language to ascribe a certain sacred quality to America. Clinton is evoking a shared "faith" that in America everyone has the ability to achieve to the extent that abilities are "God-given." The passage constitutes a subtle ingroup appeal insofar as Clinton uses first-person plural pronouns ("our") and references to America to build a sense of shared group cohesiveness in the audience. The implied group is unmistakably religious in nature because the egalitarian ideal posited by Clinton is inextricably linked with a sense of faith. As Michael Billig (2003) has argued, ambiguous references to shared identity combined with references to universal principles such as equality and freedom frequently operate to establish a sense of oneness among all message recipients. And, of course, in the American case the universal principles posited by Billig are often religious in nature. America is often portrayed as a "new Israel," endowed by God with special responsibilities and given a favored place in the world order (Fowler et al. 2004; Domke and Coe, 2010). These tenets are central to Americans' self-understanding, providing, as Robert Bellah has written, "a religious dimension for the whole fabric of American life, including the political sphere" (1967, 3). Civil religion is thus intertwined with identity, and this identity gains expression through political rhetoric.

Note that the second Clinton passage does not live up to all the criteria of Bellah's civil religion—Clinton does not specifically say that America has a special place in the world order. Clinton does, however, implicitly assert a shared belief in God and identifies "America" as a place where people have faith. Moreover, Clinton takes pains to draw his audience together in a shared concern with phrases such as "our cause" and "family and friends." In short, the second passage, in contrast with the first, unites the audience members—and all Americans—in a common cause that has something to do with religious faith, even if the substance of this faith is somewhat unspecified.

Culture wars rhetoric stands in sharp contrast to both subgroup appeals and the inclusive language of civil religion. Reagan's 1984 campaign made a point of employing this genre in the context of the debate about allowing prayer in public schools, arguing, "If our opponents were as vigorous in supporting our voluntary prayer amendment as they are in raising taxes, maybe we could get the Lord back in the schoolrooms and drugs and violence out." Several features of this passage stand out. First, it implicitly references two competing sides of an explicitly religious debate. In saying "our opponents," Reagan does not call the outgroup or the ingroup by name, instead arguing that there is some other unspecified "other" in American politics, determined to remove God from the schools (and raise taxes). Moreover, by yoking the idea of school prayer together with drugs and violence, Reagan is escalating the stakes in the debate, indicating that the absence of religion in schools is responsible for a fundamental moral breakdown.

Although it is clear that religious identities are evoked in political rhetoric, we know relatively little about how often candidates use these identities, how this has changed over time, and how these identity cues serve the interests of building a cohesive and inclusive political community. And, although it might be tempting for some to draw the simple conclusion that civil religion is "good" for democracy and that subgroup and culture wars appeals are "bad," this oversimplification would be a mistake. Religious identity rhetoric can have crosscutting and ambiguous consequences. For example, although subgroup appeals could call religious differences to mind, they could also serve an important democratic function by recognizing underserved and marginalized religious groups.[2] Likewise, although civil religion is often theorized to serve important democratic functions (Hart 2005), it is certainly possible to imagine this civil religion manifesting itself as something particular and exclusive. To the extent that civil religion rhetoric privileges a particular view of the sacred, members of excluded religious and spiritual traditions may find themselves rhetorically marginalized, not only from a religious group but also from a particular conception of American identity.

UNDERSTANDING RELIGIOUS IDENTITIES IN POLITICAL RHETORIC

To analyze how religious language is used in politics, I began by collecting a large sample of stump speeches from major party candidates, 1980–2008. There are several reasons why this data source is appropriate for capturing the overall thrust of campaign rhetoric. First, it is important to consider that I am analyzing rhetoric over multiple campaigns.

Mediums of campaign communication have changed radically in the past thirty years, with a rise in cable television and Internet use and a decline in newspaper circulation (Baum and Kernell 1999; Putnam 2000; Kaid 2003). Candidate stump speeches, in contrast, have been a relatively constant staple during this period. Scott Althaus, Peter Nardulli, and Daron Shaw (2002) find evidence of only a slight increase in candidate appearances from 1972 to 2000. Moreover, candidates have behaved in strategically similar ways during this time period (Althaus, Nardulli, and Shaw 2002, 69). This supports my using stump style speeches as a data source in that candidates can be compared on roughly even ground. Second, I avoided media interpretations of campaigns because news reports are not necessarily accurate reflections of campaign discourse; for example, media reports often accentuate negativity (Jamieson and Waldman 1997). Finally, because the later chapters in this book link candidate rhetoric with opinion changes over the months preceding a campaign, I needed to develop an indicator to capture the overall thrust of a campaign rather than episodic campaign events (Druckman 2004). For this purpose, my measuring the overall campaign climate by examining a large sample of speeches (as opposed to, say, the content of a single convention address) is preferable given what is known about preference formation. For example, James Druckman and Kjersten Nelson (2003) find evidence suggesting that the impact of a single political event is fairly short-lived.

To assess the overall thrust of a candidate's rhetoric, I began by gathering a large number of stump speeches from a variety of sources: (1) the *Annenberg/Pew Archive of Presidential Campaign Discourse* (2000), (2) the Stanford University Political Communication Lab (2000), (3) the University of California–Santa Barbara American Presidency Project, and (4) a Lexis-Nexus search of news wire transcripts of presidential campaign speeches.[3] In all, I collected 1,329 speeches made over the course of 16 campaigns.

From this large campaign speech database, I selected a sample of unambiguously religious passages that is the unit of analysis for all subsequent discussion in this book. The immediate objection to this approach is that that what seems like religious rhetoric to some might not be religious rhetoric to others. For example, Bethany Albertson (2005) has found evidence that the biblical phrase "wonder-working power" works as coded political rhetoric to persuade narrow subsets of Christians, even though this reference goes over the heads of most Americans. Although this finding supports the contention that religious rhetoric resonates with certain segments of the electorate, it also suggests that the task of identifying religious language is mired in subjectivity. To overcome this challenge, I focused on religious rhetoric that is *explicitly* religious. The choice to focus on explicit references is a design feature that clearly limits the inferences I ultimately could draw from these data; however, this sacrifice was necessary to reliably analyze the large volume of campaign speeches.

I define *explicitly religious* as any passage containing a set of religious indicator words—words that indicate or signal religion to the vast majority of Americans. Fortunately, the content analysis program Linguistic Inquiry and Word Count (LIWC) contains a predefined set of religious words that have already gone through a rigorous selection process (Pennebaker, Francis, and Booth 2001), suggesting that these indicator words are well recognized as religious.[4] This list—sixty explicitly religious indicator words in all—represents all *potential* indicators of religious rhetoric. From this list of indicator words, I eliminated words that appear infrequently, words that are religious only in certain contexts, and words that often appear as jargon. For example, I eliminated *minister* because it is usually not an indicator of religious rhetoric (e.g., prime minister or foreign minister). In other words, I developed a set of indicators that reliably mark only those passages that have meaningful religious content. These cuts yielded a list of twelve religious rhetoric indicators.[5] Using these indicators, I selected the entire passage in which that word appeared, using a set of linguistic rules to ensure that passages were sampled in the appropriate context.[6]

I performed several checks to ensure the adequacy of this sampling procedure. First, using a computer content analysis program, I compared samples drawn using different selection procedures. The samples were indistinguishable along key dimensions such as emotive language and pronoun use (Pennebaker, Mehl, and Niederhoffer 2002). Second, I qualitatively examined complete speeches to make sure this sampling procedure did not exclude any obviously religious passages. Overall, this procedure did a good job capturing the religious content of a speech. In fact, religious words that are not indicators themselves (such as *minister*) are still generally included in the sample because they typically appear in close proximity to one of the keyword indicators. This selection procedure resulted in a sample of 3,495 religious passages. From this religious rhetoric sample, I drew a random probability sample, clustered by candidate, to make the task of content analysis more manageable.

I randomly selected 75 passages per candidate, yielding a sample of 1,200. This sample is the basis of all subsequent analysis in this book.

I content-analyzed each of the 1,200 passages along several dimensions relating to identity to test my expectations about the contours of the political community (Neuendorf 2002).[7] First, each passage was coded for ingroup and outgroup references. My use of *ingroup* and *outgroup* borrow from the social psychological concepts by the same name. Essentially, ingroups are an individual's own social group attachments, whereas outgroups are social "others." The coding scheme used in this book is intended to capture the rhetorical analogs of these social psychological concepts—the cues that can bring ingroup and outgroup distinctions to the "top of the head" (Zaller 1992). Ingroup references were examined further to uncover the specific social identities to which candidates were appealing—be they religious (faithful Christians), partisan (faithful Republicans), or geographical (faithful Wisconsinites). While I analyzed religious rhetoric for numerous identities, two specific identity references are of particular interest in this chapter: *Civil religion identity* and *Subgroup identity*.[8]

The *Culture wars* variable is a subset of all outgroup references. References to outgroups were coded to discern whether the reference to the outgroup signaled a deep-seated conflict in American politics or only primed religious differences in a superficial way. In addition, only references to American political conflicts were coded as culture wars rhetoric. For example, even though the Soviet Union was the target of religious outgroup rhetoric (particularly in the early 1980s), this, if anything, was a point of unity for Americans, not evidence of a culture war.

I also coded whether candidates characterized religion as something shared by all Americans or as something personal and a matter of individual choice—essentially whether American religiosity is framed in *Shared* or *Pluralistic* terms. Religious identities have the potential to be either inclusive or exclusive. Rhetorically, candidates can emphasize the unique aspects of multiple faith traditions (or no faith tradition at all) or posit a shared American faith that is broad enough to encompass all the essential aspects of American religious diversity. Accordingly, my coding scheme assessed whether each religious passage implied a common or shared religion or God in America, or discussed religion in a way that is more pluralistic or relative.

A *Favored nation* variable was included to test the expectation that the language of civil religion identity is closely connected to many of the belief elements identified in the civil religion literature. One of the more common assertions made is that America as a kind of new Israel, "endowed . . . with special opportunities, and assigned . . . special responsibilities to do good" (Fowler et al. 2004). Given these expectations, all passages were coded to determine whether they made no reference to country, linked religion and country without ascribing a favored-nation status to the United States, or explicitly indicated that the United States is blessed in some way (Domke and Coe 2010).

Finally, a *God concept* variable tests the extent to which civil religion rhetoric privileges a particular view of the sacred. The relationship between civil religion and subgroup identities has long been a source of debate in the academic literature. Some scholars see civil religion as integrative, representing a distillation of the common elements of multiple religious faiths so as to serve as a values touchstone on which American democracy rests (Wimberley and Christenson 1981). Others, including Bellah (1967), view civil religion as transcending all subgroup beliefs, positing that a divine power is directly influencing American national affairs.

What is clear is that no matter how civil religion is conceptualized, it is generally not theorized to privilege a particular religious subgroup. Nevertheless, there is reason to suspect that civil religion rhetoric might implicitly do exactly this, particularly because adherence to civil religion ideals seem to be related to denominational traditions (Wimberley and Christenson 1981). One way to test this is to take advantage of the fact that, although most large religious traditions in America have a monotheistic belief structure, they often conceptualize God in very different ways. Methodists, for example, tend to think of God as being more distant than do Catholics or Evangelicals. Evangelicals, in contrast, think of God as being more vengeful (Noffke and McFadden 2001). George Lakoff (1996) has suggested that conservatives tend to think of God in terms of a "strict parent," whereas liberals tend to think of God with "nurturing" imagery (see also Jensen 2009). Paul Froese and Christopher Bader (2010) convincingly argue that Americans generally understand God in terms of how engaged God is the world and whether God is judgmental. These differences in God image are related to both denominational traditions and political differences.

Although God concept has been widely studied, there is relatively little guidance for reliably analyzing speeches for the image of God they project. Accordingly, I analyzed religious rhetoric for seven different conceptualizations of God deemed to reasonably approximate the variety of God images in the academic literature. *God concept* codes for "companion," "paternal," "judge," and "savior," given evidence that these images predict sociopolitical attitudes (Welch and Leege 1988). To this list I added a "maternal" God concept (Roof and Roof 1984), as well as a category for God as "provider."[9] An additional "no imagery" category was also added. To the extent that any one of these is rhetorically more prominent than the others, this will suggest that the divine elements in civil religion are more closely associated with certain religious traditions and that civil religion contains subtle elements of religious exclusivity.

SPEAKING OF FAITH IN POLITICS

The results of the content analysis provide strong confirmation of the centrality of identity in religious political rhetoric.[10] To begin, it is helpful to get a sense of how often candidates used religious language in stump speeches in general (as opposed to looking directly at the sample of religious rhetoric passages). Figure 3.1 shows the LIWC religious word

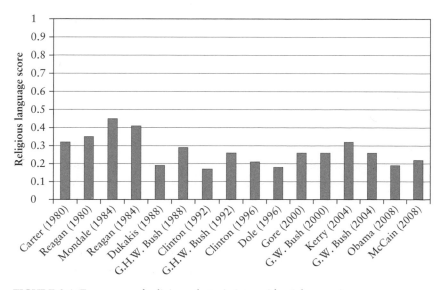

FIGURE 3.1 Frequency of religious rhetoric in presidential campaigns

Linguistic Inquiry and Word Count religious word scores for all major party presidential candidates, 1980–2008.

scores for each campaign. Several things about figure 3.1 stand out. First, although candidates are varied in their use of religious language, this variance is somewhat underwhelming, with religious words accounting for between approximately one-fifth and two-fifths of a percentage point of all total words employed in every campaign (note that the y-axis scale in figure 3.1. ranges from 0 to 1 percent).[11] This is similar to other findings in political science. For example, in analyzing political rhetoric in presidential campaigns over the past fifty years, Roderick Hart (2000, 48) finds relatively little systematic variation in the frequency of religious language use among major party candidates.

There still are some noteworthy differences between the candidates in frequency of religious word use. It is particularly interesting to note that the variation illustrated in figure 3.1 violates much of the conventional wisdom about the use of religious rhetoric in presidential campaigns. For example, John Kerry in 2004 actually scores *higher* than George W. Bush in 2004 on religious word frequency, a finding that at first blush is out of step with the widely held perception that Bush was the more regular religious communicator. Likewise, Walter Mondale's 1984 campaign had the highest rate of religious language use in the sample—a surprising finding, given that candidates such as Jimmy Carter and George W. Bush are much more well known for their public religiosity. This is further evidence that a nuanced and theoretically driven look at the language of religious identity is necessary to account for electoral and public opinion dynamics. It is not how often candidates talk about religion that matters—it is how this rhetoric is crafted.

The Centrality of Civil Religion Identity in Political Rhetoric

The evidence clearly indicates that religious rhetoric is principally used to activate a sense of group-based attachment in the mass public. Nearly 70 percent of all religious references were coupled with some sort of reference to a social ingroup—a denomination, a political party, or an undefined spiritual community. This high rate of ingroup references in religious rhetoric far eclipses any other rhetorical feature in the sample. For example, there is relatively little issue content in candidates' religious rhetoric, indicating that candidates are generally not using religious language to develop sophisticated policy-based arguments.[12] Moreover, the analysis uncovers little evidence that religious rhetoric is *consistently* coupled with any particular political issue.

To be sure, candidates have had particular issues that they were most comfortable framing in religious terms. For example, Obama often spoke of health care and education in religious terms, whereas George W. Bush in 2004 was more likely to use religious language to justify foreign policy initiatives. Nevertheless, it is important to stress that, even on occasions that Bush or Obama did frame an issue in religious terms, the use of religious rhetoric was probably more geared toward the assertion of a common identity than with a robust policy justification. For example, Obama characterized education in religious terms by arguing:

> Because I know that if we can just bring our education system into the 21st century, not only will our children be able to fulfill their God-given potential, and our families be able to live out their dreams; not only will our schools out-educate the world and our workers outcompete the world; not only will our companies innovate more and our economy grow more, but at this defining moment, we will do what previous generations of Americans have done—and unleash the promise of our people, unlock the promise of our country, and make sure that America remains a beacon of opportunity and prosperity for all the world (September 9, 2008, Dayton, Ohio, States News Service).

In this passage, Obama frames the case for education reform in religious terms. More critical, however, is that Obama deftly connects this quasi-religious sense of purpose to the larger purpose of the nation and sense of mission in the world. Although the passage is about education, its larger purpose is a clear statement of collective identity wrapped in a higher spiritualized calling. Education is necessary to fulfill "God-given potential" and the "promise of our people." Likewise, in his 2004 campaign, Bush frequently told the story of an Iraqi amputee with whom he visited in the Oval Office: "A guy took a Sharpie, folded it in his new hand, and wrote, 'God bless America,' in Arabic. You see, he said, 'God bless America' because he had been liberated from the clutches of a brutal tyrant who whimsically could cut off a hand (August 6, 2004, Washington, D.C., Federal News Service). In terms of policy, Bush was essentially using this anecdote as a rationalization for the Iraq war. But rhetorically, the passage has an aim similar to the Obama passage. America is accorded a blessed status in the world order—the Iraq invasion is portrayed as

American force acting out God's will. This is consistent with the notion that civil religion is a remarkably flexible genre. Despite vast differences in the issue content of the two passages, both assert a sense of shared spiritual identity.

Interestingly, traditional cultural issues such as abortion and same-sex marriage were almost entirely absent from the sample of religious passages.[13] This is not to say that candidates did not discuss abortion, only that they chose to do so in a way that was not explicitly religious. This finding is consistent with other research on party messaging strategies. For example, Mark Rozell and Clyde Wilcox (1996) provide an excellent discussion of the changing rhetoric of the Christian Right from the 1980s to the 1990s, arguing that the overt religious appeals have been toned down, that the thrust of the message has been mainstreamed, and that leaders now avoid overt biblical references. Although Rozell and Wilcox are analyzing Christian Right movement leaders, not presidential candidates, the logic is essentially the same: for abortion appeals to effectively resonate with a broad constituency, they need to avoid explicitly religious elements.[14]

Ingroup scores are consistently high. In addition, there is a substantial amount of interesting variation regarding which candidates linked religion with social and religious ingroups. For example, both Bush in 2004 and Clinton in 1992 yoked together religion and social groups nearly 85 percent of the time, whereas Dole did so only 53 percent of the time. Interestingly, even though Mondale used religious language overall at a higher clip than any other candidate, he comparatively rarely did so to make reference to religious ingroups (only 58 percent of the time). All this suggests that, although all candidates tended to use religious words at a roughly comparable rate, there is great variation in the manner in which they used religion to communicate identity.

It is also important to examine which identities are typically cued by religious language. In chapter 2 we found evidence that references to a distinctly American religious identity have been a powerful force across American political history, and as figure 3.2 illustrates, contemporary presidential campaigns have continued this trend, frequently invoking an American civil religion identity. Fully 55.8 percent of all passages in the religious rhetoric sample (and 80.5 percent of all ingroup-based appeals in the sample) made a reference to civil religion identity, either by referencing a common American spiritual identity or by making vague references to include the audience in a shared spiritual conception.

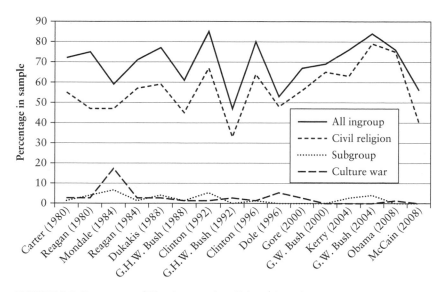

FIGURE 3.2 Frequency of identity cues in religious rhetoric

Percentage of religious rhetoric containing ingroup references (divided into civil religion and subgroup religion categories) and culture war references for all major party presidential candidates, 1980–2008.

In contrast, in the sample of 1,200 passages, only 26 actually made reference to a specific religious subgroup, and only 33 mentioned warring progressive and traditionalist groups. This does not mean that these references are unimportant—indeed, they could have a disproportionate effect on the target group. For example, culture wars rhetoric contains a disproportionate emphasis on controversial cultural issues such as prayer in public schools, whereas civil religion rhetoric is largely unused for this topic. Nevertheless, in the vast majority of presidential stump speeches, civil religion identity is clearly the dominant campaign norm. Candidates generally use religious language to excite individuals' identities as part of an American spiritual community, not as members of particular religious subgroups.[15]

The content of these group-based references is itself important, indicating that references to a civil religion identity also implies a particular belief structure. First, the evidence suggests that civil religion identity references are closely intertwined with a "minimal monotheism." When candidates make references to American civil religion they generally did so with nondenominational references to a divine creator, whereas this was not the case for either culture wars rhetoric or subgroup rhetoric.[16]

Moreover, passages cuing civil religion identity also frequently indicated that the United States is particularly "blessed" or has some special status in the world order. In the sample, 509 of the 669 civil religion passages made a nominal linkage between religion and country, and 89 of these passages did so in a way that explicitly accorded the United States a sacred status.[17] One such interesting passage comes from Bush's 2004 campaign, in which he frequently argued that "This is a time that requires firm resolve and clear vision and the deep faith in the values that makes this a great nation. And one of those—one of those deep faiths we believe and understand is that we know that freedom is not America's gift to the world, freedom is the Almighty God's gift to each man and woman in this world."(October 25, 2004, Daytona Beach, FL, Public papers of the Presidents). The passage states that a "deep faith" and "values" are part of what make America a great nation, suggesting that America owes its success to its religiosity. In terms of religious content, the phrase "deep faith" is quite diffuse, with no particular investment in any one faith tradition—what Will Herberg (1955) has characterized as an American "faith in faith." Although the passage goes out of its way to say that America is not responsible for giving freedom to the rest of the world, the American knowledge of this freedom is itself a divine gift. All this is closely connected with an assertion of collective identity— God's divine gift is something that "we believe" and "we understand" (making use of the first-person plural pronouns that Billig 2003 theorizes are essential to building a common identity). This passage rallies individuals' sense of American attachment by defining its special place in the world order.

Significantly, subgroup and culture wars identities are not connected to the idea of America having a blessed or sacred status. Of the twenty-six subgroup identity passages, only one makes a link between a specific religious identity and America as a blessed nation,[18] suggesting that, consistent with the civil religion thesis, specific religious subgroups are not typically linked to the status of America in the world order. In addition, subgroup identity actually has a negative association with the use of first-person plural pronouns, indicating that when referencing religious subgroups candidates generally did not need to make use of ambiguous pronouns to engender cohesiveness with the audience.[19] The strategic value of subgroup references lies elsewhere than in eliciting broad-based identity-laden considerations.

Likewise, culture wars rhetoric has a negative relationship with the characterization of America as blessed. This pattern makes sense. The assertion of either a progressive or orthodox identity relies on the existence of a competing group, battling (in the words of Pat Buchanan) for the "soul of America" (August 17, 1992, Republican National Convention). The status of America is thus not yet decided—should the "other side" win, the United States would cease to have any sort of divine relationship with the Creator, instead existing as a source of moral degradation in the world order. Unlike civil religion rhetoric, which gains its persuasive appeal from the assertion of the positive distinctiveness among all Americans, culture wars rhetoric gains its appeal through the definition of quasi-religious outgroups.[20]

Inclusion, Exclusion, and Religious Political Rhetoric

Above and beyond questions of persuasive appeal, each of these identity-laden rhetorical strategies has distinct consequences for defining the contours of the American political community. I first address this question by examining shared versus pluralistic conceptions of American religion, to see if candidates (either explicitly or implicitly) recognized more than one set of basic religious values. Figure 3.3 shows the percentage of shared

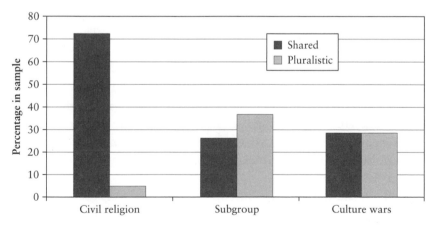

FIGURE 3.3 Pluralistic and shared religious rhetoric, by identity cue

Percentage of religious passages coded as shared or pluralistic, sorted by the type of identity invoked in the passage. Percentages do not add up to 100 percent because some passages could not be classified as shared or pluralistic. Rhetorical differences in subgroup and civil religion appeals are significant at p < .001. For details, see the online appendix, http://facstaff.uww.edu/ chappc/.

versus pluralistic religious statements classifiable into one of the three identity genres. As the graph illustrates, references to a shared religiosity were overwhelmingly used to cue a civil religion identity, whereas pluralistic statements were much more likely to reference culture wars and subgroup identities.[21]

Figure 3.3 has several important implications for the study of American religious identity. First, it is notable that when candidates made reference to civil religion identity, they normally did so in a way that attempted to build spiritual cohesion. On the surface, there is nothing exclusionary about American civil religion—rhetorically, membership is open to and shared by all. For students of church-state separation, this finding may be something of a mixed bag. Although it is certainly noteworthy that all are welcomed into a distinct vision of American religious identity, it is an open question whether this comes at a cost. Does this shared identity wash away aspects of religious uniqueness, and does it disproportionately ask members of different faiths to sacrifice different things? In other words, asserting a shared identity could potentially alienate if, instead of acting as a true religious melting pot, civil religion privileges certain ingredients in the stew. As a point of illustration, consider Bush's 2000 argument that "That's the greatness of this nation— we're all Americans, we all live in the greatest land that God has put on the face of the Earth: One nation, indivisible, under God" (October 30, 2000, Bosque Farms, New Mexico, CNN transcript). This passage is emblematic of civil religion identity rhetoric, employing the rhetorical elements identified by both Billig (2003) and Bellah (1967). Bush uses "all Americans" and "we" to build a sense of shared identity with the audience and grants America the status of "greatness" in the eyes of God. At the same time, this passage and other passages like it presuppose a particular conception of faith that is potentially alienating—a nominal nonsectarianism that, nevertheless, implies a particular religious worldview (Feldman 2005, 185).

As figure 3.3 illustrates, subgroup rhetoric rarely makes reference to a shared faith. This is consequential because it indicates that candidates for national office generally did not assert that the teachings of a specific tradition speak for the rest. In other words, it is highly uncommon to hear major party candidates for national office suggest something on the order of "this is a Christian nation." Rather, subgroup identities are typically invoked in the spirit of religious pluralism, and they recognize the coexistence of multiple faith traditions in America. Religious groups were mentioned in speeches as part of a long list of faith traditions, but the emphasis was on the ability to worship differently—not on what these traditions have in common. For example, in 2004 Bush frequently noted that "if you choose to worship an Almighty God, you're equally American if you're Jewish, Christian, Muslim, Hindu. It's the great tradition of America. And it's the tradition that must be maintained" (August 28, 2004, Lima, Ohio, FDCH Political Transcripts). Although the statement reminded individuals of their own religious identities, the message here was ultimately that all faiths can worship as they choose, or not worship at all. In a similar vein, Bill Clinton in 1992 invoked his own religious faith while at the same time endorsing the freedom to not worship at all, saying "As the great American Baptist, Roger Williams, understood so well, without the freedom to say no, the word yes is meaningless" (September 11, 1992, University of Notre Dame, Annenberg/Pew Archive of Presidential Campaign Discourse). Rather than using sectarian rhetoric to endorse a particular religious world-view, candidates thus appear to have referenced denominations (and other subgroups) to promote the inclusion of potentially marginalized groups.

Culture wars references are evenly split between shared and pluralistic concepts of American faith. These results, however, should be interpreted with caution. Unlike subgroup references, culture wars rhetoric rarely concedes the legitimacy of multiple faith traditions, and unlike civil religion rhetoric, culture wars rhetoric rarely paints a picture of spiritual cohesion. Instead, as figure 3.4 illustrates, culture wars identities are generally coupled with the recognition of some sort of a moral crisis. Whereas subgroup references acknowledge multiple faith traditions to champion religious pluralism, culture wars rhetoric sees pluralism as a moral crisis. As Reagan phrased it in his 1980 nomination acceptance speech, "The major issue of this campaign is the direct political, personal, and moral responsibility of Democratic party leadership in the White House and in Congress for this unprecedented calamity which has befallen us" (July 17, 1980, Republican National Convention, Annenberg/Pew Archive of Presidential Campaign Discourse). In this passage, Reagan asserts that the Democratic Party has a distinctly different moral vision for the country and that this vision has led to ruin.

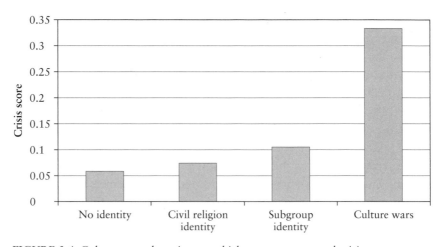

FIGURE 3.4 Culture wars rhetoric as a vehicle to convey a moral crisis

Average level of moral crisis across three identity types (as well as religious rhetoric with no identity reference at all). Differences significant at p < .001. For details, see the online appendix, http://facstaff.uww.edu/chappc/.

The Limits of Civil Religion Identity and Political Inclusion

The language of civil religion identity does much to engender a sense of a shared and cohesive religious community that permeates American politics. The evidence also suggests, however, that civil religion rhetoric may impart a sense of alienation to the message recipients. Clearly, any suggestion that God is connected to American national identity is potentially a problematic source of exclusion for atheists and agnostics, a finding that has been echoed in other research (Wimberley and Christenson 1981). Moreover, references to God could even make staunch churchgoers uncomfortable if the image of God that is conveyed is at odds with their own religious tradition. In other words, if the God of American civil religion chooses sides with certain religious traditions or ideologies, civil religion could actually be a source of political alienation.

The evidence indicates civil religion identity does seem to rhetorically privilege particular conceptions of God—that of "paternal" and that of "provider."[22] Consistent with expectations, there is an element of exclusivity to civil religion rhetoric across campaigns, insofar as the definition of a shared spiritual community is rhetorically linked to a particular image of God. This is significant because varied concepts of God have strong denominational (Froese and Bader 2010), gender (Noffke and McFadden 2001), religious-commitment (Hammersla, Andrews-Qualls, and Frease 1986), and ideological (Lakoff 1996; Froese and Bader 2010) correlates in the mass public. In particular, "paternal" and "provider" concepts are generally more consistent with an evangelical and conservative understanding of God. The "maternal" and "companion" concepts of God—a closer fit with a liberal political orientation—are extremely rare in the sample as a whole and are even less common in civil religion passages.

Inclusive and Alienating?

In political campaigns, religious rhetoric is closely intertwined with the language of identity. Candidates make religious appeals, not to forward a particular issue agenda but, rather, to form a common social bond with prospective voters. Given the unique religious history of America as a multidenominational society with a deep religious heritage, religious rhetoric is particularly adept at forwarding the three types of group identities: specific subgroup identity, civil religion identity, and cultural in-group identity codified around opposition to an outgroup.

Of these, the language of civil religion identity is by far the most common. Candidates regularly made reference to a civil religion that is shared by all Americans. Ultimately, the rhetorical expression of this identity might have produced a mixed response in the public—and also gained a mixed response from those concerned with the maintenance of healthy democratic institutions. On one hand, in asserting a shared civil religion identity, candidates were *not* asserting something that would be much more corrosive—that American is or ought to be solely concerned with upholding a particular religious tradition. Indeed, when candidates did invoke religious subgroups, they typically did so in the spirit of religious pluralism, by explicitly saying that all faiths (or no faith at all) are welcome in America. Thus, insofar as a civil religion identity truly represents a transcendent form of religious expression, it seems to be laying the foundation for social cohesion and a spirit of religious inclusivity.

Nevertheless, the evidence suggests that this is not the complete story regarding civil religion identity. Although the genre makes claims about a shared American religion, there is often an element of exclusivity not far beneath the surface. Candidates using the language of civil religion identity typically did so with a very particular image of God—as a "paternal provider"—in mind. Thus, the rhetorical expression of American identity is often exclusive and particular when expressed in religious terms (see also Marty 1987, 81–82).

Most religious rhetoric thus asserts that all Americans are included in a shared tapestry of American spirituality, even though exclusion may be implicit in much of this rhetoric. And what appears inclusive to some might feel exclusive to others. Two arguments clarify this point. First, despite evidence of the rhetorical prominence of an American civil religion, this view is not without dissent. Sociologists of religion and theologians have noted (and sometimes lamented) the degree to which the rhetoric of civil religion has mangled the distinctive aspects of religious faith traditions (for discussion, see Prothero 2007). In other words, in an effort to be nonsectarian, civil religion rhetoric may ultimately alienate devoted members of religious faith communities. Second, what claims to be nonsectarian is hardly ever so. Stephen Prothero (2007) notes the evolution from America as a Protestant nation (excluding Catholics) to America as a Christian nation (excluding Jews) to a Judeo-Christian nation (excluding Muslims, Buddhists, Hindus, and other less common traditions). Moreover, there has been some reference to the emergence of an even more inclusive "Abrahamic" or Judeo-Christian-Islamic America following 9/11 (Prothero 2007, 116). Although the trend is certainly toward inclusivity in a certain sense, it is also noteworthy that what has been claimed to be a shared American religion has always excluded individuals of certain faiths and, of course, individuals who identify with no religious tradition at all.

4

RELIGIOUS RHETORIC AND THE POLITICS OF EMOTIVE APPEALS

I'm going to fight for my cause every day as your President. I'm going to fight to make sure every American has every reason to thank God, as I thank Him: that I'm an American, a proud citizen of the greatest country on earth, and with hard work, strong faith and a little courage, great things are always within our reach.

—Senator John McCain, 2008

From Puritan jeremiads to the Bryan's populist invocations, one defining feature of religious rhetoric is its strong emotive language. But we know very little about how its use varies to suit different political demands and what the consequences of emotive religious rhetoric are on the nature of American political culture. For example, many have expressed concern that the rhetoric of a religious culture war is polluting American political discourse (Hunter 1991; Evans and Nunn 2005). To the extent that religious rhetoric is infused with the language of anger, anxiety, and hostility, it provides the possibility for a contagion effect on the mass public. At the same time, the language of American civil religion is often characterized by its glowing optimism about the future of America democracy and the place of America in the world order. Given this, it is certainly possible that religious rhetoric is more conducive to a spirit hope than to political division and exclusion.

Religious rhetoric thus lends itself to varied emotive tones, and these varied tones are clearly consequential. Given this, it is surprising that we have little systematic evidence on how emotive language is actually used in practice. The John McCain passage quoted here serves as an excellent example. The word "fight," conveys the sense that a confrontation is imminent and that the stakes are high. McCain is not fighting for a particular policy stance but, rather, for something much more fundamental—a "reason to thank God." This emotive tenor—pairing "thank God" with "fight"—is, of course, not the only option available to presidents. Both

John Kerry and George H. W. Bush regularly linked the phrase "thank God" with words such as "prosperity" and "love," signaling an intense optimism. In 1996, Bill Clinton often used the phrase "thank God" when speaking of international and domestic crises to adopt a tone of somber reverence. Religious political rhetoric readily lends itself to emotive displays and gives candidates a good deal of flexibility with respect to the affective punch of the message.

As these examples indicate, there is tremendous variety in the emotive pitch of religious rhetoric. In this chapter, I am concerned with understanding this variation. Just as the nature of identity cues informed our understanding of who is included in the rhetorical expressions of America's spiritual identity, so too can an examination of emotive cues tell us a good deal about the tone and tenor of American political discourse. Although I find that the overwhelming norm surrounding religious rhetoric is positive affect, a deeper look at the evidence suggests that the emotive thrust of a candidates' rhetoric is incredibly nuanced. Candidates adopt different emotive styles to resonate with the identities of the audience members and to accommodate existing partisan patterns of voting behavior.

RELIGION, EMOTION, AND POLITICS

Understanding emotion is of central importance to understanding the nature of religious experience, and this connection is particularly important to understanding religiosity in the American case. Psychologists have long noted a relationship between religion and emotion. William James, in *The Varieties of Religious Experience* (1902), famously theorized that "religious sentiments" were inseparable from everyday emotional experience. Contemporary psychology follows suit in affirming the centrality of emotion to religious experience. As Peter Hill and Ralph Hood conclude, "a complete analysis of religion and religiousness must necessarily involve psychological concerns, not the least of which will include both affective and unconscious processes" (1999, 1039).

The emotional impulse in American religion stems from a revivalist tradition heavily indebted to emotive rhetoric and to the related jeremiad tradition that has been fully integrated into American culture (Bercovitch 1978; Murphy 2009). Indeed, Stephen Prothero argues that the current fault lines in American Christianity can generally be understood in terms of the relative "emotionality" of adherents' faith experiences, with the religious landscape being composed of doctrinally oriented "confessionalists," emotionally oriented "experientialists," and ethically oriented "moralists." Some combination of emotion and morality, Prothero argues, tends to dominate the current religious landscape (2007, 119–20). Thus, whereas psychologists have argued that religious experience is inseparable from emotion, religious historians have provided evidence that this connection is exemplified in the case of American faith traditions.

Just as emotions are intertwined with religion, so too are emotions central to understanding political life. This observation is not a recent one. The U.S. Constitution was designed (or at least defended) out of a concern that "The *passions*, not the *reason* of the public would sit in judgment" (Madison 1788b). Similarly, Walter Lippmann (1922) famously lamented that emotion-based judgment would be the demise of democratic polities. For many years, the assumption was that emotions were inimical to effective democratic governance, despite the fact that they were fundamental facets of the human condition. In contrast to Madison and Lippmann, more recent research has substantially revised this understanding of emotions, arguing that "emotion and reason interact to produce a thoughtful and attentive citizenry" (Marcus, Neuman, and MacKuen 2000, 1). In Marcus, Neuman, and MacKuen's formulation, emotions can help individuals economize political decision making, directing attention toward threatening stimuli while influencing, when appropriate, a reliance on existing predispositions. Emotions are central to democratic life and can actually play an important and helpful role in helping individuals sort through the "blooming, buzzing confusion" of politics in a sensible manner (Lippmann, 1922, 81).

Political psychologists generally focus their attention on individuals' emotional experiences and not on the rhetorical cues that bring about these emotions in the first place.[1] Emotions are "specific sets of physiological and mental dispositions triggered by the brain in response to the perceived significance of the situation or object for an individual's goals" (Brader 2006, 51; see also Russell 2003). As such, emotions are something that exist within the individual. Language can induce or express emotions, but language use per se cannot be emotional in the same sense as an individual is emotional. Anton Marty (1908), a German linguist, has made the distinction explicit between language use and individuals' emotional states, distinguishing between "emotive communication" and "emotional communication."[2] Whereas emotional communication is a spontaneous overflowing of emotions for principally cathartic purposes, emotive communication is a "strategic signaling of affective information in speech and writing . . . in order to influence partners' interpretations of situations and reach different goals" (Caffi and Janney 1994, 328). Emotive communication is thus self-presentation with no necessary relationship to the speaker's own emotional state. Its aims are ultimately persuasive.

This distinction is critical because it suggests we need to carefully distinguish the characteristics of a message from the emotional state of an audience and a speaker. When scholars use terms such as *emotional appeals* (Rosselli, Skelly, and Mackie 1995; Brader 2006), they are typically referring to the expected emotional inducement of a particular stimuli, even though this term often confounds the fact that the qualities or characteristics of the message itself are distinct from the individual's response to that message. Indeed, because individuals can have different emotional responses to political messages, it makes sense to clearly separate message characteristics from individual emotions.

This confusion has led to an emphasis on the consequences of emotions, not their triggers. Most research studying politics and emotion, although often highly realistic, is done in a laboratory setting with little examination of the actual frequency of emotion-inducing messages in real-world campaigns. Moreover, once an emotion is successfully induced through experimental stimuli, the content of the political stimuli is reduced to secondary importance. As Jack Glaser and Peter Salovey summarize, "Although we have seen no shortage of investigations of the role of affect in social judgment, some even bearing, however indirectly, on the influence of target affect, the vast majority of research and theory has focused on the moods or emotions of the person making the judgment . . . investigating how the affective behavior of targets of judgments influences those judgments may prove crucial" (1998, 167).

Most of the available evidence suggests that emotions are incredibly important to politics, although we know very little about what induces these emotions in the first place. And, as we have already seen, religious rhetoric is often distinguished by its unique emotive content. It thus makes sense to turn to religious rhetoric to look for the origins of this important psychological process. Understanding these dynamics is important for several reasons. First, as already suggested, the emotive character of religious rhetoric may have distinct consequences in terms of how individuals ultimately make political decisions. Second, in more general terms, the emotive characteristics of religious rhetoric should tell an important story about the treatment of religion by candidates for elected office. Is religious rhetoric crafted so as to goad people into a culture war or to bring about optimism about the future? This question also raises larger questions of political representation. Given the ability of enthusiasm, anger, and anxiety to make religious electoral cleavages salient, the coupling of emotion with religion could create challenges to governing in a cohesive manner.

THEORIZING THE ROLE OF EMOTIVE RELIGIOUS RHETORIC IN CONTEMPORARY CAMPAIGNS

Given what we have already learned about the nature of religious rhetoric, its emotive content is expected to exhibit several key characteristics. First, as previously discussed, religious rhetoric is expected to be readily distinguishable from other types of political speech. Moreover, the jeremiad tradition (discussed in chap. 2) suggests that there is room in religious rhetoric for it to manifest both positive and negative emotive characteristics (Murphy 2009). On the one hand, emotive religious rhetoric may call to mind "fire and brimstone" lamentations, such as Jonathan Edwards's (1741) depiction of sinful humanity as a spider dangling over a fire by a single strand of web. This image suggests negative emotive characteristics, such as fear, threat, and anxiety. This same sort of negative language is instantiated in the "threats" identified by political pundits and politicians, such as "Godless communism" in the 1980s or "homosexuality" in the 1990s (an emotive impulse bearing some degree of similarity to culture wars theorizations).

On the other hand, there is evidence to suggest that American spirituality is moving away from images of sin and depravity, and has come "to dwell on a lighter, more pleasurable plane, one on which good feelings [are] augmented and good spiritual times encountered without a haunting sense of sin and disgrace" (Albanese 2001, 181). In addition, whereas more polarized figures such as Pat Robertson may benefit, in some sense, from blaming the Hurricane Katrina disaster on godlessness, mainstream political candidates do not have an incentive to rely heavily on negative images. Indeed, some evidence suggests that audiences tend to adopt the emotions conveyed by speakers (Salovey and Birnbaum 1989; Bower 1991)—a transfer of affect from the speaker to the message recipient

(Ladd and Lenz 2008). In this case, using positive emotive characteristics in religious rhetoric makes strategic sense; if candidates choose to employ a genre that is inherently emotion inducing, it makes sense to do so in such a way that it triggers the recall of positive memories. Thus, it is likely that religious political rhetoric will be more apt to exhibit positive emotive characteristics than does other political speech and less likely to exhibit negative emotive characteristics.

This expectation does not, of course, preclude that possibility that candidates do, at times, use religion to induce negative emotions. Indeed, the findings in chapter 3 serve as evidence that different forms of religious rhetoric are tailored to specific electoral purposes. Given this, we can expect that negative religious rhetoric should be used almost exclusively to forward a vision of a cultural war, whereas positive and optimistic rhetoric should be coupled with American civil religion identity. Consistent with the notion that the purpose of civil religion is to build a sense of positive distinctiveness across a wide range of message recipients, this rhetorical style should be principally concerned with presenting a spiritualized version of American identity by optimistically arguing that the nation has a special role to play in the world order.

Culture wars theorists, of course, do not just argue that the rhetoric of a culture war is uniquely distinguishable. The argument—and concern—is that this rhetorical style is growing and that this has negative consequences on healthy political discourse. Specifically, culture wars theorists argue that there has been a growing polarization between the progressive and orthodox factions, with 1992 being a critical election year in drawing this line in the sand (Bolce and De Maio 1999). Given that culture wars are typically understood to be an elite-driven phenomenon, one sensible hypothesis is that the religious rhetoric used by presidential candidates has been growing steadily more hostile. Thus, it is important to test whether religious rhetoric has grown significantly negative over time. Moreover, it is important to know what the precise emotive composition of culture wars rhetoric is. If culture wars rhetoric uses negativity to convey anger and hostility, it may signal to religious factions a need to dig in their heels and prepare for battle (DeSteno, Dasgupta, et al. 2004). In contrast, if culture wars rhetoric tends to be more anxious in character, it may ultimately persuade people to reconsider their political options and seek more information about candidates (Brader 2006). The conclusions we draw about a culture wars statement ought to be informed by its exact emotive construction in the public sphere.

Finally, all of this so far has been painted with a rather broad brush, not taking stock of the fact that, in the time period under scrutiny (1980–2008), the Republican Party has enjoyed a considerable edge among religious voters. Indeed, research indicates that voters are more likely to see religious people and Evangelicals as being mainly Republicans, indicating that, for many, religious groups have a clear partisan profile (Campbell, Green, and Layman 2011). Because an association exists between party and religiosity, I expect this alignment to be related to strategic rhetorical choices. And because this association exists in the minds of voters, strategic actors will take advantage of it. Republican candidates have an incentive to use language that will facilitate a reliance on existing predispositions and group-based associations, and Democratic candidates should strive to create distance from voters' religion-based standing decisions. Thus, we can expect that Republican candidates should score higher on measures of positively valenced emotions because they are thought to increase a reliance on habitual and group-based decision making and that Democratic candidates should use more anxiety and sadness to de-emphasize existing religious associations. Specifically, because anxiety can signal uncertainty and a need to further explore options, anxious religious rhetoric may be Democrats' best option to persuade voters that the strong association between religion and party is an erroneous one.

THE EMOTIVE CHARACTER OF RELIGIOUS RHETORIC

These expectations are informed in part by the assumption that there is a relationship between the emotive character of religious rhetoric and the emotions of the people who hear these messages—the voters. This assumption should not be controversial. Volumes of psychological research have used language (and other message characteristics such as music, pitch, and facial expressions) to induce emotions in research participants. In short, it is possible to craft speech so as to bring about emotions—psychologists and candidates alike engage in this regularly.

What is less clear is how to measure a message according to the likely emotional effect it will have on audience members. Ultimately, to make a claim about the emotive character of religious rhetoric, any measure of emotive character ought to bear a relationship with the emotions it induces in message recipients. No tools exist to determine expected emotional inducement; however, several content analysis computer programs have been developed to assess the emotional state of the message source. These tools have been widely applied in a number of contexts. For example, James Pennebaker's Linguistic Inquiry and Word Count (LIWC) (Pennebaker, Francis, and Booth 2001) software was initially designed to analyze emotional writing (Rude, Gortner, and Pennebaker 2004). Since its development, however, LIWC has also been used to analyze a number of political phenomena. For example, LIWC has been used to track the psychological state of presidential candidates, finding that John Kerry used many more negatively valenced words than his running mate, John Edwards (Pennebaker, Slatcher, and Chung, 2005).[3] Likewise, Whissell's Dictionary of Affect in Language (WDAL) is a computerized content analysis tool used for assessing the emotions of speakers (Duhamel and Whissell 1998; Whissell 1994). Like LIWC, WDAL has been used to assess the emotions of political figures. For example, Cynthia Whissell and Lee Sigelman (2001) find that "power language" (which is language characterized, in part, by positive affect words) in presidential speech has increased with the advent of television.[4]

Content analysis software is thus a reliable tool to draw speaker personality inferences—at least when the text being analyzed represents the speaker's own mental disposition (and not that of speechwriters). In addition, there are several reasons why these programs should be good tools to determine the mood induced by public utterances. Theories of emotional contagion hold that when a speaker expresses an emotion, a corresponding emotion can be induced in the message recipient—speakers and audiences essentially converge emotionally (Hatfield, Cacioppo, and Rapson 1994, 153–54).[5] These effects should be particularly strong in the case of political speech, when the speakers are experienced at conveying mood and the messages are crafted to do so. In fact, given that campaign rhetoric is often crafted to bring about specific emotional effects, LIWC and WDAL may be more effective tools for determining induced mood than the genuine emotional state of the speaker.[6]

Both LIWC and WDAL are essentially word count programs that contain large dictionaries of "emotional words." In both cases, words were rigorously scored by teams of coders for their emotional character.[7] Although each program computes emotion scores in a slightly different manner, in both the logic is essentially the same. Scores are computed by counting the number of emotion words in a particular speech or text, and dividing by the total number of words in that text. Because these tools were not designed with the aforementioned expectations in mind, there is some disconnect between the measures included in the software and the actual emotional constructs detailed in my hypotheses. For example, neither WDAL nor LIWC contains a direct measure of enthusiasm—an emotion that is theorized to be quite important politically. To address this, I examined the data across all available measures, aiming to arrive at robust conclusions across both computer programs. This also provided an important cross-validation between the two measurement tools.[8]

THE EMOTIVE APPEAL OF RELIGIOUS RHETORIC

Although the findings in chapter 2 suggest that the appeal of religious rhetoric in politics has been derived historically from its emotive character, in a sense all political rhetoric could be thought of as emotionally evocative. It follows that to develop a better sense of the role of religious rhetoric in elections, we need to first ask what makes religious rhetoric stand apart. Understanding the unique emotive distinctions that characterize religious appeals in presidential campaigns provides substantial insights into how religion shapes electoral politics and American political culture in general.

Religious Rhetoric and Secular Campaign Speech

As a first look at the emotive content of religious rhetoric, let us examine LIWC and WDAL emotion scores for our sample, comparing the average for all candidates' speeches with the average for all passages using explicitly religious language. If emotive language is as closely intertwined with religious rhetoric as theory suggests, the religious rhetoric sample should distinguish itself along emotive lines. Consistent with these predictions, religious campaign rhetoric tends to be overwhelmingly positive, providing candidates with a vehicle to deliver optimistic messages to the electorate. As figure 4.1 illustrates, religious rhetoric scores are higher for all positive emotive cues and lower for all negative emotive cues compared with campaign speech in general. These differences are relatively large in magnitude, and statistically significant ($p < .05$) for eight of the eleven measures examined. Thus, although this approach glosses over some of the differences between discrete emotive cues, it is safe to conclude that voters hearing rhetoric steeped in religious language hear something much more positive than they do in typical campaign rhetoric.

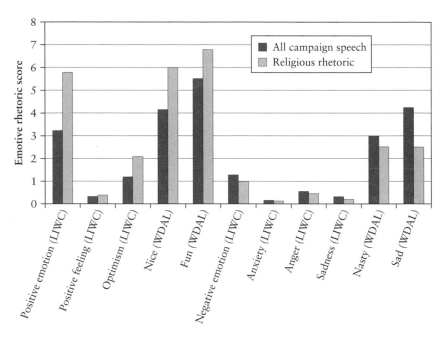

FIGURE 4.1 Emotive appeals in religious rhetoric and secular campaign speech

Comparison of religious and secular campaign speech on all available measures of emotive language. Across all variables, religious rhetoric tends to be more positive and less negative than secular campaign speech. All differences significant at p < .05, except "positive feeling," "anxiety," and "anger." LIWC, Linguistic Inquiry and Word Count; WDAL, Whissell's Dictionary of Affect in Language

The magnitude of these differences itself requires some examination because it is not at all obvious how a passage with a score of 3.1 (the mean "positive emotion" score across all speeches) is substantively different from a passage with a score of 5.41 (the mean "positive emotion" score in the religious rhetoric sample). To illustrate what figure 4.1 means in practice, I examine next two passages emblematic of typical emotive content. Consider first Reagan's comment in 1984 that:

> We must do more than talk about these values; we must restore them and protect them against challenge. And we must use our resources in and out of government to allow our historic values to enrich the lives of all who follow us—allowing our faith to be heard and to be felt, infusing our schools with the finest of quality, giving law enforcement all the tools they need to fight crime and drugs, and never limiting the opportunities for any American. All those

belong to the future that we will build. And we didn't come all this way as a nation without such values, and we can't step into tomorrow without the continued strength and moral stamina they give us (September 3, 1984, Fountain Valley, California, Annenberg/Pew Archive of Presidential Campaign Discourse).

LIWC scores this passage at 4.92 on "positive emotion" and 0.82 on "negative emotion," which is approximately the positive and negative emotive average for our sample of religious rhetoric. Although the word "fight" is recognized by LIWC as a "negative emotion" and "anger" word, the overwhelming thrust of the passage conveys a sense of positive emotion. Not only are some religious words, such as "faith," used in a very positive sense but words such as "quality," "tools," and "future" convey a message of hope. In contrast, consider the following passage from McCain's 2008 stump speech, which approximates the average positive and negative emotion for campaign rhetoric in general:

So I need to make health care—that is obviously your key and prime concern right now for you—available and affordable, and I'm willing to have the federal government step in and help. But second of all, because these people with chronic illnesses or preexisting conditions cannot get it, we will have government-approved plans that provide them for it. We will create jobs, and we will help small businesses by keeping their taxes low. (October 2, 2008, Denver, Colorado, Federal News Service).

This passage is noticeably less optimistic than the Reagan passage, and although it is not a political attack, it also contains more cues that might induce negative emotions. While phrases such as "affordable" and "create" may certainly induce positive emotions in the audience, the passage is considerably more sedate than the Regan passage, a distinction that is captured by the LIWC scores (LIWC gives the passage a positive emotion score of 2.6). In addition, the passage contains more negative emotion words than would be typical in a religious passage (LIWC gives the passage a negative emotion score of 1.3). Words such as "concern" and "illnesses," although not at all unusual in political speech in general, would be out of place in religious rhetoric. To summarize, the contrast in emotive tone between these two passages is quite striking and suggests that the magnitude of the difference between a typical religious passage and typical general campaign speech is substantively important. These passages illustrate that the significant differences illustrated in figure 4.1 are also substantively consequential in terms of the overall tone conveyed by a candidate, suggesting that religious rhetoric may ultimately have a different emotional effect on voters than campaign rhetoric generally.

The genre of religious campaign rhetoric thus tends to be much more positive than typical campaign speech. Although there are significant exceptions to this generalization (as we see in the remainder of this chapter), it is safe to conclude that, on balance, when candidates invoke religion, they do so to make voters enthusiastic and happy, not angry or fearful. This finding comports with Marcus, Neuman, and MacKuen's (2000) work on emotions, which finds that enthusiasm tends to be highly effective at mobilizing core supporters. Insofar as the vast majority of voters report some type of religious adherence, it makes sense for candidates to adopt strategies that are psychologically compatible with mobilizing this adherence.

Civil Religion Identity and the Question of a Culture War

Although positive emotive communication clearly exceeds the negative in religious campaign rhetoric, there is also good reason to expect this changes depending on the type of identity being cued in the passage. In particular, we expect the language of American civil religion to be glowingly optimistic and culture wars rhetoric to excel in inducing negative emotions. The results of this study bear out this prediction, with an interesting twist—culture wars rhetoric is best characterized by its anxiety-laden character, not by its anger.

Figure 4.2 displays the levels of positive and negative emotive cues in religious rhetoric, sorted by civil religion, subgroup, and culture wars rhetoric. As figure 4.2 illustrates, civil religion appeals tend to paint a remarkably positive picture of a shared religious ethos. For example, Obama frequently remarked that "I believed that Democrats and Republicans and Americans of every political stripe were hungry for new ideas, new leadership, and a new kind of politics—one that favors common sense over ideology; one that focuses on those values and ideals we hold in common as Americans."(November 3, 2008, Jacksonville, FL, Federal News Service) This statement is typical of the emotive thrust of civil religion appeals across the sample. A nonspecific version of American spirituality ("values") is held to be something that is common to all Americans ("Republicans and Democrats") and is defined in positive terms ("common sense," "ideals," and "newness").

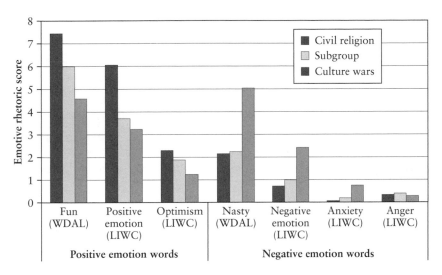

FIGURE 4.2 Emotive appeals by identity type

How emotive rhetoric is paired with different religious identities. The language of American civil religion stands out as a particularly positive emotive genre. Although culture wars rhetoric is considerably more negative, this negativity is defined by its anxiety-arousing elements, not anger. An ANOVA indicates that between-identity variance is significant at p < .05 for every emotion variable except anger. LIWC, Linguistic Inquiry and Word Count; WDAL, Whissell's Dictionary of Affect in Language

Culture wars rhetoric is nearly the polar opposite of civil religion rhetoric. Culture wars rhetoric tends to be considerably more negative than either its civil religion or subgroup counterparts. This negativity is overwhelmingly anxious, not angry. In identifying cultural and religious schisms, candidates tend frame the argument in terms of fear and uncertainty about the future, not acrimonious outrage. The rhetoric of the culture war is not so much an angry call to arms as the identification of some sort of corrosive element within American political culture. For example, in an illustrative passage in 1988 George H. W. Bush located the "unreasonableness" with "intellectuals" who were trying to squelch "legitimate rights": "I do not recoil in horror from the idea of a child saying a prayer in a school. I support a moment of voluntary prayer or silent prayer. I know this is a difficult issue for some people. But the intellectuals have, in my friend Bill Bennett's phrase, "fastidious disdain" for public expressions of religious sentiment that is, to my mind, unreasonable and ungenerous. The overwhelming majority of the people feel a moment of silence or silent prayer is a legitimate right" (September 27, 1988, Columbus, Ohio,

Annenberg/Pew Archive of Presidential Campaign Discourse). Bush's tone here is negative, but it is not angry.[9] Rather, his point is to raise doubts about another group of people who represent a challenge to a supposedly cherished right—individuals should be afraid about what might be coming if the other party gains power. As Brader (2006) observes, this type of appeal gains its power by "stimulating attentiveness" on threatening political cues. The power of the culture wars rhetoric thus comes from engendering fear of some political outgroup, not in conveying anger per se.

There is a good deal of academic debate over whether a culture war (or some form of opinion polarization) exists at all, how best to conceptualize it, and whether it has been increasing over time (Wolfe 1998; Abramowitz and Saunders 2005; Evans and Nunn 2005; Fiorina, Abrams, and Pope 2010). Although my aim in this book is not to address the degree of polarization in the American public, given that many culture wars theories rely on some transmission of cultural tension from political elites to the rank and file, the data in this chapter provide an interesting test of whether elite rhetoric has been becoming more provocative. Accordingly, I also examined the frequency in religious rhetoric of outgroup references, culture wars references, negative emotion, and anxiety, as they have appeared from 1980 to 2008.[10]

The evidence indicates that there is a substantial amount of variation in the extent to which candidates employ these rhetorical elements; nevertheless, there is virtually no evidence of an increase in the hostility of religious rhetoric or in the extent to which religious rhetoric has been used to call attention to cultural others. In addition, there is no evidence of a spike in 1992, which is often put forth as a critical year in hastening the growth of an orthodox-progressive divide in the public (Bolce and De Maio 1999).

Although there has been no steady increase in culture wars rhetoric over time, the use of culture wars and negative religious rhetoric does appear to follow a pattern. Specifically, a candidate's decision to use negative religious rhetoric depended in large part on what his or her opponent was saying. For three of the four indicators I examined (culture wars rhetoric, outgroup references, and negativity), the candidates' rhetoric scores during a political campaign varied in tandem.[11] That is, neither Obama nor McCain spent much time referencing outgroups in 2008, but Mondale and Reagan both did in 1984. In other words, culture wars rhetoric begets more culture wars rhetoric.

It is impossible to know whether these culture wars references represent the candidates' calculated responses to one another or whether they are spurious, with the candidates both responding to some exogenous political event that is prominent in a given year. In all likelihood, some combination of factors explains the prominence or absence of a culture wars–driven campaign. For example, much of the negative outgroup rhetoric in 1984 involved attacks and counterattacks over a proposed school prayer amendment. Neither candidate originated this debate—it had been raging long before the 1984 campaign. Each made the choice, however, to integrate the issue into his campaign and to frame the issue in a manner consistent with the notion of a culture war.

Thus, all the evidence in this study indicates that the rhetoric of a culture war has not been on the rise since 1980. It is necessary to add one significant caveat. The present study examines the rhetoric only of the major party presidential candidates and only the rhetoric framed in expressly religious terms. Accordingly, these data miss much of the abortion debate, for example, which is often framed in secular terms by unelected political elites. What can be said with certainty, however, is that presidential candidates are not leading the charge in polarizing mass opinion through the use of religious rhetoric.

Religious Rhetoric and Partisan Differences

Thus far, the evidence is clear that religious rhetoric defines itself through a remarkably positive tone and that this tone is particularly evident in civil religion rhetoric. Nevertheless, although candidates' using positive language makes sense, especially in a country marked by high rates of religious adherence, positive emotion is only one part of the story. A second part of this story involves the extent to which the emotive character of religious rhetoric interacts with standing party affiliations. The Republican Party has enjoyed a long-standing advantage among more religious voters, whether we conceive of religiosity as "religious commitment," "orthodoxy," or "church attenders" (Layman 2001; Olson and Green 2006). Given this, we expect that Republicans should embrace a different emotive tone in their religious appeals, specifically adopting a more positive and optimistic tone. This is consistent with psychological theories of emotion and politics, and it also makes intuitive sense. When Republicans reach out to religious voters, their main aim is to drum up a higher voter turnout by encouraging a decision calculus consistent with standing heuristic decision making. They are, in a sense, preaching to the converted, and it is sensible for them to embrace a rhetorical strategy centered around encouraging people to rely on what they already "know to be true" about religion and partisanship (see also Campbell, Green, and Layman 2011). We expect Democratic candidates, on the other hand, to be more apt to use religious language to encourage voters to think through and complicate standing links between party affiliation and religiosity. To sway the religious electorate, Democratic candidates need to convince voters that what they might presuppose about religion and partisanship is wrong. Negative rhetoric—and in particular anxiety cues—are well equipped to do this.

As figure 4.3 illustrates, candidate rhetoric in our sample generally meets these expectations. Republicans scored higher on all measures of positive emotion, and all these differences are statistically significant at $p < .05$.[12] As displayed in figure 4.3, this positivity peaked for George W. Bush and Reagan. This finding generally fits with the conventional wisdom about Bush's and Reagan's rhetorical styles, which often steeped religious descriptions of American achievement in positive emotive exuberance. As Reagan frequently said during his 1984 campaign, "if we can strengthen our economy, our security, strengthen the values that bind us, then America will become

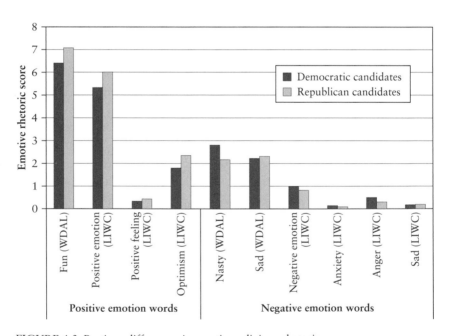

FIGURE 4.3 Partisan differences in emotive religious rhetoric

Linguistic Inquiry and Word Count (LIWC) and Whissell's Dictionary of Affect in Language (WDAL) emotion scores for presidential candidates, sorted by party affiliation. Republican candidates score higher on all positive emotion variables (left) and lower on all negative emotion variables (right). All differences are statistically significant at $p < .05$.

a nation even greater in art and learning, greater in the love and worship of the God who made us and who's blessed us as no other people on Earth have ever been blessed" (October 26, 1984, Fairfield, CT, Annenberg/Pew Archive of Presidential Campaign Discourse).

In contrast, Democratic religious rhetoric tended to be considerably more negative than that of Republicans. This is particularly interesting, given that secular speech did not follow this pattern. In fact, when we examine the secular campaign stump speeches, it is clear that Republicans tended to be the more negative party of the two, outscoring the Democrats on every single measure of negative emotion. Nevertheless, this pattern was reversed when the parties spoke to voters in religious terms.

This reversal is expected, particularly in the case of Democrats' anxious religious rhetoric. Insofar as Democrats can arouse anxiety surrounding religious issues and identities, they can create uncertainty in the minds of voters regarding the traditional association between the Republican Party and faith. Interestingly, Democratic candidates also tended to adopt an angrier tone in their religious appeals. This is somewhat surprising, given that anger is typically associated with strong group dynamics—angry people tend to dig in their heels and show resistance to opinion change.

A qualitative examination of Democratic religious rhetoric high in anger provides some guidance for interpreting these results. Angry Democratic rhetoric appears to have been of two types. First, much of the rhetoric was a direct response to the Republican monopoly on the religious vote. For example, in the 1984 campaign Mondale frequently responded to attacks from the Religious Right: "But I am alarmed by the rise of what a former Republican congressman has called "moral McCarthyism." A determined band is raising doubts about our people's faith" (September 6, 1984, Washington, DC, Annenberg/Pew Archive of Presidential Campaign Discourse). As this passage indicates, much of the angry Democratic religious rhetoric was in response to the relationship between religion and the Republican Party. This defensive posture has characterized much of the Democratic religious rhetoric from 1980 to 2004.

The second type of angry Democratic Party rhetoric was due to the party adopting a posture of moral outrage with regard to particular issues. For Clinton in 1996, it was church burnings—an issue that is obviously impossible to discuss in nonreligious terms. For Gore in 2000, it was health-care reform—insurers were frequently described as "playing God." Mondale in 1984 also employed this strategy regarding the social safety net, coupling anger-inducing rhetoric with a reference to the Republican outgroup: "If you pull their lever, you'll put their values in charge of the most vulnerable people in our nation: the elderly, the handicapped, the disadvantaged, the unemployed" (October 11, 1984, Miami, FL, Annenberg/Pew Archive of Presidential Campaign Discourse). This rhetorical strategy is interesting because it appears that Democratic candidates were trying to reframe traditionally Democratic issues—from hate crime to health care to disability—in religious terms.

Because a good deal of attention has been devoted to Obama's appeal with religious voters, it might be somewhat surprising that he did not score particularly high on optimism, anger, or anxiety—emotions that typically garner the interest of political psychologists interested in persuasion. Interestingly, Obama's religious rhetoric stood out in one category considerably less studied by psychologists and political scientists—sadness. Obama's WDAL sad score is 4.7, well above the sample average of 2.5.[13] Obama used sadness in a unique and systematic manner, comparable only with Reagan in the sample of presidential candidates. Obama lamented the possibility of an American fall from greatness while at the same time offering a message of hope for the future. Interestingly, Obama's LIWC sadness score correlates positively (and significantly) with his optimism score. In other words, a lament rarely occurred without a promise that a spiritualized version of American greatness would return.[14] For example, Obama regularly remarked: "We can build new partnerships to defeat the threats of the 21st century and restore our moral standing; that America, once again, is that last, best hope for all those who are called to the cause of freedom and who long for lives of peace and who yearn for a better future" (October 28, 2008, Harrisonburg, VA, Federal News Service). In this passage, moral standing has been lost, suggesting an America that has, in a certain sense, broken its covenant. At the same time, Obama sees a restoration of this moral standing in the future, bringing with it peace and freedom. Of all the candidates studied, Obama's emotive tone is quite remarkable—not for its positivity alone but, like the eighteenth-century jeremiad, for its positivity in the face of tribulation.

THE TENOR AND TONE OF RELIGIOUS POLITICAL RHETORIC

So far we have seen not only that candidate religious rhetoric is distinguished by its unique emotive characteristics but that candidates have used religious rhetoric in systematic and predictable ways, given their electoral goals. Religious rhetoric is, on the balance, a positive genre, marked by optimistic rhetorical flourishes about American ideals. But this general conclusion masks much of the nuance used in crafting religious messages. Candidates often pair emotive language with specific identity cues to craft messages with ramifications that crosscut cultural groups. Culture wars rhetoric, for example, is quite negative, designed to fuel existing cultural tensions. The overarching message of culture wars rhetoric is that "there is another side out there, and you should fear it." Culture wars arguments are framed specifically to suggest that a cultural or religious outgroup represents a very real threat to the ingroup's beliefs and values. In contrast, American civil religion identity rhetoric is characterized in positive terms, infusing a distinctly spiritual identity with a sense of optimism and purpose about the future. Audiences exposed to this rhetorical mode will certainly walk away with the sense that the future of America is full of promise—at least for those who find a point of common identification with the main tenets of civil religiosity.

This rhetorical mode was used in a particularly interesting manner by then-candidate Obama, who combined the optimism of American civil religion with lamentations about spiritual and moral greatness lost. Many have noted Obama's particular appeal with religious audiences, making inroads with the faithful where other Democrats have failed. Part of this, no doubt, involved Obama's comfort in quoting scripture and preaching the social gospel. Nevertheless, other Democrats have tried this rhetorical strategy with little success. For example, Kerry's 2004 stump speech regularly urged voters that "It's time to reach for that future. It's time to hear and heed the ancient proverb that should guide us today: When you pray, move your feet" (March 28, 2004, St. Louis, MO, PR Newswire Association). Despite this explicitly religious call to action, Kerry gained little notoriety for his use of religious language. What sets Obama apart from Kerry—and really every other presidential since Reagan—is his unique emotive style. Obama deftly lamented American greatness lost but combined this with a message of hope about the future in a style not unlike a Puritan jeremiad.

Although the Obama example helps make some sense of the 2008 election, there is an even more important general conclusion that should not be lost. That is, a candidate's self-presentation as religious was largely due to the emotive framing of his message. This is not to say that the candidates did not have substantive differences in their messages—they did.

However, much of what distinguished a candidate as religious appears to be the emotive tools used to carry that message. This certainly appears to be part of what distinguished Bush from Kerry in 2004; Bush's religious optimism score was dramatically higher than that of Kerry, despite the fact that both used comparable amounts of religious language.[15] Given that the defining features of a candidate's religious self-presentation may be as much emotive as issue-based, these findings raise questions about the nature of political representation and what governance should look like after candidates take office.

The strategic deployment of emotive religious rhetoric also reminds us that the rhetorical choices candidates make always occur in the context of existing partisan constraints. Overall, Republicans tended to use more positive religious rhetoric, whereas Democrats used more negative religious rhetoric—strategies that make sense, given the desires of the parties to emphasize or deemphasize the connections religiously predisposed voters are likely to draw. This suggests a self-conscious awareness on the part of candidates to use religious rhetoric to influence existing patterns of partisan voting behavior. The emotive tone connected to a reference to God or prayer is not incidental but, rather, calculated to make inroads with religious voters.

The evidence presented here does not indicate that religious political rhetoric is an inherently impassioned rhetorical form. Indeed, there is considerable variance in the emotive characteristics of candidate rhetoric. Nevertheless, religious rhetoric in recent presidential campaigns (across candidates) stands apart from other forms of campaign rhetoric with a distinctly positive emotive valence. Thus, contrary to the hopes of Madison and Lippmann, mass emotions may stem from (rather than run opposed to) elite opinion leadership. This finding should not, however, be taken as a lament about the role of emotion in democratic decision making, nor should it be taken as a criticism of how religion is rhetorically employed. As recent research (Marcus, Newman, and MacKuen 2000) has demonstrated, emotions play a measured and important role in the process of assessing and economizing political information. Consistent with this growing literature on emotions, these findings indicate that emotive religious rhetoric may play an important role in democratic decision making, signaling to voters the appropriateness of relying on their religious predispositions at times while critically engaging the political environment at others.

5

THE CONSEQUENCES OF RELIGIOUS LANGUAGE ON PRESIDENTIAL CANDIDATE EVALUATIONS

This is the source of our confidence—the knowledge that God calls on us to shape an uncertain destiny. This is the meaning of our liberty and our creed.

—President Barack Obama, 2009 Inaugural Address

In this passage, President Obama is invoking a by now familiar genre. Even in the midst of great uncertainty, America has a divinely inspired place in the world order. But when a president speaks, do Americans listen? Does invoking this creed have a special resonance with the American mass public—a strong enough pull to influence the manner in which Americans evaluate candidates and elected officials? Addressing this question not only helps us understand the place of religious rhetoric in American politics but also how campaigns influence political behavior more generally.

Political scientists have debated the extent of the influence of rhetoric on the electoral process since the advent of the modern campaign. One of the more enduring points of contention has been whether stable predispositions govern political decision making from one election to the next or whether contextual factors such as campaign advertising and political debates exert a significant and varied influence. One scholarly tradition has long claimed that news media and advertising actually exert minimal effects on individuals' attitudes (Klapper 1960). Moreover, evidence suggests that certain predispositions—partisan identification in particular—are unmoved movers that are incredibly important in determining electoral attitudes and that are resistant to persuasive forces (Campbell et al. 1960; Green, Palmquist, and Schickler 2002). These predispositions preclude the possibility of substantial campaign effects (through advertising, media coverage, etc.) because the relationship between stable attitudes and vote choice is unwavering.

On the other hand, recent research has produced, through both improved measurement (Bartels 1993) and nuanced theorization (Druckman 2005), substantial evidence that campaigns have measurable effects on citizen attitudes and electoral outcomes (Kinder 1998). In particular, evidence shows that contextual forces can prime the importance of numerous factors, including identity, on political evaluations (Transue 2007). Likewise, increased attention to the role of emotion in politics has shed light on the electoral decision calculus. For example, Brader (2006) has produced evidence that campaign advertising works by influencing individuals' affective states, which in turn has consequences on (among other things) the extent to which voters rely on existing predispositions in electoral decision making (Marcus, Neuman, and MacKuen 2000).

Religious rhetoric provides the penultimate test case study in the stability versus change debate. Religion is among individuals' most stable predispositions (Sherkat 2001; Jennings and Stoker 2007).[1] That an individual's religiosity is so stable suggests that the extent to which religion matters in a given campaign ought to remain relatively consistent between elections. But, at the same time, the relationship between religious and political attitudes in the electorate *is* changing (Kohut et al. 2000; Olson and Green 2006). Somewhat paradoxically, then, there are reasons both to view religion as an unmoved mover and as a force that can exert a variable impact from election to election.

To understand the role of religiosity in electoral behavior, it is helpful to begin by making a distinction between *affiliation* with a particular denomination or tradition, *beliefs* about the divine, and level of religious *commitment* or involvement (Olson and Green 2006).[2] Affiliation is perhaps the most intuitive way to think about religiously based electoral behavior (Herberg 1955). Religious communities have long coalesced around a particular party, due to a shared identity with candidates from that party, a platform consistent with the doctrine of that religious community, or policies that would otherwise benefit members of that religious group. For example, mid-twentieth-century Catholic support for the Democratic Party arose in part because of prominent Catholic party leaders such as Al Smith and John F. Kennedy. Moreover, the party of Franklin Delano Roosevelt offered Catholics a vision of economic equality and an immigration policy more amenable to Catholic social mobility while at the same time opposing anti-Catholic bigotry (Wald and Calhoun-Brown 2006).

Although affiliation is still an important force in American politics, recent scholarship suggests that new belief-based fault lines may be re-shaping traditionally affiliation-based divisions. Specifically, evidence suggests that an individual's level of religious orthodoxy might now be a more important predictor of party identification than his or her denominational affiliation (Wuthnow 1988; Hunter 1991; Leege and Kellstedt 1993; Kohut et al. 2000; Layman 2001; Leege et al. 2002). Catholics are, again, an excellent case in point. Catholics, in this view, are now divided into a more conservative-orthodox wing, which tends to be most concerned with issues such as same-sex marriage and abortion, and a liberal-progressive wing, which is concerned with social justice issues. Republicans have attracted orthodox Catholics (along with evangelical Protestants and more conservative mainline Protestants), and Democrats have attracted progressive Catholics (along with most Jews, African American Protestants, liberal mainline Protestants, and seculars) (Kohut et al. 2000). As Geoffrey Layman (2001) adeptly argues, this fault line is an increasingly significant factor in American elections.

Finally, as the 2004 church attendance gap suggests, individuals' level of religious commitment can be an important predictor of voting behavior, with more committed individuals tending to vote for conservative Republican candidates. Scholars suggest multiple reasons for this. For example, Paul Djupe and Christopher Gilbert (2003) argue that frequent church attenders are exposed to a more regular stream of information (sermons and conversations with fellow attenders) that might make religious political connections salient. It also may be the case that religious commitment is a proxy for belief and affiliation factors in vote choice. As Laura Olson and John Green speculate, "It may be, for instance, that weekly attenders are concentrated in some religious communities and not in others, or it might be that less-frequent attenders are not particularly influenced by the distinctive values of religious communities" (2006, 458).

Clearly, affiliation, belief, and commitment combined help explain patterns of religiously based political behavior. Layman's (2001) account is particularly convincing, carefully documenting how the orthodox–progressive divide was leveraged by strategic politicians though position-taking on cultural issues and how this gradually reshaped party coalitions.[3] For this reason, regardless of candidates' rhetorical style, Republicans generally enter electoral contests with considerable advantages among orthodox voters. Nevertheless, each of these theories still struggles to account for the dramatic ebb and flow of religious salience from election to election. For example, although belief-oriented divisions were evident in the 2004 election, the election did not represent a simple stepwise increase in the gradual move toward a permanent division between religiously committed and secular Americans. By 2008, the 64-35 split between the most frequent church attenders and seculars had receded to 55-43. Thus, although a persistent religion gap is a significant feature in American politics, we cannot yet explain what divides religious voters from one election to the next. In short, research supports the contention that religion influences how people see the political world, but we do not have a complete understanding of how these connections emerge and recede in different electoral contexts.

To compensate for this shortcoming, many accounts argue that religious cleavages in politics are issue-driven and are therefore transitory and election-specific. There is little doubt that certain issues have the potential to resonate more with specific religious groups (Leege et al. 2002); however, there are several problems with giving high-salience religious issues singular credit for driving voting patterns. First, issue-oriented explanations are often post hoc and, accordingly, have difficulty predicting which issues will matter and when. Second, issue-oriented explanations run the risk of overgeneralizing religious subgroups. Frequent church attenders are a diverse bunch. Whereas some church attenders might be particularly concerned about gay marriage and abortion, others might be concerned about entirely different issues, or even endorse pro-choice and pro-same-sex marriage positions. Jim Wallis, a progressive pastor, lamented as much during the 2004 presidential campaign, decrying accounts of religious voters as monolithic.[4] Of course, frequent church attenders did actually vote in a remarkably consistent way. But, as the Wallis example illustrates, it would be a mistake to assume that issues alone were driving this pattern of voting behavior.

Empirical evidence is consistent with the argument that issues are only a part of the story, with 2004 again providing a telling case in point. The 2004 election represents the high-water mark for religious cleavages in electoral politics, and a high-profile exit poll indicating that 22 percent of the public cited "moral values" as the most important electoral issue is often taken as evidence that the religious vote was issue-driven. Even in 2004, however, it is doubtful that religious individuals voted solely on the basis of traditional religious or moral issues. Analyzing independent survey results, D. Sunshine Hillygus and Todd Shields (2005) convincingly argue that domestic terrorism and Iraq were considerably more important in the minds of voters than were the moral values issues such as same-sex marriage and abortion. Although Hillygus and Shields do not examine the independent effect of religiosity on vote choice, the fact that abortion and same-sex marriage had only a modest effect suggests that other factors may be responsible for the religion gap. Daniel Smith, Matthew DeSantis, and Jason Kassel (2006) reach a similar conclusion after examining county-level election returns in same-sex marriage initiative states. Although some counties with high concentrations of evangelicals tended to support George W. Bush at higher than expected levels, the evidence indicates that same-sex marriage did not drive turnout among religious voters.

My own analyses are consistent with the argument that salient cultural issues did not drive the 2004 religion gap. I examined a large survey conducted by the Pew Research Center shortly before the 2004 election (Pew Research Center for the People and the Press 2004)[5] to assess whether the significant gap between frequent and infrequent church attenders persisted, even when I had statistically controlled for factors such as the importance of same-sex marriage, abortion, and moral values. Although I found some evidence that these factors were predictive of voting behavior, it is clear that cultural issues tell only part of the story. Even when the analysis accounted for a long list of cultural issues,[6] frequent church attenders were still considerably more supportive of Bush than secularly inclined voters. In other words, even taking the salience of cultural issues into consideration, a large gulf still persisted between frequent and infrequent church attenders. In fact, even in the eleven states with a same-sex marriage ballot initiative, only 23 percent of the sample knew that there was a same-sex marriage initiative on the ballot, and frequent church attenders were no more likely to know about the initiative than infrequent attenders. This suggests that even in the most moral values–saturated environment possible, moral issues alone were probably not driving a wedge between religious and secular voters.[7] All this indicates that salient moral values issues were not driving the religion gap in 2004, and other forces—including rhetorical expressions of emotion and identity—may be responsible for pushing religious and secular Americans in different directions.

Although the religion and politics literature provides a convincing account of many of the factors involved in shaping the patterns of religious voting behavior, we still have much to learn about how the role of religion can change dramatically from one election to the next and whether these changes are rhetorically instigated.[8] One key contribution of the literature previously discussed is the consensus that multiple conceptualizations of religious orientation are necessary to account for the dynamics of American political behavior. Denominational affiliation, orthodoxy, level of commitment, and other types of orientations can all plausibly factor into voters' decision calculus, given the right electoral circumstances. It stands to reason that variations in how candidates strategically employ religious rhetoric to leverage these varied orientations may help explain the fluctuating role of religion in American elections.[9]

UNDERSTANDING WHEN RELIGION BECOMES A FACTOR

If issues do not explain the varying influence of religious factors from one election to the next, then what does? The dual theories of identity priming and emotive communication provide a powerful explanation. The key observation here is that the two defining features of religious rhetoric—emotion and identity—have an important parallel in the psychology of persuasion. Neither of these mechanisms requires fundamentally retheorizing the enduring nature of religious predispositions or insisting that religious attachments are in some way fickle. Rather, identity and emotion-based models of persuasion imply that religious attachments are deep and enduring, but that campaign rhetoric is capable of making latent religiosity salient to the task of political evaluation. Religious rhetoric can prime religious considerations both by increasing the weight given to religious *identity* in political evaluation and by inducing *emotions* relevant to political judgment, causing individuals to rely to a greater or lesser extent on religious predispositions.

Individuals can hold multiple (and potentially crosscutting) identities at any given time, and the activation of these identities depends largely on context (Hogg 2006; see also Roccas and Brewer 2002). For example, imagine a Catholic woman, deeply attached to her local parish. She sends checks to Focus on the Family and generally considers herself an orthodox Christian. Although these social groups might be mutually reinforcing, there may be cases in which these identities have crosscutting, opposing political implications. If a fellow member of her local parish is running for a seat on the school board and his central campaign issue is the free distribution of contraceptives in schools, we can certainly imagine a tension between the woman's parish-based bond to the candidate and her attachment to a broader national movement. The question becomes: Which of these identities will have the most electoral pull? Ultimately, there is no right answer to this question. Political judgment depends on which identity is effectively primed, or made cognitively accessible and germane to the task of political evaluation.[10]

All this suggests that any prediction about the religious basis of voting behavior needs to grapple with precisely which identities are being primed in a given electoral context. In the previous chapters, I suggest three main ways in which religious identities are invoked: civil religion identity appeals, subgroup identity appeals, and appeals to a culture war. Recall that, of these three, civil religion appeals are clearly the most common in presidential election campaigns. As an example of how civil religion appeals work, consider Bob Dole's 1996 argument that a "moral understanding is the source of *our* certainty. Drug use is wrong because it destroys individual character and responsibility. It is wrong because it leaves *us* useless to God and *our* neighbor" (September 18, 1996, West Hills, CA, Annenberg/Pew Archive of Presidential Campaign Discourse; italics added). Although he never explicitly mentions a group, Dole is implying a shared sense of group identity by his use of "us" and "our." Moreover, this identity is connected to a shared religious and moral ethos that has policy implications (antidrug), lifestyle implications (we must make ourselves useful to the community), and theological implications (God exists). To use drugs is not just to commit a crime but also to violate a certain moral and religious commitment that all Americans have with God.

Although it is clear that Dole was appealing to some social group, it is less clear how to empirically identify the members of this group. Theoretically, civil religion rhetoric has its greatest appeal among those who feel a deep sense of attachment to a spiritualized understanding of America and who hold a sense of shared fate with other Americans who belong to this community. Dole's rhetoric is noteworthy for its lack of sectarian content. It is likely that appeals such as this have persuasive force among the religiously committed generally rather than to a specific religious tradition.

The second class of identity is distinct subgroup identities such as Christian or Baptist. Priming religious identity in the narrower sense has advantages in its own right. From a psychological perspective, this might mean rhetorically inducing a sense of "positive distinctiveness" by distinguishing a particular religious group identity from a superordinate identity category. As Marilynn Brewer summarizes, "Particularly for individuals who are vested in a single group identity, the threat of lost distinctiveness may override the pursuit of superordinate goals" (1999, 437). In addition to being a psychologically viable option, priming more specific religious identities might have distinct political advantages. Subgroup loyalties could be experienced more intensely than civil religion identity, and these groups might have built-in networks for disseminating political information. In addition, particular ingroup identities may lend themselves more readily to concrete political issue positions, such as anti-death penalty or anti-abortion.

Finally, like subgroup appeals, culture wars rhetoric should theoretically appeal to more narrowly defined religious groups—self-identified religious progressives and the religiously orthodox. But culture wars rhetoric takes a very different path than subgroup appeals to make these identities salient; it emphasizes outgroups and religious conflicts. Psychologists have long questioned whether outgroup differentiation is a critical component of ingroup attachment (Brewer 1999), and culture wars rhetoric represents an important test case of this debate. If the rhetoric of a religious war in American politics is an effective tool for the activation of strong ingroup favoritism, then a rhetorical call to arms could be more persuasive than simple subgroup appeals.

Evidence thus indicates that civil religion, subgroup, and culture wars appeals activate different identities in the mass public. And research has indicated that rhetoric can influence the religious patterns of political behavior. For example, Leege and colleagues (2002) argue that culturally charged messages influence different segments of the electorate. But, rather than arguing that religious rhetoric activates different segments of *the electorate*, I contend that religious rhetoric works by activating different parts of *the individual*. Any single individual can simultaneously hold multiple religious identities (as well as numerous secular identities), any of which can become prominent in a given situation. The real question is: How does political rhetoric prime these latent group attachments and make them germane to vote choice?

Accordingly, the relationship between religious rhetoric and identity-based voting should theoretically follow a distinct pattern. First, references to civil religion identity should prime very general religious considerations across denominational divides and other religious subgroups. In contrast, we expect more tailored references to specific subgroups to have stronger effects, limited to the specific ingroup to which candidates appeal. Although I expect this basic process to hold across a number of denominational identities (e.g., frequent references to Southern Baptists should make individuals' own Southern Baptist identity salient), there is insufficient data to test this hypothesis across all elections. Thus, I have used a measure of orthodoxy, a concept that is theoretically related to a sense of religious exclusivity (Iannaccone 1997; Smith 1998). Calling specific group-based distinctions to mind activates this evaluative dimension.[11] Culture wars appeals are also expected to prime the orthodox-progressive scale as an evaluative criterion (with orthodox individuals responding more favorably to culture wars rhetoric). But my expectations about the effects of culture wars rhetoric are somewhat mixed. It is unclear whether outgroup differentiation is the best strategy to form ingroup cohesion. Moreover, because candidates often employ surrogates to serve as campaign "attack dogs," I am not as confident that the culture wars measure would adequately capture the overall tenor of the campaign.

Like religious identities, different emotive cues will likely have varied consequences on how positively or negatively individuals evaluate candidates and even on the extent to which an individual's own religious predispositions become germane to political evaluation. All else being equal, positive emotive rhetoric has a positive impact on overall judgment, whereas candidates who are, on the balance, more negative, are evaluated less favorably. At the same time, different emotions are also linked to different processing styles, and because the emotive rhetoric in our sample is explicitly religious in nature, it follows that it may activate religious evaluative criteria in voters for use in political judgment. In short, I expect that both anger and enthusiasm cues should activate religious commitment as a basis for a favorable candidate evaluation. In very different ways, both of these emotional states tend to increase people's reliance on standing predispositions, including religiosity. For example, when in 2000 Bush promised to set "a positive, optimistic tone" and linked this message of enthusiasm with taking an oath "on the Bible" and the honoring the integrity of the office "so help me God" (August 1, 2000, Harrisburg, PA, FDCH Political Transcripts), he was communicating to voters that they should bring religious standards to bear on his candidacy. By inducing enthusiasm, Bush was telling the public that there was no need to look beyond religious heuristics as the basis of how to vote.

Anxiety, in contrast, is related to cognitive evaluative strategies and political behaviors such as increased information search. Although the available data do not provide a direct test of whether anxiety-inducing religious rhetoric had these predicted effects, I expect that, unlike anger and enthusiasm, anxiety cues would not activate standing religious predispositions as a basis for candidate evaluation.

THE EFFECTS OF RELIGIOUS RHETORIC ON CANDIDATE EVALUATION

To capture a candidate's religious rhetoric style, I examined the effects of the subgroup,[12] civil religion, and culture wars variables from chapter 3, along with the LIWC anger and anxiety scores and a scaled measure of candidate enthusiasm from chapter 4.[13] Averaging these measures over the courses of an entire campaign provided a good estimate of the thrust of the candidate's rhetorical approach to religious identity rhetoric and emotive language (see Druckman 2004).[14]

To examine the impact of religious campaign rhetoric on individual preferences, I pooled seven American National Election Surveys (the 1980, 1984, 1988, 1992, 1996, 2000, and 2004 ANES) from 1980 to 2004.[15] The use of ANES data is appropriate for several reasons. First, the survey is administered in the context of the presidential election campaigns in our sample, and it contains both pre- and postelection questionnaires. Thus, it is possible to examine how individual attitudes have changed over the course of the campaign. Second, the ANES contains several measures of individual religiosity. As suggested earlier, persuasion can work indirectly by priming latent considerations, but only among those who already have some form of religious attachment. It is thus important to examine the variation in the extent to which religious predispositions become predictors of attitude change, as a function of religious rhetoric.

To truly capture the effects of religious rhetoric on the political process, it is not enough to simply measure the evaluation of a candidate at one particular time. Voters enter the election season with a host of preconceived notions about candidates; what is ultimately of interest is the extent to which a candidate's rhetorical choices shape the basis of these beliefs. Accordingly, I examine the candidate assessments of survey respondents *after* the election while statistically controlling for preelection feelings. This allows me to examine how well campaign rhetoric can predict changes in individuals' feelings toward candidates over the course of electoral campaigns.[16]

The theory of identity priming suggests that different dimensions of religiosity should be activated or deactivated depending on the rhetorical thrust of a given campaign. I examined two specific dimensions of interest. *Religious commitment* was measured as church attendance and the importance of religion in an individual's life.[17] Given that religious commitment is a nondenominational measure of religious adherence, I expect that civil religion rhetoric should activate religious commitment as an evaluative dimension. Of course, religious commitment is a highly imperfect approximation of civil religion identity; however, given the need for a consistent measure of nondeminational religiosity across several elections, religious commitment is the best available indicator. Second, I expect that subgroup and culture wars rhetoric should activate *Religious orthodoxy*. The ANES is somewhat limited in its ability to consistently measure religious orthodoxy spanning 1980–2004.[18] Therefore, I replicated a measure of religious orthodoxy developed by Layman (2001, 78–87) that involves using religious tradition to rank individuals' denominational orthodoxy and then further differentiated respondents based on church attendance.

The model contains several control variables of theoretical importance in assessing campaign effects. I controlled for *Partisan identification*, *Race*, and *Gender* because each of these variables can ultimately exist as other identities that can be activated or deactivated over the course of a campaign. I also controlled for the *Date of the survey interview* because individuals surveyed two months before an election have theoretically been exposed to less religious rhetoric than those surveyed the day before the election.[19] In addition, I controlled for *Media exposure* because religious rhetoric could disproportionally affect those individuals most exposed to religious messages across levels of religiosity (Zaller 1992).[20]

Religion's Varied Role from Election to Election

In this chapter, I use an analytical strategy called multilevel modeling to analyze how the religious rhetoric unique to a candidate influences vote choice. These models can be complex;[21] however, the logic underlying this statistical method is a fairly straightforward way to test for identity priming and emotive rhetoric in campaigns. Specifically, we are interested in whether the strength of the relationship between religiosity and change in candidate evaluation is related to systematic differences in candidate rhetoric.

Consider figure 5.1. If we ignore whether the lines are dashed or solid, figure 5.1 looks like little more than a random array of lines. But this figure actually provides valuable information about the role of religion in campaigns. Aligned along the y axis are the survey respondents' changes in candidate evaluation for all presidential candidates from 1980 to 2004. A positive value indicates that the respondents evaluations of the candidate improved over the course of the campaign, whereas a negative value indicates that the voters came to see the candidate less favorably. Along the x axis I have plotted individuals' levels of religious commitment. Thus, if religiosity was never activated by campaign dynamics (i.e., if it made no difference in the evaluation of candidates), we would expect to see fourteen horizontal lines. To be sure, people's opinions of candidates might get better or worse over the course of a campaign

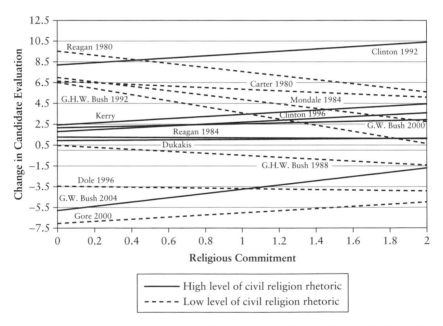

FIGURE 5.1 Religious commitment and change in candidate evaluation by level of civil religion rhetoric, 1980–2004

Relationship between religious commitment and change in candidate evaluation for all Republican and Democratic presidential candidates from 1980 to 2004. In most cases, more religious voters showed a larger, more positive change in their evaluation of candidates when the candidates frequently invoked American civil religion than did less religious voters.

(as reflected in the y intercepts of these horizontal lines). But a line with a slope of 0 for any candidate would indicate that the religiously committed did not display any more (or less) change in opinion than the uncommitted and that, in all likelihood, religious factors were not activated by campaign rhetoric.

Figure 5.1 should make it clear that religiosity did play a markedly different role from one campaign to the next. For example, consistent with conventional wisdom, religious voters came to see George W. Bush *much more positively* as the campaign progressed—suggesting that Bush's rhetoric changed perceptions in a way that resonated with voters. In other words, while Bush generally fared poorly over the course of the campaign, the slope of the line for Bush is steeper than for Kerry, suggesting that Bush successfully activated religious commitment as an evaluative criterion. While Bush's lower overall numbers could be due to any number of factors (related to foreign policy, educational policy, et cetera), the damage was abated considerably among religiously committed respondents. Interestingly, the findings in figure 5.1 also rule out the possibility that the effect of religion on candidate evaluation is limited to a candidate's partisanship. For example, all else being equal, George H. W. Bush actually fared worse with religious than non-religious voters over the course of the 1992 campaign (a negative slope), whereas Clinton garnered comparatively more favor with the religiously committed as the election progressed (a positive slope). Keeping in mind that the y-axis is *change* in candidate evaluation, figure 5.1 illustrates that campaigns do not universally reinforce existing partisan allegiances between Republicans and the religiously committed.

In technical terms, my central purpose in this chapter is to explain the variance in the slopes of the lines (Raudenbush and Byrk 2002). The question is: Why do religiosity committed (or orthodox) voters warm up to some candidates over the course of an election but sour on others? Or stated differently, what activates religious cleavages in some elections? Multilevel models allow us to address precisely this question by bringing order to the cacophony of lines in figure 5.1 by modeling the varied slopes as a function of candidate rhetoric. Accordingly, I have also distinguished the lines in figure 5.1 by the level of civil religion rhetoric the candidate used in that campaign. Although the figure breaks candidate rhetoric into only two very rough categories (low and high), a clear trend is nevertheless evident. When candidates used high levels of civil religion rhetoric (solid lines), the more religiously committed voters changed their evaluation more favorably than did less religious voters (i.e., the slope is positive). When candidates failed to do so (dashed lines), the less religiously committed voters changed their evaluation more favorably than did more religious voters (i.e., the slope is negative). (The exception is Gore in 2000, who had the highest level of civil religion rhetoric in the "low" category.) Thus, the level of candidate rhetoric can be used to meaningfully interpret the relationship between religious commitment and candidate evaluation. The data indicate that, when candidates use religious language, voters respond in predictable and politically powerful ways.

THE NUANCED ROLE OF RELIGIOUS RHETORIC
IN PRESIDENTIAL ELECTIONS

We know that religious rhetoric plays an important role in defining the boundaries of the political community and in setting the tone for political discourse. But we generally do not think of candidates as centrally preoccupied with trailblazing new standards of religious discourse or codifying a particular vision of the American creed. Candidates are, instead, "single minded seekers of reelection" (Mayhew 1974, 5), principally concerned with crafting speech in a way that will garner electoral favor (Jacobs and Shapiro 1994).

Understood this way, the evidence strongly supports the conclusion that emotive and identity-laden cues are persistent elements in religious rhetoric largely because they are effective means to gain electoral support among religious voters. Let us begin by addressing the identity question, examining subgroup, civil religion, and culture wars identities in separate multilevel models. These models allow us to examine how the relationship between candidate evaluation and religiosity changes as a function of religious rhetoric, while controlling for other factors typically thought to play a role in candidate evaluation.[22] Figure 5.2 summarizes the results, providing evidence that the language of identity influences change in candidate evaluation in complex and varied ways, activating different dimensions of religiosity under different circumstances.

Panel A of figure 5.2 illustrates the interaction between religious commitment in the electorate and civil religion identity rhetoric during a campaign. As the graph illustrates, at high levels of civil religion rhetoric (held at the 75th percentile), religiously committed voters substantially improved their evaluations of candidates. When candidates failed to invoke this rhetorical style (low levels of civil religion rhetoric, held at the 25th percentile), the opposite effect holds—committed voters actually lowered their evaluation of the candidate. This can be thought of as a sort of "sin of omission." When candidates failed to invoke the language of civil religion identity—the norm in campaign religious rhetoric—religiously committed voters essentially punished them at the polls. Consistent with our expectations, the opposite effect holds when we consider the relationship between religious orthodoxy in the electorate and the language of civil religion identity (panel C). All else being equal, orthodox individuals responded to civil religion rhetoric by actually lowering their opinion of the candidate. When candidates refrained from references to American civil religion, however, the orthodox tended to improve their overall evaluation of them. It is plausible that, whereas nonsectarian religious language appeals to the religiously committed in a very general way, these watered-down nonsectarian versions of religious faith are ultimately threatening to the most orthodox individuals. This is consistent with many theoretical accounts of religious orthodoxy as an orientation toward religious exclusivity. Civil religion rhetoric ultimately exists to paint American spirituality with a broad brush, distilling commonalities across religious worldviews. Accordingly, this rhetorical construction may ultimately threaten identities that define themselves through contrasts with secular society and other religions.

The opposite pattern holds for Christian subgroup rhetoric. All else being equal, the religiously committed tended to have less favorable opinions of candidates who used Christian subgroup rhetoric, and their opinions improved substantially when candidates refrained from subgroup references (panel B). This finding makes sense, especially if candidates tend to have some sort of bias in the particular subgroup that they rhetorically privilege. For example, in his 1984 campaign, Mondale repeatedly made reference to his Methodist faith and upbringing. Although he certainly never suggested that Methodism was the "one true faith" in any sense, this rhetorical strategy may have reminded many committed individuals of their differences with the candidate rather than establishing a point of shared identity.

The interaction between Christian subgroup rhetoric and orthodoxy displayed in panel D is not statistically significant, although for orthodox individuals, the picture does tend to improve slightly when candidates regularly referenced Christian subgroups. These results fit with the

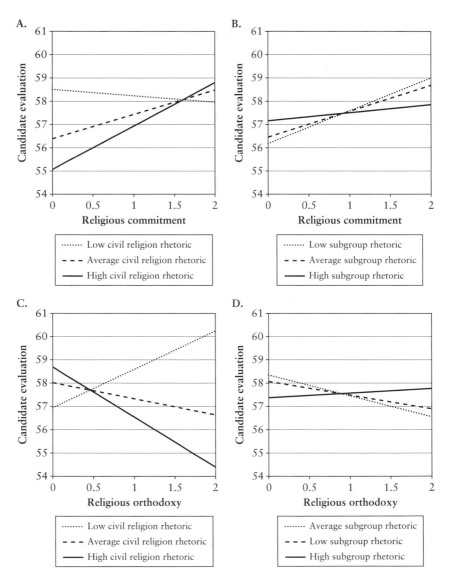

FIGURE 5.2 Religious rhetoric and change in candidate evaluation

Relationship between type of religious rhetoric and postelection feeling thermometer scores, by level of religious commitment (panels A and B) and level of religiosity or orthodoxy (panels C and D). All models control for preelection feeling thermometer scores and a host of control variables. Civil religion rhetoric significantly interacts with religious commitment (panel A) and orthodoxy (panel C) (p < .01). Christian subgroup rhetoric interacts significantly with religious commitment at p < .1 (panel B). The Christian subgroup rhetoric interaction with orthodoxy is not significant (panel D). For full model details, see the online appendix, http://facstaff.uww. edu/chappc/.

expectation that subgroup appeals work very differently than civil religion rhetoric. Unlike rhetoric linking religion to country, references to specific Christian denominations (e.g., Catholicism and Protestantism) and to Christianity tended to lower the most religiously committed individuals' opinions of candidates. This makes sense. Because religious commitment transcends faith traditions, language privileging a particular tradition may seem threatening to many committed individuals. And, while the candidate evaluations and orthodoxy do not vary significantly as a function of Christian subgroup rhetoric, it is at least possible to conclude that orthodox Christians are not turned off by sectarian rhetoric in the same way the religiously committed are.

Figure 5.2 provides evidence that religious ingroup appeals interact with religious identity in nuanced ways. Interestingly, culture wars rhetoric does *not* have a significant relationship to any of the measures of individual religious identity under scrutiny. There are several interpretations possible of this nonfinding. At one level, the null finding could simply be a product of the methodological approach adopted in this chapter. I examined only presidential stump speeches, and evidence indicates that under many circumstances presidential candidates avoid going "on the attack"; they relinquish this duty to campaign surrogates (Sigelman and Buell 2003). Thus, the campaigns might have activated religious predispositions through culture wars rhetoric in a way that the present study simply does not observe.

Despite the fact that campaign surrogates might be primarily responsible for waging culture wars, there is still considerable variation in the extent to which presidential candidates used religious language to identify outgroups. It is thus important to grapple with why the data do not show the public reacting to this variation in any significant way. Social psychology provides one good response to this question. Although many have assumed that the construction of social ingroups necessitates the definition of outgroups (Sumner 1906), numerous studies have demonstrated that this is not in fact the case—ingroup identification need not go hand in hand with outgroup differentiation (see Brewer 1999 for a review). Although the case of culture wars rhetoric is theoretically consistent with many of the conditions that tend to increase the likelihood of negative reciprocity, there are also reasons to suspect that culture wars rhetoric will not actively differentiate outgroups in the ways its practitioners hope (Brewer 1999). Specifically, Brewer (1999) argues that "concentric loyalties" can mitigate the effects of negative outgroup feelings. As we have already seen, American religiosity is nothing if not a rich tapestry of crosscutting identities. It is certainly possible that the effects of culture wars rhetoric are greatly diminished by the activation of a superordinate identification with American civil religion. In this way, the potentially divisive elements of culture wars rhetoric could be mitigated by the effects of other religious genres.

As with the identity models, I examined the effects of each of my emotion variables separately. The cross-level interaction between individual religiosity and a specific emotive rhetoric indicates the extent to which that rhetorical mode induced an emotional state consistent with a reliance on religious predispositions. The direct effects of an emotive style on the intercept are, in contrast, more consistent with the idea of mood congruent judgment. In other words, if emotive style is influencing the *relationship* between religiosity and evaluation, this suggests that emotive religious rhetoric is influencing the religious basis of candidate evaluation. If the emotive style impacts individuals regardless of their level of religious commitment, it suggests that religious rhetoric is probably best seen as a vehicle used to express emotions in a more general sense.

Let us begin by exploring the effects of two negative emotions, anxiety and anger. I examined the effects of these rhetorical elements in conjunction with one other feature—references to the candidate's opponent. Negative emotive rhetoric can be directed at a specific target, or negative emotive rhetoric can be characteristic of a candidate's style more generally. Angry rhetoric can be directed at a candidate's opposition, or it can be a more general lamentation about the state of the country. It is important to make a distinction between these rhetorical choices, controlling for emotive rhetoric directed at an opponent from a more general negative emotive style. The anxiety and anger models thus contain control variables for opponent references.

Several results of this analysis stand out. First, religious opponent references are very important to how candidates are evaluated; however, the effects are not necessarily straightforward. Figures 5.3 and 5.4 display the results of the anger and anxiety analyses, isolating the impact of references to the opponent. When we compare the pairs of lines in each model, we can see that religious references to the opponent are generally a useful rhetorical strategy. The lines that correspond to high levels of opponent rhetoric are consistently (and significantly) higher than the low opponent lines, indicating that candidates who "called out" their opponents on religious grounds were, on balance, more favorably evaluated. Interestingly, religious references to the opponent do not appear to play differently for religiously committed versus uncommitted voters, as the small slopes for the solid and dashed lines illustrate. When religious rhetoric about the opponent was kept to a minimum, religiously committed voters tended to evaluate the candidate more favorably than did the nonreligious voters in the same rhetorical context. In contrast, when candidates went on the attack using religious language, there was little difference in how this message was heard by religious versus nonreligious voters. This unexpected finding suggests that, in general, candidates can help their own standing by characterizing their opponent in negative religious terms—and that the this religious appeal will be effective with voters regardless of their religious predispositions. Candidates who refrain from using religious language as an attack device, however, do not pay as steep a price among religious voters as among nonreligious voters. To explain this finding, we may speculate refraining from opponent-centered religious language may be consistent with a "righteous" religious image—an image that might resonate more with religious voters.

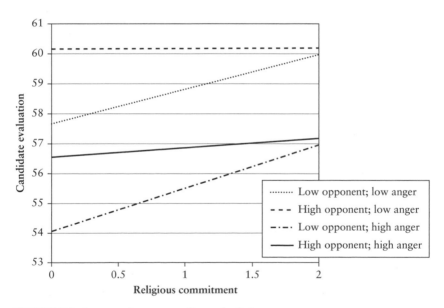

FIGURE 5.3 Angry and opponent-directed religious cues

Relationship between religious commitment and postelection candidate evaluation at different levels of angry and opponent-directed rhetoric. The graph displays effects with anger and opponent-directed rhetoric held at the 25th and 75th percentiles. The interaction of opponent-directed rhetoric and religious commitment is significant (p < .01), whereas the interaction with anger is not. For full model details, see the online appendix, http://facstaff.uww.edu/chappc/.

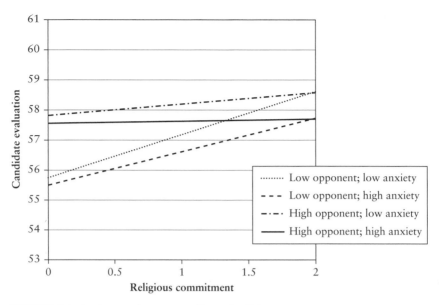

FIGURE 5.4 Anxious and opponent-directed religious cues

Relationship between religious commitment and postelection candidate evaluation at different levels of anxiety and opponent-directed rhetoric. The graph displays effects with anxiety and opponent-directed rhetoric held at the 25th and 75th percentiles. The interaction of opponent-directed rhetoric and religious commitment is significant (p < .01), whereas the interaction with anxiety is not. For full model details, see the online appendix, http://facstaff.uww.edu/chappc/.

Angry appeals, illustrated in figure 5.3, do little to win the hearts of voters, and in fact, there is little difference in how religiously committed and uncommitted voters responded to angry religious messages (the differences in slopes of the lines in figure 5.3 are not statistically significant). Interestingly, candidates who conveyed anger through religious rhetoric actually tended to be evaluated less favorably by the electorate as a whole as a campaign progressed. This is consistent with the concept of affect transfer, whereby the negativity expressed by a candidate is adopted by the message recipients (with both religious and secular voters responding to anger in a similar manner). All this suggests that religious rhetoric is more of a vehicle to convey emotion to a general audience, not a means to reach out to a religious constituency (or possibly that candidates who are losing ground tend to adopt an angrier rhetorical style).

The anxiety-inducing character of religious rhetoric does not correspond with any significant differences in the slopes of the lines graphing candidate evaluation against religious commitment or with the intercepts in the model (figure 5.4). In the case of the slope, this null finding was expected. Anxiety was not expected to activate religious predispositions as an evaluative criterion because it is typically associated with an increased information search, not a reliance on existing predispositions. Nevertheless, it is interesting to note that, whereas an angry mood tends to lower a candidate's overall standing, anxiety does not have a similar effect.[23]

Finally, I examined whether enthusiastic religious rhetoric activates religious commitment as an evaluative criteria. The results, displayed in figure 5.5, indicate that enthusiastic religious rhetoric tended to activate religious commitment as an evaluative criteria. This is consistent with the idea that emotive rhetoric can indirectly influence the basis of political evaluation rather than transferring to all message recipients. Rather sedate expressions of religious identity did little to fire up religious voters. In contrast, and consistent with the work of Marcus, Neuman, and MacKuen (2000), religious voters responded to enthusiastic expressions of religious identity by drawing on this identity in the process of candidate evaluation.

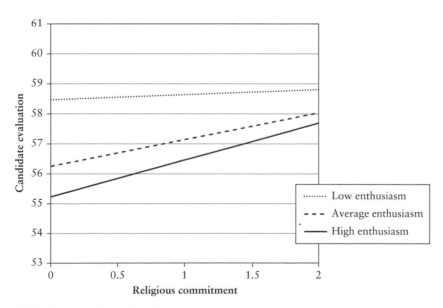

FIGURE 5.5 Enthusiastic religious cues

Relationship between religious commitment and postelection candidate evaluation at different levels of enthusiasm. The graph displays the effects with enthusiasm held at the 25th, 50th, and 75th percentiles. Note that, although the intercepts run counter to expectations, this difference is not significant. In contrast, the cross-level interaction between enthusiasm and religious commitment is significant at p < .05. For full model details, see the online appendix, http://facstaff.uww.edu/chappcl/.

These results indicate that emotive forms of religious expression have non-negligible consequences on the electorate but that these effects are quite nuanced. Religious rhetoric appears to operate as a vehicle to convey anger, although religiously committed and uncommitted voters respond to this style in similar ways. Enthusiastic religious language, in contrast, appeals to religious predispositions, activating religious commitment as an evaluative criterion, which is consistent with evidence that enthusiasm can activate group-based evaluations.

RELIGIOUS RHETORIC AND CANDIDATE EVALUATION

The results presented in this chapter provide evidence of how religious rhetoric influences voters' decision calculus, and in doing so, they raise a series of important questions about how political representation is understood within the context of an ostensibly secular democratic state. The data indicate that religious rhetoric plays an important role in candidate evaluation; however, it generally does so indirectly. Emotive and identity rhetoric can activate very specific dimensions of individual religiosity. Civil religion identity tends to increase the extent to which individuals use religious commitment as a basis for candidate evaluation, but it tends to decrease the effects of orthodoxy on candidate evaluation. In the case of Christian subgroup rhetoric, the opposite pattern holds. Christian group references tend to make those who are religiously committed, across religious group affiliations, evaluate a candidate less favorably. These results make intuitive sense. Language intended to excite religious predispositions in a nonsectarian manner affects candidate evaluations for those most committed to religion—across denominations and across levels of orthodoxy. On the other hand, when the rhetoric cues specific Christian denominations, this pattern reverses itself.

Likewise, the emotive character of a campaign is important to understanding how voters evaluate candidates. Enthusiastic religious rhetoric activates religious evaluative criteria. This finding makes sense, given what is known about the nature of emotions and political decision making. Enthusiastic individuals have little incentive to cast off their predispositions and engage in the effort of an information search. When a candidate sends an enthusiasm-inducing religious message, this signals both that the candidate shares a common religious group orientation and that this common orientation is an adequate basis for political preference formation. In contrast, when a candidate uses a high degree of angry rhetorical cues, this induces negative feelings toward that candidate, but it does not make religion salient. Thus, controlling for the strategically advantageous use of references to the opponent, anger-inducing religious rhetoric is an ill-advised campaign strategy.

These findings indicate that the religious dynamics of a campaign matters, but they also stress the need for a nuanced understanding of religious rhetoric. Indeed, when I replicated these analyses for frequency of religious word use, I found that the frequency of religious words used in a campaign alone does not predict opinion change, either directly or indirectly. When we try to explain how religious rhetoric works, then, it is important to begin with the theoretical basis for preference formation. Identity priming and emotion are two such mechanisms. These mechanisms make sense in terms of what we know about the psychology of religion: it is intertwined with an individual's identity, and it has the potential to be a tremendously emotional experience.

At one level, the findings in this chapter speak to the utility of religious rhetoric as a campaign strategy, and from this perspective we have reached several definitive conclusions. At the same time, these results ask as many questions as they answer. Insofar as religious identity becomes the basis for vote choice, it raises the question of whether this rhetorically primed constituency has expectations about political leadership. In other words, religious voting complicates the representative task considerably—particularly in a democracy characterized by a wall of separation between church and state. In the next chapter, I turn to this question, asking how religious rhetoric impacts the representational dynamics of American politics.

6

CIVIL RELIGION IDENTITY AND THE TASK OF POLITICAL REPRESENTATION

> *It's not about the Republicans sending hecklers to my rally. It's about Jerry Falwell picking the next justices of the Supreme Court. And this election is about leadership. It's about what we expect a president to do when he represents American values and dreams.*
> —Vice President Walter Mondale, 1984

Hanna Pitkin defines *to represent* as to "make present again." In American politics, elected representatives go about the task of making their constituencies present again in varied and complex ways. A representative might, for example, deliver what Pitkin calls "substantive representation," advocating on behalf of policies that his or her constituency desires. A representative might also deliver "descriptive representation" by, essentially, looking like his or her own constituency. Or representation can be symbolic, centered on a common identification between rulers and the ruled—what Pitkin calls an "alignment of wills" (1967, 108).

When analyzing the relationship between an elected leader and a *religious* constituency, we often ignore important symbolic aspects of representation. Instead, scholars, politicians, and pundits alike are often quick to focus on substantive aspects of representation. For example, when Bush won the 2004 election, the victory was often taken to suggest a substantive policy mandate focused on issues such as abortion and same-sex marriage. Likewise, the media are often mesmerized by descriptive accounts of religious representation. When Sonya Sotomayor was nominated to the Supreme Court, the national news media devoted significant attention to the fact that six of the nine Justices would be Catholic, asking how the descriptive composition of the Court might affect judicial decision making.

These substantive and descriptive accounts of representation have led to a number of important insights about the role of religion in American politics.[1] But, as we have seen in previous chapters, religious communication in American campaigns is not generally remarkable in its substantive issue content. Rather, religious rhetoric is a genre that is best characterized by the way in which candidates invoke identity and emotion; it is focused more on aligning the hearts and minds of candidate and constituent than on asserting a religious policy platform. Voters swayed by religious appeals may ultimately be more interested in a candidate's identity and symbolic vision of the American state than in any particular policy prescription. When Walter Mondale, in the speech quoted here, contrasted Jerry Falwell with American values and dreams, he wasn't persuading via a substantive policy platform but was, instead, locating a point of common identification with the audience and asking voters to evaluate his candidacy by thinking about the type of leadership he offered.

To fully understand the role of religion in the dynamics of political representation, it is thus important to know whether voters' expectations are primarily substantive or symbolic. Unfortunately, relatively little research has examined what citizens' expectations of government actually are when they cast a ballot based on a candidate's religious self-presentation. Do voters, swayed by a candidate's religious appeals, expect a certain set of policies or are their desires more closely related to specific symbolic concerns? Moreover, the American public is not of one mind when it comes to religion, and many voters will find little to agree with in religious rhetoric. Given that some religious rhetoric contains a distinctly exclusivist element, it follows that for some voters a religious representational style does little to make them feel "present again." Indeed, religious rhetoric may leave some voters feeling alienated from the political system altogether.

THE CENTRALITY OF CIVIL RELIGION IDENTITY

Understanding the American religious landscape requires grappling with the multiple and crosscutting religious identities that coexist in the American public. For example, culture war theorists have argued that many American denominations are divided within by warring orthodox and progressive factions. Civil religion theorists have a different point of emphasis, arguing that common spiritual denominators unite individuals across religious traditions, transcend multiple traditions to see God at work in American democracy, and serve as a cultural glue and point of political unity.[2] Although a definite tension exists between the culture war and civil religion perspectives, the evidence indicates that no one viewpoint is descriptively right or wrong. Instead, different religious orientations—for example, as a Baptist, a Protestant, an orthodox Christian, or a member of the American civil religion—can all coexist as latent religious identities in a single individual, and these identities are made politically salient through the use of religious political rhetoric.

No one religious identity tells the complete story of American political life and culture, but an identification with American civil religion clearly is a prominent part of the story. The rhetoric of American civil religion— with its constituent emotive and identity-laden elements—has been a dominant mode of public religious expression for hundreds of years. For political elites, this rhetorical choice makes strategic sense. America is characterized by both high rates of religious adherence and a high degree of religious pluralism. Civil religion rhetoric theoretically allows elites to make effective appeals to a broad and diverse constituency.

This said, much remains to be learned about American civil religion and its effects. First, it is important to know something about the citizens for whom this genre has its greatest appeal. Unlike denominational or ideological orientations, identity with the American civil religion remains a poorly understood concept, in part because the boundaries of this community are so mutable and amorphous. Consider the example of John F. Kennedy's inaugural address, often considered to be an ideal-type example of American civil religion rhetoric. If Kennedy had told American Catholics that they had a special standing in God's divine plan, Kennedy would have activated denominational affiliations as a basis of political evaluation. But Kennedy said no such thing. Instead, he said that "the same revolutionary beliefs for which our forebears fought are still at issue around the globe—the belief that the rights of man come not from the generosity of the state but from the hand of God" (January 20, 1961, Inaugural Address, American Presidency Project). It is important to understand which religious identity, if any, Kennedy's rhetorical move made salient. Did voters find in this statement a point of common identification with Kennedy? If so, for most voters it was certainly not a point of common identification as a Catholic, or as any other denomination for that matter. And given the overwhelming message of quasi-religious unity, it is unlikely that this statement made the orthodox-progressive divide salient. Instead, the likely point of common identification was a spiritually infused understanding of nation. All Americans are, in Kennedy's rhetorical formulation, united as recipients of God's special favor and connected to the same revolutionary point of origin.

Whereas most previous research conceptualizes American civil religion as a type of political rhetoric (Hart 2005), the theory of civil religion identity priming indicates that appeals such as Kennedy's should have an important analog in the American public mind. Relatively little research, however, has treated civil religion as an individual religious orientation. One important exception to this gap in the literature is a series of papers authored by Ronald Wimberley and colleagues in the late 1970s and early 1980s (Wimberley 1979, 1980; Wimberley and Christenson 1980, 1981). Like the present work, Wimberley conceptualizes civil religion as an individual orientation that can be activated by campaign communication. For example, Richard Nixon effectively projected civil religious imagery in the 1972 presidential campaign and also received a disproportionate share of the civil religion vote (Wimberley 1980). Wimberley (1979) also finds strong evidence that civil religion is distinct from other political and religious constructs.[3] His findings suggest that a sizable portion of the American public identifies with the basic tenets of American civil religion, and that these individuals respond to cues from officeholders. This interplay has important consequences for understanding the role of religion in political representation and for understanding the contours of political culture more generally.

Incorporating Wimberley's research with research on the nature of social identities, I define *civil religion identity* as a self-awareness of membership in the civil religion tradition and a sense of attachment to this tradition.[4] Civil religion identifiers see themselves as part of a nondenominational religious tradition, and they draw on this group membership to define their social selves. Membership accords a certain positive distinctiveness, drawn from the sense that God has blessed their group—the American nation—and afforded it special privileges and responsibilities.

Examining civil religion identity in the American public presents several challenges. The civil religion is, in many ways, a social group in the same way that Christian religion is a social group. It has members who adhere to a basic belief structure and who draw meaning from attachment to the group. But civil religion lacks an institutional structure (and even a formal name) that many denominations and traditions have. Accordingly, it is challenging to design survey items that capture the extent to which people see themselves as objective members of this group. To address these challenges, I began with the battery of civil religion questions used by Ronald Wimberley and James Christenson (1981) and Sergei Flere and Miran Lavrič (2007) and then modified the items to incorporate aspects of social identity, such as a sense of shared fate and group attachment. For example, respondents were asked to agree or disagree that "As Americans, we are blessed with special opportunities." Using the *we* voice taps into the idea of shared responsibility. Likewise, individuals were asked if they agreed that "America, as a nation, holds a special higher power," an item again designed to measure whether people draw meaning from this group attachment. In addition, consistent with the notion that social identities are often characterized by a particular worldview (Abdelal et al. 2006), individuals were asked several belief-oriented items, such as "The U.S. Constitution is a holy document." Thus, I operationalized civil religion identity as including a group attachment component, as well as beliefs that accord America and Americans a sacred place in the world order.

In this chapter, I investigate the properties of civil religion identity and how individuals who scored high on a civil religion identity (CRI) scale respond to religious cues in two studies. Most evidence comes from the National Civil Religion Identity Study, conducted in summer 2010, in which four hundred adults were surveyed to assess (1) the extent to which they identified as a member of the American civil religion and (2) how they evaluated political candidates. This study provides critical evidence about how an identification with American civil religion can inform our understanding of political representation. In addition, this study contains a question-order experiment, whereby some respondents were randomly selected to respond to political items immediately following a religious question battery, with the expectation that religious cues would prime a different basis of candidate evaluation. The second study, conducted on four hundred undergraduate college students in fall 2008, looks more directly at how rhetoric primes different evaluative criteria as a basis of vote choice. After answering a series of questions about politics and religion, students were asked to evaluate a candidate's web page which had been specifically altered to prime certain religious evaluative criteria. Each of these studies is described more completely in this chapter and in the online appendix (http://facstaff.uww.edu/chappc/).

A Portrait of Civil Religion Identity

The results of the National Civil Religion Identity Study indicate that many Americans deeply identify with American civil religion but also that civil religion identification is not uniformly accepted across the electorate. Even though civil religion is theoretically a nondenominational religion, in practice its adherents are primarily Christians, suggesting limits to the ability of civil religion to serve as a transcendent cultural glue.

Many American agree with the basic tenets of American civil religion and see themselves as members of this spiritual community (figure 6.1). Between one-third and one-half of the individuals surveyed saw the basic American institutional framework as infused with religious elements. About 35 percent of Americans somewhat agreed or strongly agreed that the United States has entered into a special covenant with God, and 32 percent saw the U.S. Constitution as a holy document. Likewise, given that presidents regularly (and often famously) make strong religious appeals, we might expect a sizable percentage of the public to see this institution as having a religious element.[5] The data enforce this prediction—about 57 percent agreed that "The office of the presidency is a sacred position."

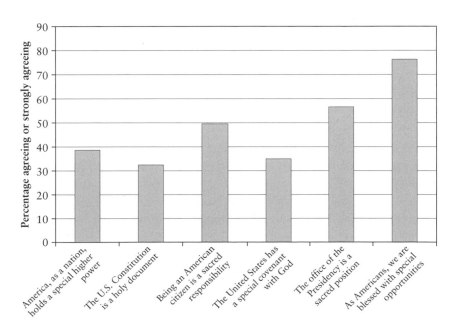

FIGURE 6.1 Civil religion identity in the American public

Weighted agreement with the six civil religion identity (CRI) indicators. Bars represent the percentage of respondents who "somewhat" or "strongly agree" with the statement on a 5-point scale.

A sizable percentage of respondents also agreed with the survey items that explicitly tap into the group-membership aspects of civil religion identity by making references to citizenship, using the *we* voice, and making references to shared responsibility. Fully 76 percent of the public agreed or strongly agreed that "As Americans, we are blessed with special opportunities." Likewise, almost half of Americans saw citizenship as a sacred responsibility, and 39 percent thought that America, collectively, holds a "special higher power."

Together these results indicate that a large portion of the American public identifies themselves as members of an American civil religion and agrees with its basic tenets. Critically, these survey items all appear to be measuring the same underlying religious dimension; that is, individuals who agreed with one question tended to agree with all the questions, and the opposite is also true.[6] This is important because it suggests that the group-membership aspects of civil religion are closely intertwined with beliefs about the privileged place of American institutions. If you agree that America has entered into a special compact with God, you also probably have a spiritualized sense of attachment to the United States and understand your own citizenship in quasi-religious terms.[7]

To further explore the composition of this identity, I created a scale from these six survey question, and compared this CRI scale with other important political and demographic characteristics. Even though civil religion identity is not entirely uniformly represented across the political spectrum, the data indicate that no single nonreligious demographic group has a monopoly on civil religion adherents. For example, among different racial groups, whites were only slightly more likely to strongly identify with civil religion identity, Hispanics slightly less, and African Americans are roughly evenly split between high- and low-CRI individuals.[8] Overall, the differences in the racial composition of civil religion identifiers are far from staggering. Likewise, a slightly higher percentage of men identified with American civil religion, although the difference between men and women is not statistically significant. Older Americans generally scored higher on the CRI scale, although the difference between young and old is relatively modest.[9] Finally, although Republicans did score significantly higher on the CRI scale than did self-identified Independents and Democrats, civil religion identity is still present in all partisan groups. About 20 percent of Democrats and 35 percent of Independents still averaged an "agree" response on all six items on the CRI scale.

The most striking and normatively consequential differences in civil religion identity adherence are those between different religious traditions. Civil religion rhetoric theoretically aspires to transcend faith traditions and engender a sense of inclusivity in the political community. However, *rhetorically* civil religion might not always perform as promised. For example, as we see in chapter 3, references to God tend to privilege an image of God as parent-provider, which runs counter to the understanding of some traditions. This raises the question of whether America is accorded a unique quasi-religious status among those who find little to agree with in the substance of these beliefs.

The results of the National Civil Religion Identity survey indicate that Americans do not equally identify with civil religion across all religious traditions.[10] Catholics, Protestants, and Mormons strongly identify with American civil religion, whereas Muslims, Jews, agnostics, and atheists find little to agree or identify with on the CRI scale.[11]

This finding presents something of a paradox. Membership in the American civil religion is characterized as being open to everyone—being a common denominator of all faith traditions. Civil religion theoretically exists as a solution to American religious diversity, providing common moral and ethical denominators that can serve as a basis for political unity. And, throughout history, the rhetorical construction of the identity has been trending toward greater inclusiveness. Prothero (2007) concurs, noting that the rhetorical expressions of American nonsectarianism has evolved from just including Christian denominations to referencing the Judeo-Christian tradition and to, much more recently, referencing the "Abrahamic" tradition.

Although trending toward greater inclusivity, however, civil religion has always been an exclusive group, and this exclusivity may have observable consequences in the American public.[12] Regardless of whether civil religion rhetoric is trending toward universal inclusivity, Americans who are non-Christian certainly do not feel included—a finding that may have its origins in religious political rhetoric. This presents a challenge to theorists who claim that civil religion identity can effectively embrace the full religious diversity of the United States. Although the aim of civil religion may be to unite, in practice this identity reveals deep divisions along religious lines.[13]

Two important conclusions can be drawn from the previous section. First, in the American electorate, civil religion identity is unevenly distributed across religious traditions. It is striking that members of many faith traditions uniformly reject an identity that is commonly invoked in presidential political rhetoric. Insofar as symbolic representation involves the active "alignment of wills" between rulers and the ruled, it seems that large portions of the American electorate are not being adequately represented along these lines.

Second, despite these divisions, a large portion of the American electorate—particularly Christians—strongly identify with American civil religion. This has important representational consequences when we consider high-CRI individuals as a voting bloc, potentially united to make political demands. On one hand, if high-CRI voters have a substantive issue agenda in mind, then leaders who rhetorically embrace the language of American civil religion have a mandate to enact specific policies. This issue-based hypothesis often dominates electoral interpretations when we ask which issues the "religious vote" cares most about. On the other hand, it is not entirely clear what the substantive issue agenda for high-CRI voters would actually look like. After all, the language of civil religion has been used to rally support behind a number of political causes across American history. For those who identify with the civil religion tradition, the true basis of political representation involves electing a leader who appears to be a prototypical group member—a candidate with whom citizens feel a common sense of identity and shared fate. According to this hypothesis, high-CRI voters may desire a specific symbolic representational style, not any particular issue agenda.

If this latter hypothesis is correct, this has important consequences for how we understand the role of religion American elections. Specifically, if high-CRI voters are more concerned with a candidate's religious image than with particular issues, leaders in government should use caution in aggressively promoting a culture war–style policy platform or in claiming any sort of religious policy mandate. Consider the 2004 presidential campaign, in which Bush frequently and deftly employed the language of American civil religion. When Bush achieved a lopsided victory over Kerry among (church-attending) religious voters, many suggested that this electoral division signaled a political agenda the president should pursue. Bush advisor Karl Rove, being interviewed by Fox News's Jim Angle shortly after the election, made this case explicitly. After Rove trumpeted the significant victory among religious voters, Angle followed up by asking what policy consequences this electoral cleavage would have:

ANGLE: Will the president press the issue now and push for a constitutional amendment defining marriage?

ROVE: Well, look, the president has this old fashioned notion that when you run on something in a campaign, you attempt to do it in office. He ran in 1999 and 2000 on a certain series of issues. And once in office, pursued each and every one of those issues. I think the American people can have confidence that he treats the things that he said in the campaign as significant promises and pledges, which he will now attempt to fulfill.

ANGLE: So the answer is yes?

ROVE: Absolutely.

Rove here makes the assumption that religious voters prioritize issues such as same-sex marriage, a view consistent with theories of a culture war in American politics. For Rove, this policy mandate is justified on the grounds that Bush performed exceedingly well among frequent church attenders. Nevertheless, insofar as Bush's rhetoric was actually activating civil religion as the relevant evaluative dimension, there is good reason to challenge Rove's assumption. It stands to reason that what civil religion voters saw in Bush was a leader who, like they did, viewed America as having a special place in a divine plan and a sacred set of responsibilities. Despite Bush's personal opposition to same-sex marriage, it is not clear that this issue was salient for high-CRI voters.[14]

Data from the National Civil Religion Identity Survey supports the hypothesis that high-CRI voters prefer a leader who symbolizes moral clarity and a sense of American spiritual values but who does not necessarily have a substantive issue platform.[15] To address this, let us begin by examining the rival issues hypothesis to determine whether civil religion voters are particularly concerned with traditional moral issues, such as abortion and same-sex marriage (figure 6.2). As the graph illustrates, voters who score high on the CRI index were only modestly more likely to see abortion and same-sex marriage as important issues when evaluating candidates. This indicates that the extent to which individuals embrace membership in American civil religion does not greatly influence the salience they attach to issues typically thought to be the fodder of the culture war.

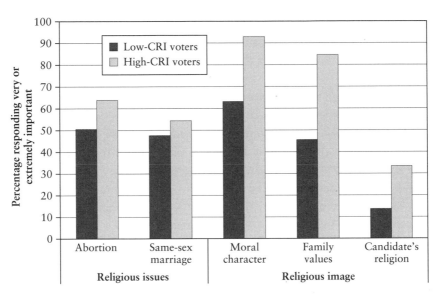

FIGURE 6.2 Issue and image salience by level of civil religion identity

Above: Figure 6.3 reports the Importance of a candidate's stance on abortion, same-sex marriage, moral character, family values, and religion in assessing candidates. There is a relatively small difference between high- and low-CRI respondents on abortion and same-sex marriage issue salience, but there is a large significant difference between high- and low-CRI respondents on each of the image variables (p < .01). For a multivariate test of these relationships, see the online appendix, http://facstaff.uww.edu/chappc/. CRI, civil religion identity

In contrast, high-CRI voters do think about candidates differently when image is taken into consideration (figure 6.2). Civil religion identifiers were far more likely than their low-CRI counterparts to acknowledge that a candidate's religion and moral character are important and to say that it is important for a candidate have strong family values. It is clear that civil religion identifiers were not evaluating candidates on the issues any more than low-CRI voters were but, rather, desired candidates who appeared to be the rightful inheritors of the civil religion tradition and who led in a manner that communicated a sense of moral purpose. Civil religion identifiers were nearly 20 points more likely to say that a candidate's religion is important, 30 points more likely to say that moral character is important, and 39 points more likely to say that family values are important. In contrast, high-CRI voters were only modestly more concerned with the dominant religious issues of the day—abortion (13 points) and same-sex marriage (7 points).[16] Clearly, voters who endorse and identify with the core principles of civil religion are more likely to desire a certain type of leader, although this does not necessarily trans-late into a substantive issue platform. This is consistent with the work of Larry Bartels (2008), who finds that frequent churchgoers attach rela-tively little importance to cultural issues, compared with economic issues such as job creation and economic spending, and that the salience of cul-tural issues does little to differentiate frequent versus infrequent church attenders. But even though cultural issue salience do little to distinguish voters along religious lines, the evidence presented here indicates that high-CRI individuals are distinguished by their symbolic concern that candidates be of a certain moral pedigree and hold certain values.[17]

Additional evidence from the National Civil Religion Identity Study suggests that adherents of this identity are most concerned with a particu-lar symbolic representative style. As figure 6.3 illustrates, high-CRI voters were 36 percentage points more likely to desire a candidate that makes them proud of their country and were twice as likely as low-CRI voters to say that it is important to elect a candidate like themselves. This supports the contention that high-CRI voters do not evaluate candidates along the

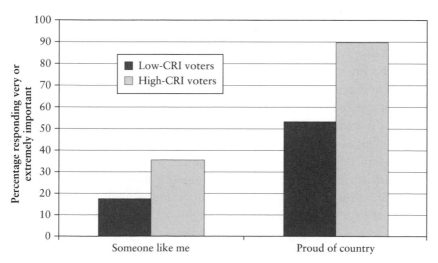

FIGURE 6.3 "Pride in country" and "a candidate like me" by level of civil religion identity

Importance of "the candidate makes me proud of my country" and "the candidate is someone like me" in assessing candidates. There is a large significant difference between high- and low-CRI voters on each of these variables (p < .01). These differences persist when the analysis controls for national identity and partisan identification. For a multivariate test of these rela-tionships, see the online appendix, http://facstaff.uww.edu/chappc/. CRI, civil religion identity lines of issue positions; rather, they want candidates who fit a specific group prototype consistent with a spiritualized sense of national identity. Moreover, these relationships hold up even when the analysis controlled for other factors such as national identity.[18] Civil religion identity is closely intertwined with concern for both pride in country and common identity.

One potential objection to this line of reasoning questions the utility of the concept of civil religion identity. Perhaps the CRI index is simply measuring secular national identity, or perhaps the CRI index is a redundancy, too similar to other measures of religiosity to be conceptually important. There are both empirical and theoretical responses to these objections. Empirically, data from the National Civil Religion Identity Survey provide a strong refutation to both these concerns. Using multiple regression, I examined the relationship between the CRI index and concerns about a candidate's moral character while statistically holding constant other factors, such as party identification, religious fundamentalism,[19] and national identity. The data indicate that CRI is the best available predictor of the importance people attach to a candidate's moral character. All else being equal, neither national identity, religious fundamentalism, religious commitment, nor party identification have a statistically significant relationship with evaluations of a candidate's moral character. And, although social conservatives were moderately more likely to say that moral character is important, civil religion identity is still the strongest predictor in the model.[20]

This finding makes theoretical sense. Civil religion identity is distinct from secular measures of national identity, as well as from measures of religious identity such as fundamentalism that specifically imply a specific set of religious beliefs (e.g., biblical inerrancy). Civil religion identity is a highly spiritualized sense of national identity that requires not that its followers adopt specific positions on religious matters but, rather, that they believe that the United States itself is intertwined with the sacred. In fact, the survey data indicate that high-CRI individuals and religious fundamentalists ultimately evaluate candidates on different grounds. For religious fundamentalists and others with a more traditional religious orientation, clearly issues (e.g., abortion and same-sex marriage), not representational style, drive political evaluations. Whereas high-CRI voters attached relatively little importance to these issues compared to low-CRI voters, voters identifying with religious fundamentalism were highly likely to see these issues as politically salient.[21]

Thus, the importance that religious voters attach to these traditional cultural issues depends on exactly what is meant by *religious*. The evidence indicates that individuals who strongly identify as religious fundamentalists evaluated candidates based on the candidates' positions on the traditional cultural issues; this is consistent with accounts of limited but salient religious divisions in American politics (Layman and Green 2005). However, *fundamentalists* does not describe most voters.[22] In contrast, a sizable portion of the electorate—particularly the Christian electorate—strongly identifies as members of American civil religion. These voters are not fundamentally concerned with cultural issues but, rather, representational style. They prioritize a specific vision of moral leadership intertwined with pride in country.

This analysis is consistent with the notion that that an issue-laden culture war is *not* driving American elections, except perhaps for a small group of religious fundamentalists. This finding has important representational implications, recasting our understanding of religious voting in American elections. It is a mistake to suppose that religious cleavages are always issue-driven, as many analysts and politicians did following the 2004 election. Indeed, a concern with moral values may have had very little to do with substantive issues for many voters. In actuality, many voters—those who strongly identified with American civil religion but not necessarily religious fundamentalism—were probably attracted to Bush (over Kerry) because of the type of symbolic leadership his rhetoric conveyed, not because of any particular issue stance. In other words, Kerry's problem with frequent church attenders was not that he was pro-choice, although some voters might have rationalized their vote choice in these terms (Lodge, McGraw, and Stroh 1989; Rahn, Krosnick, and Breuning 1994). Rather, Kerry's problem was that he did not seem like he could authentically steer the nation in a spiritually righteous direction.

CIVIL RELIGION IDENTITY, POLITICAL RHETORIC, AND AMERICAN POLITICAL CULTURE

Political representation involves not only the evaluative standards that individuals bring to bear on political candidates but also how voters respond to rhetorical cues. Does religious rhetoric shift the basis of candidate evaluation, and what role do religious cues play in defining American political culture? Given an ostensible separation of church and state, it is important to know whether religious rhetoric is driving a wedge between voters or whether it is working to weave diverse faith traditions together. In other words, how are rhetorical choices influencing American political culture?

I investigated this question using a question-order experiment embedded in the National Civil Religion Identity Study, as well an experiment with undergraduates that exposed participants to various types of religious rhetoric. Both studies employed a similar strategy, designed to mimic the rhetorical cues present in a real campaign, albeit under controlled conditions. In this way, I was able to examine how nuanced rhetorical choices affect the basis of vote choice. I primed participants with various religious cues before asking them a series of questions about how they evaluate political candidates. The results suggest that civil religion rhetoric is a powerful force in American elections but that the effectiveness of the appeal depends a good deal on the religious identity of the individual voter. That is, even though civil religion aims to be nonsectarian, it is clearly not a panacea for greater inclusivity.

Varied Responses to Religious Messages

Just as Christians and non-Christians display markedly different patterns of identification with civil religion identity, these two groups also respond to message cues in different ways. Christians, on the whole, tend to evaluate candidates more favorably when primed with religious cues. Understanding this interaction between religious beliefs (or group membership) and message cues can help us assess the extent to which political leadership is providing symbolic representation for the entire polity or potentially alienating key segments of the electorate.

The first piece of evidence to support this contention comes from an experiment administered to college undergraduates in fall 2008. After filling out a background questionnaire that included the CRI scale,[23] individuals read a one-page description of a candidate's position on "working families," designed to look like a web page from an actual ongoing campaign.[24] The web pages were modified to mimic one of three rhetorical styles: (1) a control condition, containing no religious language; (2) a civil religion condition, containing references to a collective American spirituality; and (3) a subgroup religion condition, containing religious language that singled out specific religious subgroups. For example, for the civil religion condition the candidate's issue statement said, "My parents taught me about faith, responsibility, hard work, and the importance of a family to a child's well-being. Our shared faith in these enduring values is what makes this nation great." In contrast, for the subgroup religion condition the candidate's issue statement said, "My parents taught me about faith, responsibility, hard work, and the importance of a family to a child's well-being. No matter what your racial, ethnic, or religious background—whether you're a Baptist, a Catholic, a Lutheran, or whatever—these values are enduring." Like subgroup campaign rhetoric, this condition mentioned other faith traditions but did so in a pluralistic manner. The subgroups were rhetorically cued but not explicitly privileged.[25]

The results of the experiment are striking. As expected, in the control condition Christian and non-Christian respondents are equally likely to express support for the candidate. As figure 6.4 illustrates, support among non-Christian respondents dropped off considerably in both the civil religion and subgroup religion conditions. Two features of figure 6.4

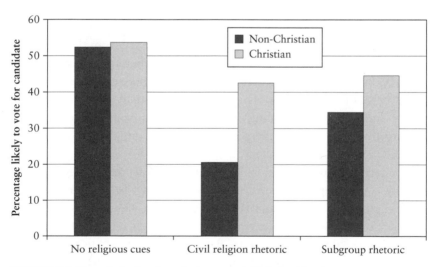

FIGURE 6.4 Vote choice by rhetorical cues and Christian identity

Percentage of individuals likely to vote for a hypothetical candidate (scoring 5 or higher on a 7-point scale) by rhetorical condition and Christian self-identification. The overall decrease in candidate support in both the civil religion and subgroup religion conditions is probably due to this being a student sample. Most notably, Christians and non-Christians have significant differences in their levels of support in the civil religion condition, suggesting its appeal is not universal ($p < .05$). For a multivariate test of this relationship, see the online appendix, http://facstaff.uww.edu/chappc/.

deserve our attention. First, note that, although candidate support for all groups went down considerably in the two religious conditions, this is largely the product of a very secularly inclined student sample. Compared with the results of the National Civil Religion Study, even self-identified Christian respondents in the student sample had markedly lower levels of religious commitment, civil religion identity, and fundamentalist orientations. Thus, the drop in Christian support in both religious conditions should not be taken as a sign that these rhetorical choices are a poor strategy in general.

The more important feature of figure 6.4 is the gap in support between Christian and non-Christian students in the civil religion condition. Strikingly, when the candidate employed the language of civil religion, Christian and non-Christian respondents moved in opposite directions. Civil religion may function as a point of common identification for Christians, but for non-Christians candidate support drops considerably (difference significant at $p < .05$). This suggests that for non-Christian respondents civil religion may serve to alienate rather than bridge differences—an understandable response, given that civil religion contains an element of exclusivity. It is also worth reiterating that although both the civil religion and subgroup religion conditions used religious language, this treatment was a far cry from the explicitly divisive language of the culture war. Even a rather subtle reference to "shared faith" produces a divergent response between Christian and non-Christian respondents. This suggests that there is a fine line between sufficiently broadening identity-laden appeals to be inclusive and making appeals with the presumption that one does in fact speak for all.

The results from the National Civil Religion Identity Survey make an equally compelling case that Christians and non-Christians respond to civil religion rhetoric in distinctly different ways. This survey contained a rather subtle question-order manipulation, designed to prime subgroup religion and civil religion identities. Before answering questions about the importance of religion, morals, abortion, and so on, participants were asked to respond to one of three question sets: (1) a series of questions about the economy (control), (2) the six-item civil religion question battery, or (3) a series of questions addressing denominational and subgroup religious affiliations. Thus, rather than receiving message primes in the form of candidate rhetoric, individuals were simply exposed to questions designed to tap different aspects of religious identity.

First, it should be noted that, regardless of question-order condition, Christian adherents scored nearly all the religious and quasi-religious issues as significantly more important in evaluating candidates. In addition, in almost every case, the religious prime accentuated this difference between Christians and non-Christians on religious issue importance. In other words, the gap between Christians and non-Christians regarding the relative importance of morals, family values, and religion grew when respondents were primed with questions about civil religion or subgroup religion affiliation. Although these differences did not generally reach standard threshold for statistical significance, one notable exception existed. When no religious prime was present, Christians and non-Christians were about equally likely to say that it is important to elect a candidate who makes them "proud of their country." However, for survey respondents who received a civil religion cue, the responses from Christians and non-Christians diverged significantly. Christian respondents in this condition tended to strongly agree that it is more important to elect a candidate who makes them proud of their country, whereas non-Christians see this criterion as much less important.[26] This finding makes sense. Civil religion rhetoric puts forward a particular monotheistic understanding of American national identity and claims that this identity applies to all citizens. Non-Christian respondents are less apt to desire a leader who makes them proud of their country when country itself is infused with a set of religious ideals that are often used to exclude.

This evidence suggests that American civil religion—an identity often expressed in political rhetoric—has the potential to be a divisive force in American politics. Merely asking individuals six questions about identification with American civil religion is enough to encourage many Americans to place less value on a candidate who makes them proud of their country. Civil religion rhetoric may provide an important form of symbolic representation for many Americans, but for those rhetorically marginalized from this identity, strong civil religion rhetoric may actually lead to negativity toward country more generally. Interestingly, theoretical approaches to civil religion often focus on its role in serving as a legitimizing force for the state itself (Wald and Calhoun-Brown 2006). Although these data do not speak to the issue of political legitimacy directly, the notion that a subtle question-order experiment could make individuals have less desire for a candidate who makes them feel pride in their country is significant. When the civil religion net is not cast sufficiently wide, it could actually delegitimize certain aspects of the political process.

Persuasive Appeal of Civil Religion

In chapter 5, I present evidence that presidential candidates who use civil religion rhetoric tend to activate religious evaluative criteria as a basis for vote choice. Although the data in chapter 5 have the advantage of analyzing actual voters immersed in actual campaigns, the data lack the precision of an experimental analysis. The two studies used in this chapter compensate for this weakness, exposing individuals to religious cues under controlled conditions and obtaining more accurate measures of civil religion identity. The results from these studies are consistent with (and extend) the results from chapter 5, indicating that civil religion rhetoric directs attention to religious evaluative criteria. For high-CRI respondents, civil religion rhetoric effectively induces positive emotions and provides a point of common religious identification between candidates and voters.

Data from the undergraduate civil religion experiment provide a strong test of how candidate rhetoric interacts with individuals' religious predispositions. Figure 6.5 displays the likelihood of respondents

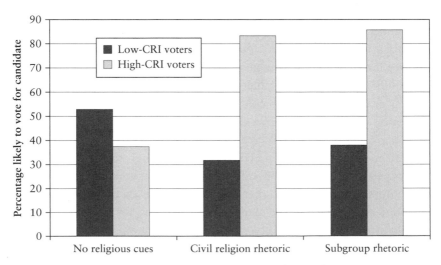

FIGURE 6.5 Vote choice by rhetorical cues and civil religion identity

Percentage of Christians likely to vote for a hypothetical candidate (scoring 5 or higher on a 7-point scale) by rhetorical condition (no cues, civil religion rhetoric, or subgroup religion rhetoric) and level of civil religion identity. Consistent with chapter 5, candidates were evaluated less favorably by high-CRI voters when no religious cues were present (p < .05). For a multivariate test of this relationship, see the online appendix, http://facstaff.uww.edu/chappc/. CRI, civil religion identity voting for the hypothetical candidate in each of the three rhetorical conditions. As the graph illustrates, high-CRI respondents were significantly more likely than low-CRI respondents to endorse a candidate whose message contained some sort of religious cue. Interestingly, high-CRI voters also appeared to punish candidates who failed to use civil religion rhetoric, whereas low-CRI voters viewed these candidates more favorably. This parallels the negative slope shown in figure 5.2 (panel A) in the previous chapter, where candidates who failed to cue American civil religion were punished by more religiously committed voters.[27]

Evidence from the National Civil Religion Identity Study also indicates that civil religion identity has a unique persuasive power. And, consistent with the previous discussion, its persuasive force is more closely connected to a symbolic assessment of leadership than to a substantive issue stance. Table 6.1 shows the results from two multivariate regressions, illustrating how question-order priming interacts with religious identity to predict the salience of religious voting criteria. I consider here two broad measures of political evaluation (as in figure 6.2). The first, religious image, combines the importance that individuals attach to a candidate's moral character, religion, and family values and is designed to approximate symbolic expectations about representative performance. The second, religious issues, combines the importance that individuals place on a candidate's stance on abortion and same-sex marriage, and is intended to approximate a substantive representation dynamic.

Just as figure 6.2 shows that high-CRI voters are more concerned with religious images than with issues, table 6.1 indicates that religious cues play an important role in activating these image-laden evaluative criteria. High-CRI individuals who were exposed to subtle civil religion cues were significantly more likely to report that image-laden concerns are important in evaluating candidates. And, consistent with the findings from chapter 5, not all religious orientations reacted in the same way. In fact, all else being equal, self-described religious fundamentalists were actually *less likely* to say that these factors are important in the civil religion condition. Moreover, the regression predicting religious issue salience does not obtain similar results. Civil religion priming did little to encourage voters to desire a substantive issue agenda—the effects of civil religion rhetoric were entirely symbolic.

TABLE 6.1 Religious cues and the religious basis of candidate evaluation

		Religious image	Religious issues
	(Constant)	.430** (.043)	.391** (.073)
Individual-level variables	Party identification	.01 (.006)	.009 (.010)
	Ideology	.06** (.014)	.054** (.024)
	Civil religion identity	.068 (.295)	−.063 (.112)
	Religious fundamentalism	.103** (.019)	.074** (.032)
Question order	Civil religion condition	.022 (.026)	.038 (.044)
	Subgroup religion condition	.024 (.025)	.058 (.042)
Interactions	CRI * Civil religion	.17* (.098)	.112 (.169)
	CRI * Subgroup religion	.054 (.092)	−.089 (.159)
	Fundamentalism * Civil religion	−.05** (.025)	−.036 (.043)
	Fundamentalism * Subgroup religion	−.031 (.027)	.072 (.047)
	R-square	0.462	0.194

Notes: All entries are unstandardized regression coefficients. All components of interaction terms are grand mean centered. Dependent variables are the *Religious image* and *Religious issues* scales. Standard errors are in parentheses.

* significant at $p < .1$, ** significant at $p < .05$.

Religious Rhetoric and Religious Identity for Non-Christians

Religious cues can be a powerful rhetorical tool to induce positive emotions and activate identity-relevant concerns in Christians; however, non-Christian Americans have a markedly different response. To begin, note that not all non-Christian respondents have the same reaction to religious cues. Although non-Christians from a variety of religious affiliations (e.g., Judaism and Islam) tended to have significantly lower levels of support for candidates who used religious language, this drop was particularly pronounced for individuals with no religious affiliation. For individuals who did not identify with any organized religious tradition (primarily self-identified agnostics and atheists), civil religion rhetoric appears to be a particularly substantial turnoff. This nosedive in support among nonidentifiers makes sense. Even though civil religion has been described as a "minimal monotheism," it is theism nonetheless. Given that civil religion purports to be speaking for all Americans, it makes sense that those who remain excluded from this vision of the American community would evaluate the candidate negatively. Among individuals from non-Christian faith traditions, the subgroup priming actually improved support compared to the control. This suggests that the mere mention of multiple faith traditions in this condition was enough to generate broad-based support, even when the traditions mentioned were not their own.[28]

Just as previous findings illustrate that Christians exposed to civil religion rhetoric are ultimately primed to evaluate the candidate on different terms, so too did non-Christians come to see civil religion candidates in a fundamentally different light. I examined this by looking at both the traits ascribed to the candidates and the emotions that the rhetoric induced.[29] Two findings stand out. First, non-Christians tended to view candidates in both the civil religion and subgroup religion conditions as more religious. But after being primed with a civil religion cue, the perceived candidate religiosity had a strong negative correlation with vote choice ($r = -.425$, $p < .01$). Thus, among non-Christians in the sample, a strong civil religion candidate was viewed as being more of a liability than an asset. Perceived religiosity was not, however, a liability in the subgroup religion condition.

This pattern can be explained by the specific identities cued in the experiment. The subgroup religion priming made reference to multiple faith traditions: "No matter what your racial, ethnic, or religious background—whether you're a Baptist, a Catholic, a Pentecostal, or whatever—these values are enduring." Even when the non-Christians did not fall into any of these denominational groups, this rhetorical style was apparently inclusive enough such that religiosity was not made germane to vote choice. For non-Christians, subgroup and civil religion rhetoric appear to give different impressions of the candidate's own religious tolerance. Subgroup religion rhetoric signals a pluralistic and open religiosity, whereas civil religion rhetoric appears to signal a less tolerant religiosity that is threatening to non-Christians. Thus, religious rhetoric always makes candidates appear more religious to audiences, but the specific religious image that a candidate projects makes a substantial difference in whether it will garner support or create opposition among non-Christian constituents.

In addition to seeing subgroup and civil religion candidates as more religious, non-Christians also had a different emotional response to the religious cues and made different inferences about the candidate's empathy.[30] More than 85 percent of non-Christian respondents in the control condition felt that "caring" described the candidate either "quite a bit" or "extremely well." In contrast, only 67 percent of respondents in the civil religion condition and 60 percent of respondents in the subgroup religion condition felt similarly. Likewise, when candidates invoked the genre of American civil religion, non-Christians reported feeling significantly more irritated and less proud, hopeful, and excited.[31] Although a candidate compassion gap was also present in the Christian sample, it was considerably smaller. This large Christian/non-Christian difference says volumes about how religiously infused leadership is understood by the mass public. Relatively nondescript campaign platitudes lead non-Christian voters to see candidates as less compassionate, even when the rhetoric is gesturing toward inclusivity. Non-Christian voters react to civil religion and subgroup religion cues in a dramatically different way than Christian voters. Whereas civil religion rhetoric has tremendous appeal among Christians (particularly those who scored high on the CRI scale), it can be a liability among non-Christian Americans, inducing negative emotions and creating the impression that the candidates lack compassion. Religious rhetoric need not speak of a culture war to foster divisions.

THE PSYCHOLOGICAL UNDERPINNINGS OF CIVIL RELIGION

Representatives are not just agents who enact specific policies but are symbolic carriers of the American creed, expected to uphold certain standards of moral righteousness. This representative dynamic begins, in many ways, with the rhetorical context established in political campaigns. This is not to suggest that voters have quasi-religious expectations of leaders who invoke the language of a civil religion in every political culture. In American politics, however, the expectations about representatives are steeped in a normative context that places religious imperatives on candidates' self-presentation.[32]

The argument, then, is that in American politics voters—and particularly civil religion identifiers—have a set of quasi-religious expectations about political leadership. These expectations exist because of norms that are deeply ingrained in American political life. Although explicitly crossing the wall of separation between church and state is prohibited, civil religion provides a vehicle through which religious evaluative standards become acceptable or even desirable. When candidates invoke the civil religion, they magnify the effects of this evaluative standard on their own candidacy.

Definitively testing a thesis that involves the transmission of cultural norms is inherently challenging. Data from the National Civil Religion Identity Survey, however, provide one interesting way to approach the problem. The survey contains a short battery of questions adapted from Mark Snyder's (1974) self-monitoring scale (see also Gangestad and Snyder 2002). *Self-monitoring* refers to the tendency of individuals to differ in the extent to which they monitor and regulate their self-presentation in public appearances. High self-monitors are highly responsive to social cues and norms about appropriateness. The concept of self-monitoring can help shed light on the extent to which civil religion rhetoric works by cueing expectations about religious political norms. If civil religion works by creating the expectation that religious evaluative standards are politically and culturally appropriate, then high self-monitors who identify as members of the American civil religion should be especially likely to weigh religious considerations more heavily when exposed to civil religion cues. In other words, because high self-monitors tend to place a greater weight on public appearances, they should be particularly sensitive to the language of civil religion.

To test this, I looked at two evaluative standards that bear several conceptual similarities. I examined the use of family values and the same-sex marriage issue, which is often framed by political conservatives as a family values issue, as evaluative criteria. In this way, I could examine whether civil religion rhetoric primed the expectation that a religious image was a desirable quality in a candidate and whether this extended to religious issues as well. To begin, figure 6.6, panel A, displays the relationship between CRI score and the importance of the same-sex marriage issue in the control condition. The three lines correspond to different levels of self-monitoring. As expected, the graph shows very little difference between high and low self-monitors. This essentially replicates what we see in figure 6.2—high-CRI voters were not any more concerned with cultural issues than low-CRI voters were. Interestingly, the negative slope for high self-monitors indicates that, if anything, civil religion

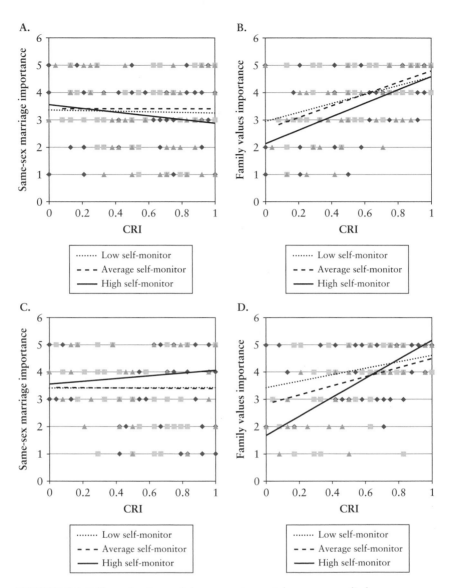

FIGURE 6.6 Self-monitoring and the normative social pressure applied by civil religion rhetoric

Scatterplots of CRI scores (x axis) and the importance of either same-sex marriage (panels A and C) or family values (panels B and D) scores (y-axis), with regression lines added for levels of self-monitoring. Separate plots are displayed for control (no religious cue; panels A and B) and civil religion (panels C and D) conditions. The interaction between CRI scores and self-monitoring is significant only in panel D, suggesting that, when high-CRI individuals encounter civil religion rhetoric, they take this as a cue that it is normatively appropriate to evaluate the candidate on quasi-religious grounds. The dotted lines are linear regression lines for low self-monitors (diamonds). Dashed lines are linear regression lines for average self-monitors (squares). Solid lines are linear regression lines for high self-monitors (triangles). For multivariate tests of these relationships, see the online appendix, http://facstaff.uww.edu/chappcl. CRI, civil religion identity

identity voters worried about public appearances were actually *less* likely to report that same-sex marriage is an important issue. In the absence of religious cues, the expectation of high-CRI voters is that the same-sex marriage issue should not matter in candidate evaluation.

Figure 6.6, panel C, displays the same set of relationships in the civil religion condition. For high self-monitors, the slope of the self-monitoring line is now positive. This suggests that even a cue as subtle as the question-order experiment can create the expectation that candidates ought to be evaluated based on religious issues. Nevertheless, the difference between high and low self-monitors in panel C is far from staggering (and not significant), indicating that, although civil religion cues might create a modest imperative to evaluate candidates on cultural issues, this social expectation is quite slight.

The story was different when individuals were asked whether a candidate's family values were an important part of their evaluative process. When no religious cue was present (figure 6.6, panel B), all levels of self-monitors follow a similar (and by now familiar) pattern—higher levels of civil religion identity translate into a greater perceived importance of a candidate's family values. Moreover, when first exposed to a civil religion cue (panel D), a significant gap emerges between high and low self-monitors. That is, high civil religion identifiers who were most concerned with maintaining a public presentation consistent with cultural norms nearly universally endorsed the notion that family values was an important component of candidate evaluation. In contrast, high self-monitors who did not endorse the tenets of civil religion (low-CRI voters) were more likely to reject family values as an important voting rationale. Priming American civil religion identity tends to push those most sensitive to social pressures in different directions.

This indicates that part of the reason for the success of civil religion rhetoric is because it engenders the expectation among many voters that representation based in a religious candidate image is culturally and socially desirable. Thus, when Bush regularly invoked the language of civil religion in the 2004 campaign, he reinforced a social norm that religion— or at least quasi-religious values—have a place in politics. High-CRI voters making a decision in the 2004 electoral context would have had the distinct impression that religious voting was entirely appropriate. Note, however, that this evaluative standard did not apply to religious issue positions but only to vague character appraisals such as the candidate's family values.

Although the U.S. Constitution erects a wall of separation between church and state, voters regularly bring religious standards to bear on political figures. The dynamics of this complex representational process depends on the religious standards in question, the voters' own religious identity, and the nature of candidate rhetoric. Although many have interpreted religious voting patterns as placing a substantive issue-based mandate on the officeholder, most religious voters are actually more concerned with a symbolic representational style. Indeed, the most common style of religious rhetoric—American civil religion—tends to direct many voters' attention to the religious image, not any particular religious policy platform. It does so by promoting the view that, in American politics, religious evaluative criteria are social acceptable and normatively desirable.

On one hand, these findings are an effective counterexample to the view that a rhetorical cultural war is driving cultural cleavages in the United States. Although self-identified religious fundamentalists may be overwhelmingly concerned with abortion and same-sex marriage, *fundamentalist* does not describe most of the American electorate. Thus, consistent with Geoffrey Layman and John Green (2005), we find that an issue-driven culture war is real but is being "waged by limited religious troops on narrow policy fronts" (83). On the other hand, the analysis also reveals deep tensions with respect to the way religious political rhetoric is normally expressed. Candidates' characterizations of America as a blessed nation resonate with many, but they leave many others unhappy with these candidates and less likely to weigh religious evaluative criteria. Thus, although civil religion is properly considered a broad superordinate identity, it is far from an identity with universal appeal.

7

THE RHETORICAL CONSTRUCTION
OF RELIGIOUS CONSTITUENCIES

*With a good conscience our only sure reward, with history the final
judge of our deeds, let us go forth to lead the land we love, asking His
blessing and His help, but knowing that here on earth God's work
must truly be our own.*
—President John F. Kennedy, 1961 Inaugural Address

Religious rhetoric is a defining feature of the American political campaign. Although the contours of the genre have changed over time, it
contains two enduring elements that make it well suited to be a highly
persuasive tool given the unique American religious landscape. Specifically, the genre is defined by the rhetorical expression of politically salient collective identities and the use of highly emotive rhetorical cues. By
rhetorically leveraging emotions and identity, political elites have thus
used—and will continue to use—this genre to their electoral advantage.
The evidence is clear that, for vast segments of the American public, religious rhetoric is a desirable, if not necessary, component of a candidate's
public self-presentation. Nevertheless, the prevalence of this genre in the
public sphere produces crosscutting effects on the ability of candidates to
deliver adequate representation to all constituents and on the meaning of
an inclusive and tolerant democracy.

In this chapter, I explore the interconnections among religious persuasion, representation, and culture. The evidence suggests that to fully
understand the politics of religious appeals we need to fundamentally
retheorize the nature of religious constituencies. Religious rhetoric
should be thought of less in terms of appealing to stable preexisting religious groups and more in terms of rhetorically activating latent religious
identities. Of particular importance is the activation of an American civil
religion identity. Even though the tenets of civil religion have a broad
adherence in the American public, civil religion is also quite exclusive,
putting forward an explicitly religious conception of American national

identity. Moreover, a candidate's invoking American civil religion recasts the relationship between the representative and voter, bringing symbolic representational demands to bear on the political process. In the end, *separation of church and state* may ultimately be a misnomer in American electoral politics, in that religious rhetoric is responsible for actively creating religious constituencies that can drive election results.

RELIGIOUS RHETORIC AND POLITICAL PERSUASION

It is no accident that religious rhetoric is such a robust feature of American election campaigns. In American politics, religious rhetoric provides a unique solution to the convergence of three challenges faced by candidates. That is, in a winner-take-all electoral system, candidates need to develop a rhetorical style with broad appeal to a religiously diverse constituency that leverages the psychological underpinnings of persuasion. Religious rhetoric, as it has evolved across American history, sits comfortably at the intersection of all these forces.

Of particular importance is the civil religion tradition, which is used to activate a spiritualized sense of collective identity in the American public. As demonstrated in chapter 6, civil religion finds broad identification in the American public, and candidate rhetoric routinely makes this identity electorally salient. It should not be lost on us that civil religion identity gains its power from unique religious makeup of America. In a marketplace of competing religious traditions, civil religion identity attempts to unify an otherwise diverse set of religious affiliations and orientations. Along these lines, however, civil religion rhetoric is not the only choice for candidates. In different electoral environments, candidates have sought to make denominational identities salient and even to activate a schism between orthodox and progressive religious factions.

The key observation here is that religious constituencies are not permanent facts in American elections, defined by bright lines and intractable group allegiances. Rather, individuals have numerous and crosscutting religious identities, and religious political rhetoric works by strategically making these identities politically salient. Scholars of electoral behavior have long understood that individuals hold an array of competing considerations on matters of foreign and domestic policy, and which considerations are brought to the forefront of political evaluation has much to do with how skilled politicians make their case. The process of religious identity priming follows a similar course. To fully understand the role of religion in voting, we should not ask just how campaigns activate religious groups in the electorate but also how campaigns activate different religious identities in the individual.

This has important implications for understanding and interpreting elections. It cautions us not to perceive the religious vote as monolithic but, rather, as a diverse group with multiple interests and desires. It also informs our understanding of candidate strategy. Previous research has found substantial evidence that candidates craft their rhetoric to strategically prime the issues on which they will be favorably evaluated (Jacobs and Shapiro 1994). The present research adds to this understanding of campaign dynamics by showing that candidates also actively construct a common group identity with voters in the electorate. This social group identity need not be formed around any particular issue in the way that farmers might unite around agriculture subsidy policies or union members might unite around changes in labor law. Identity itself can be grounds for persuasion—it need not have a substantive basis in political issues.

This ultimately may be the best explanation for the difference in the religious vote from 2004 to 2008. George W. Bush made significant gains with religiously committed voters during the course of the 2004 election, accentuating the already sizable religion gap enjoyed by Republican candidates. Bush's rhetoric deserves the credit for this. His religious self-presentation was not sectarian but, rather, cast American greatness in religious terms, thus appealing to the identities of a broad array of voters. Although John McCain used religious rhetoric, he did not do so in a manner consistent with the activation of religious identity. In contrast, Obama deftly primed civil religion identity, lamenting the loss of U.S. status in the world order while, at the same time, offering a promise of American greatness. Even though McCain still enjoyed an advantage among religious voters, Obama's rhetorical style was probably responsible for closing the large gap that had been present four years earlier.

FROM PERSUASION TO REPRESENTATION

After the election is over, the active yoking of religion to politics in political campaigns leaves an indelible imprint on the American social fabric. When candidates use religious rhetoric to actively promote civil religion identity as a basis of vote choice, the effect is that many voters understand political leadership in symbolic terms. Given the right rhetorical cues, electoral behavior becomes more about a candidate's image of moral character and less about substantive issues. This is consistent with Pitkin's (1967) understanding of symbolic representation, in which political elites are conceived of as active symbol-makers rather than passive agents who simply stand for their constituents. Pitkin has serious concerns about this representational style, writing that symbolic representation is not "merely ritual activity. Rather, it is a kind of activity to foster belief, loyalty, satisfaction with their leaders, among the people. . . . Since there can be no rational justification of the symbolic representative's position as leader, the emphasis (as with symbols) must fall on the nonrational or emotive elements in belief, and on leadership techniques which exploit such elements" (1967, 107).

Given how subtle and ecumenical religious rhetoric often is in practice, "exploit" may be too strong of a word to describe most candidates' use of rhetorical style. Moreover, although religious rhetoric can shift vote choice, the evidence is clear that, even in religiously charged environments, many other factors (e.g., party identification) remain important. Nevertheless, Pitkin's analysis directs our attention to the normatively problematic aspects of a rhetorical style steeped in religious language. Voters may rush to the polling place unaware that their preferred candidate may not ultimately stand for (or even care about) their substantive interests. Religious rhetoric can thus create representational disjointedness, whereby purely symbolic behavior is taken to imply a substantive mandate.

On top of this representational challenge for those who do identify with civil religion is the question of representation for those who do not. As Murray Edelman notes, "Signs evoke an intense response only for those already taking the roles that make them sensitive to the cues that are given off" (1964, 122). The case of civil religion rhetoric is interesting in that it clearly does not stand for everyone but purports to do exactly that. This rhetorical exclusion has observable consequences. Many Americans simply do not feel represented by candidates who employ the language of civil religion identity. This represents a major challenge, especially considering the growing religious diversity of Americans' religious faiths. As a result, civil religion rhetoric has changed over time to become more inclusive, although exclusion is still a part of the genre. One representational challenge for political elites wielding the language of religious identity is whether the genre can expand once again to offer an even more inclusive definition of the American civil religion.

All this paints a fairly negative portrayal of the representational thrust of American civil religion; however, this portrayal needs to be tempered by our recalling that, theoretically, civil religion exists as a solution to the complex representational challenge posed by a religious constituency that is both diverse and highly committed. For all its potential representational drawbacks, civil religion still stands as a clear alternative to the rhetoric of culture wars, which seeks to actively deepen religious differences. Political observers should take some comfort in the fact that the vast majority of religious rhetoric is not preoccupied with fostering deep societal divisions; in fact, the vast majority of religious language seeks to assert a point of shared collective identity. Moreover, as many have noted, civil religion also plays a role in providing basic political legitimacy for American institutions (Wald and Calhoun Brown 2006). It has helped to rhetorically construct a movement identity for diverse constituencies, as was the case with the Populist movement (Williams and Alexander 1994). And it has been used to direct national attention toward moral shortcomings and to urge reform, as Obama's campaign rhetoric frequently did.

In sum, civil religion plays a complex representation role, engendering a collective identity in a diverse public while, at the same time, directing the electorate toward largely image-based standards of political evaluation. Multiple layers of evidence indicate that, for all its purported attributes, civil religion rhetoric creates serious representational challenges in a pluralistic religious society. Ultimately, perhaps the genre defies an assessment painted with a broad brush. Civil religion rhetoric plays an important representational role, but in doing so it produces serious normative challenges that must be acknowledged as well.

FROM PERSUASION TO AMERICAN POLITICAL CULTURE

In appealing to voters, presidential candidates typically invoke one of three religious identities: subgroup religion references to specific denominations and faith traditions; references to American civil religion, which involves spiritualized, yet banal expressions of American national identity; and divisive references to a culture war in American political life. The expression of these religious identities has important consequences for how faith and American national identity are understood in the public sphere. The concept of an American civil religion, for example, is often theorized to play a positive role in the maintenance of democratic institutions. Jean-Jacques Rousseau famously theorized that a "civil profession of faith" legitimizes democratic institutions (1762). In the American case, Tocqueville asserted a variant of the Rousseauian argument. Even though Americans, Alexis de Tocqueville argues, are divided into numerous sects, "they all see their religion in the same light" (1840, 449). The unity and the general moral wherewithal provided by religion is indispensable to American democracy: "Every religion . . . imposes on each man some obligations toward mankind, to be performed in common with the rest of mankind, and so it draws him away, from time to time, from thinking about himself. . . . Thus religious people are naturally strong just at the point where democratic peoples are weak" (Tocqueville 1840, 445).

If Tocqueville and Rousseau are correct, civil religion is indispensable to American democracy. At the same time, the evidence in this book raises serious doubts about whether the American civil religion casts a wide enough net to generate an inclusive and tolerant political culture. If it does not, civil religion may have a corrosive effect on religious freedom. As Rousseau (1762) himself recognized, civil religion is closely intertwined with intolerance for those who do not ascribe to its basic tenets. In chapter 3, I have shown that civil religion rhetoric has potentially divisive undercurrents. Of its adherents, it requires not only a belief in God but a belief in a very specific conception of God. This detailed attention to God image is not just a theoretical exercise. Evidence presented in chapter 6 suggests that these rhetorical nuances have observable consequences for the American public, making some feel suspicious of and distant from political candidates. In this way, civil religion rhetoric, although politically persuasive, does not live up to its billing as a source of political cohesion.

Even though the cultural impact of civil religion is potentially problematic, it is important not to oversell the negatives. Consider Kennedy's remarks quoted at the outset of this chapter. Kennedy evokes this strong statement of American civil religion from the vantage of a religious outgroup facing substantial religious prejudice. Months earlier in his campaign, Kennedy worked to assure voters that "I am not the Catholic candidate for president. I am the Democratic Party's candidate for president, who happens also to be a Catholic" (September 12, 1960, Houston, TX, Annenberg/Pew Archive of Presidential Campaign Discourse). Rhetorically, Kennedy supplanted fears that he would deliver descriptive representation that privileged Catholics with a symbolic alignment of wills. In this sense, the idea that leaders are active symbol-makers can be seen as potentially working to overcome virulent religious discrimination, insofar as the leader reconstitutes the symbol in the spirit of civil inclusivity. Even though American civil religion can marginalizes some voters, history suggests that the genre is adaptive enough to rhetorically accommodate a growing diversity of citizens. Ultimately, the future of religious rhetoric will be assessed on these terms—on how well it manages to carve out a rhetorical space that accommodates diversity and promotes tolerance while still managing to offer meaning and vision.

NOTES

Chapter 1. A Theory of Religious Rhetoric in American Campaigns

1. For exit poll results, see http://www.cnn.com/ELECTION/2008/results/polls.main/ and http://www.cnn.com/ELECTION/2004/pages/results/states/US/P/00/epolls.0.html.

2. For example, on a Pew Research Center for the People and the Press (2004) survey administered shortly before the 2004 election, 96 percent of those surveyed responded that "the economy" was "very important" or "somewhat important" in how they voted; 94 percent responded "very" or "somewhat important" for "Iraq," 94 percent for "terrorism," 90 percent for "taxes," and 95 percent for "education."

3. The prominence of religion in 2008 was not just limited to Palin and Wright. That year also featured a candidate forum at the Saddleback Church hosted by Pastor Rick Warren. In contrast, an explicitly religious debate format was entirely absent in 2004. Like 2004, 2008 featured several high-profile gay marriage amendments on state ballots. Clergy made news in 2008 when many declared a willingness to lose their tax-exempt status by endorsing a candidate (McCain). And misinformation about Obama's own religious affiliation received regular treatment in the press and the blogosphere.

4. Other scholars have identified similar dichotomies. For example, Putnam and Campbell's (2010) exhaustive work on the role of religion in American society fundamentally grapples with the tensions between religious polarization and pluralism. This dichotomy bears a conceptual similarity to rhetorical expressions of a "culture war" and a "civil religion."

5. For example, certain conceptions of spirituality may be particularly individualistic in nature and self-consciously devoid of any social identity–relevant component. Nevertheless, religious practices in the United States frequently *do* imply substantial group commitments and behaviors.

6. For example, Evans and Nunn (2005) have described culture wars rhetoric as "form of communication does not lend itself to the formation of a consensus position that can be supported by the electorate," a conclusion that speaks to the contrast between culture wars and civil religion modes of discourse.

7. Lerner and Keltner (2000) specifically distinguish anger from fear, finding the latter to be more associated with assessments of uncertainty in the environment and thus to lead to more pessimistic judgments. See also Sengupta and Johar (2001) for a nuanced discussion of the impact of anxiety on information processing.

8. This claim is consistent with other work (i.e., Fiorina, Abrams, and Pope 2010) that argues that culture wars issues have limited appeal for most voters. The present work extends this claim by arguing that, rhetorically, religious language is actually used to unify diverse coalitions by activating symbolic concerns (and by actually avoiding framing issues along religious lines). Indeed, Hillygus and Shields (2008) have convincingly argued that the utility of culture wars rhetoric may actually involve fracturing opposing-party coalitions. Given that civil religion rhetoric is unlikely to be a significant source of inter-

party division, it makes sense that the utility of civil religion involves broader appeals to symbolic cohesion.

Chapter 2. Religious Rhetoric in American Political History

1. The critical biblical passages interpreted by Puritan leadership, according to Bercovitch (1978), are Jeremiah 50:5 and Jeremiah 31:31–33: "They shall ask the way to Zion with their faces thitherward, saying, Come, and let us join ourselves to the LORD in a perpetual covenant that shall not be forgotten" (Jeremiah 50:5, King James version). "Behold, the days come, saith the LORD, that I will make a new covenant with the house of Israel, and with the house of Judah. Not according to the covenant that I made with their fathers in the day that I took them by the hand to bring them out of the land of Egypt; which my covenant they brake, although I was an husband unto them, saith the LORD. But this shall be the covenant that I will make with the house of Israel; After those days, saith the LORD, I will put my law in their inward parts, and write it in their hearts; and will be their God, and they shall be my people" (Jeremiah 31:31–33).

2. Winthrop cites the prophet Micah on this matter. Micah offered Israel a complex message of guilt and repentance, consistent with the notion that the Puritans' mission was parallel with Israel's covenant with God. The "shipwracke" metaphor in this passage is also worth noting because the sermon was most likely delivered aboard a ship crossing the Atlantic.

3. For example, in *A History of the Work of Redemption* (1739, sermon 24) Edwards locates the introduction of the Gospels to the American continent as "one way by which divine providence is preparing the way for future glorious times of the church when Satan's kingdom shall be overthrown . . . . When those times come, the doubtless the gospel which is already brought over into America shall have glorious success, and all the inhabitants of this new-discovered world shall be brought over into the kingdom of Christ." See also Ahlstrom (1972, 311).

4. In Bercovitch's words, "Edwards *discovered* America in scripture" (1978, 99), a move that, despite differences with the first-generation Puritans, was ultimately based "on the figural precedents of the Israelites' covenant renewals under Joshua and Nehemiah" (104).

5. Although Edwards was highly innovative in this regard, he was by no means its sole practitioner, and examples of Americans as God's chosen people are frequent from the 1730s onward. See, for example, Samuel Dunbar's (1760) election-day sermon in Massachusetts, entitled "The Presence of God with His People." Dunbar frames the sermon by directly comparing the "British American provinces and colonies" with King Asa, who realizes that his fate and the fate of his people is intertwined with faith in God (Dunbar 1760, 211; see also 2 Chronicles XV). The reference to "American provinces and colonies" is significant, indicating that, despite being an address specific to the Massachusetts government, Dunbar was viewing the fate of the colonies as shared and the colonies as a whole as having a relationship with God.

6. The case can also be made that this newfound identity was also critically important in putting forward the ideals of the American Revolution. For example, Wise's 1717 "Vindication of the Government of New England Churches" viewed America (and particularly New England) as blessed by God's grace and destined for providential greatness (Rossiter 1949, 21). As Rossiter writes, had Wise been writing in 1776, "he would have outdone Paine and Jefferson in proclaiming the necessity of rebellion" (1949, 29).

7. Examples of this rhetorical style are common. For example, Samuel Langdon's "The Republic of the Israelites as an Example to the American States" (1788), preached as an election-day sermon in New Hampshire at the height of the ratification debate, illustrates how the status of "favored nation" applied to constitutional ratification. According to Langdon, "If I am not mistaken, instead of twelve tribes of Israel, we may substitute the thirteen states of the American union, and see this application plainly offering itself, viz.— That as God in the course of his providence hath given you an excellent constitution of government, founded on the most equitable, and liberal principles, by which all that liberty is secured which a people can reasonably claim, and you are empowered to make righteous laws for promoting public order and good morals (1788, 957). Langdon proceeds to note that this duty is particularly incumbent following the birth of Christ, who is "far superior to Moses" (957). It is interesting to note the overlap of religious and republican principles. The U.S. Constitution was viewed as a gift from God, which ultimately existed to promote a republican sense of public virtue. Rhetorically, Langdon is building on his religious predecessors to create a sense of national identity under God. The sermon contains a litany of God's many blessings on the American people (including General Washington), as well as a sense of shared fate and a common threat in England, concluding that "we cannot but acknowledge that God hath graciously patronized our cause, and taken us under his special care, as he did his ancient covenant people" (958). This sermon also has a significant ecumenical slant (964), suggesting that the developing identity is self-consciously nonsectarian (that is, a very general American Protestantism).

8. This rhetorical style emerged long before the ratification debate itself. Ezra Stiles's 1783 election-day sermon in Connecticut draws on Israel's covenant with God "as introductory to a discourse upon the political welfare of God's American Israel; and as allusively prophetic of the future prosperity and splendor of the United States" (1783, 7). Stiles endorses a nonsectarian America at length: "The united states will embosom all the religious sects or denominations in christendom" (1983, 54). America is, moreover, seen as a paragon of religious virtue, with a distinct place in the millennial unfolding of history: "They will then search all Christendom for the best model, the purest exemplification of the christian church, with the fewest human mixtures. And when God in his providence shall convert the world, should the newly christianized nations assume our form of religion; should american missionaries be blessed to succeed in the work of christianizing the heathen, in which the romanists and sovereign protestants have failed, it would be an unexpected wonder, and a great honor to the united states. And thus the american republic, by illuminating the world with TRUTH and LIBERTY, would be exalted and made high among the nations in praise, and in name, and in honor" (1783, 68–69). See also Meacham (2006).

9. See also Noah Webster (1787) and Pelatiah Webster (1788). Also, see Winthrop (1788) for one example of the use of the "chosen people" narrative to argue against the adoption of Constitution.

10. The dissent in Numbers that Franklin refers to revolves around whether the Israelites should return to Egypt, not constitutional government, as Franklin suggests. Franklin's use of "thirteen tribes" also draws a parallel with the American states; however, there are typically thought to be twelve tribes, descending from the twelve sons of Jacob recorded in Genesis.

11. A distinction should be made between explicitly religious justifications for the Constitution and religious language used to frame ostensibly secular issues. For example, Riker's sophisticated analysis places great importance on the persuasiveness of the Federalist argument that "crisis necessitates reform," as well as strategic positioning in swing-state conventions (1996, 258). With regard to religion, Riker (using content analysis) finds only

a modest amount of discussion regarding the religious provisions in the Constitution (266) and that the argument that "God favors the Constitution" occurred infrequently (273). At first glance, Riker's content analysis seems to do some damage to the claim that religious rhetoric held any sway in the ratification debate. The scope of Riker's analysis, however, is different than the perspective taken in the present investigation. Riker's methodology involved summarizing the arguments made in campaign material—typically at the paragraph level (30). Although these summary sentences are an excellent way to assess the overall themes of a campaign, religious political rhetoric need not be a campaign theme per se. Instead, religious language can be used to frame any number of political themes or to prime a sense of shared identity. Religious rhetoric may not be an "argument" at all but may, instead, color a speech so as to engender a sense of shared identity.

12. In addition to playing a role in the construction of collective identity, religious rhetoric also played an important (and related) role in abolitionist and pro-slavery rhetoric. See especially Noll (2006) and Genovese (1998).

13. Noll (2006) calls this a "theological crisis." The problem was not, Noll argues, that Americans trusted in providence. This concept was highly ingrained in the American mind. The problem was how "narrowly defined" this concept became. Despite the outcome of the Civil War, when both North and South were confronted with the gruesome realities of war, it was difficult to see the workings of God in history (Noll 2006, 94). See also Miller, Stout, and Wilson (1998).

14. This section owes much to Bates (2004) and Aiello (2005), who provide valuable insights into the nature of anticommunist rhetoric and who directed my attention to several revealing sources, such as the *American Mercury* articles of the 1950s.

15. The defining characteristics of American identity thus remained similar to previous rhetorical constructions, enhanced by stark contrasts to an external threat—one actively seeking to destroy the status of America in the world order. Bates makes a similar claim, arguing that the introduction of "godless communism" into the rhetoric of civil religion represents a fundamental shift in rhetorical style: "Civil religion predated American independence, and anticommunism had existed since the birth of communism. But the linkage of the two, and the parallel linkage of atheism and communism, represented something new in American politics" (2004, 30).

16. Specifically, McCarthy said, "As you know, very recently the Secretary of State proclaimed his loyalty to a man guilty of what has always been considered as the most abominable of all crimes of being a traitor to the people who gave him a position of great trust. The Secretary of State in attempting to justify his continued devotion to the man who sold out the Christian world to the atheistic world, referred to Christ's Sermon on the Mount as a justification and reason therefore, and the reaction of the American people to this would have made the heart of Abraham Lincoln happy. When this pompous diplomat in striped pants, with a phony British accent, proclaimed to the American people that Christ on the Mount endorsed communism, high treason, and betrayal of a sacred trust, the blasphemy was so great that it awakened the dormant indignation of the American people" (1950). McCarthy was referring to the Secretary of State Dean Acheson's refusal to condemn Alger Hiss, an accused communist spy (who was convicted of perjury).

17. See also Putnam and Campbell (2010, 86–90).

18. Noting that this argument runs into problems with individuals who do not believe in God at all, Docherty develops an interesting way of dealing with atheism. Atheist Americans are, according to Docherty, a "contradiction in terms" because what makes an American is a belief in God. Atheists, then, are "spiritual parasites . . . living on the accumulated Spiritual Capital of a Judeo-Christian civilization" (Docherty 1954).

19. Marty (1987, 84) notes that Eisenhower was a "particularly gifted priest" of the civil religion and suggests that his rhetoric may have ultimately transformed the cold war into a sort of "holy war."

20. The *jeremiad* is a type of sermon employed by American Puritans, characterized by three principal components: the stating of a "doctrine," usually from the Jeremiah or Isaiah; the "reasons," or an elaboration of the doctrine; and the "applications," or how the doctrine applies to daily life (Miller 1953, 29). The term is derived from the Old Testament lamentations of Jeremiah.

21. A cursory look at the existing literature might suggest, however, that the early generations of Puritan colonists *avoided* explicitly emotive persuasive techniques, instead focusing on the logical implications of scriptural mandates (White 1972). The Great Awakening evangelists certainly ramped up the emotional tenor of religious activities; nevertheless, Berkovitch (1978) has persuasively documented important affective impulses that predate the Great Awakening.

22. The revivalist departure from earlier Puritan rhetoric was a watershed moment in religious language and caused considerable controversy within religious circles, dividing the religious establishment into rationalist "Old Light" Calvinists and evangelical/emotional "New Light" Calvinists, who were in most other ways doctrinally orthodox.

23. Edwards argued that in religious communication there is a problematic disconnect between an abstract theological idea and the words we use to communicate that idea (Miller 1956, 179). For example, in describing the "joy" that enabled early Christians to endure persecution, Edwards contends that "Their Joy was full of *Glory* . . . . the Joy was unspeakable, and no words sufficient to describe it" (1746, 123). As Miller summarizes, Edwards "was ready to maintain that an emotional response [to words] is also intellectual. . . . A passionate grasping of meaning from a thing or a word is as much an idea—a more clear and distinct idea—as a theoretical grasping" (1956, 181). It is interesting to note that Edwards appears to predate the work of contemporary functional theories of emotions in some respects. Edwards gives emotions a role alongside rational thought, arguing that "the mind is the proper seat of the affections" (Miller 1956, 211).

24. "The Omaha Platform" was adopted at the first national convention of the Populist Party.

25. See also Marty (1987, 80) on the malleability of civil religion rhetoric.

Chapter 3. *Religious Rhetoric and the Politics of Identity*

1. According to the 2007 Pew U.S. Religious Landscape Survey, 16.1 percent of Americans consider themselves "unaffiliated," and another 4.7 percent consider themselves members of non-Christian denominations (Pew Research Center for the People and the Press 2007).

2. Overby and Barth (2006) find that radio advertising that is narrowcast to marginalized groups actually tends to increase those individuals' optimism in democracy because their concerns are being directly addressed by the candidates. In a similar way, candidates might stump in a locale with a relatively monolithic religious minority audience, using subgroup rhetoric to make these individuals feel efficacious and included in the political process. Subgroup appeals thus have the potential to enhance the dynamics of religious pluralism by including marginalized groups.

3. In compiling these data, I am particularly indebted to the work of Roderick Hart and Kathleen Hall Jamieson, and to the efforts of the Campaign Mapping Project, as well as the Stanford University Political Communication Lab.

4. To this list, I have added one theoretically motivated religious word—*values*—based on evidence that moral values are of central importance to voting behavior and that voters who report that moral values are important typically attend church at higher rates (Olson and Green 2006). Although values need not be religious, because this word was on the tip of the tongue of frequent church attendees, I deemed it important to explore its rhetorical use.

5. These indicators include all forms of the words: (1) church, churches; (2) faith, faithful, faithfully, faiths; (3) God, God's, Lord, Lord's; (4) moral, morality, morals; (5) pray, prayer, prayers, prays; (6) religion, religions; (7) religious, religiously; (8) sacred; (9) soul, souls; (10) spirit, spiritual, spirituality; (11) values; (12) worship, worships.

6. In other words, I used these indicators to point to spots in candidate speeches where religious language is used; however, even when I identified rhetoric as religious, there is no natural stopping and starting point for a religious passage. Although I could simply have chosen to sample only the sentence in which the indicator word appears, these passages then would be lacking in context and richness. In addition, because much of my sample came from audio transcripts, the sentence is itself a somewhat arbitrary marker. Consequently, I adopted the following rules for sampling rhetoric. First, I sampled all sentences in which an indicator word appeared. Second, if the sentence contained demonstrative or personal pronouns, I also selected up to (but no more than) three prior sentences in order to identify the noun to which the pronouns referred. Third, I made slight modifications to the punctuation where awkward periods and dashes from a speech transcript obscured the meaning. Fourth, if the indicator sentence was part of a quotation, I included the entire quotation.

7. Interested readers can find a more detailed explanation of the coding scheme in the online appendix, http://facstaff.uww.edu/chappc/.

8. The civil religion and subgroup categories were created by collapsing several different subcategories together. Civil religion identity combines all religious references to American identity with unspecified references using first-person plural pronouns. This fits with the theoretical specification outlined, which suggests that civil religion identity works primarily through its appeal to a broad nondenominational religious constituency. Subgroup identity collapses all references to the Judeo-Christian tradition, specific religious denominations, and nondenominational groups. The vast majority of these sectarian references are to Judeo-Christian faith traditions. For further coding details, see the online appendix, available at http://facstaff.uww.edu/chappc/.

9. The provider category was motivated by the frequency of this imagery in candidate rhetoric, which was uncovered in the pretesting for codebook development. Even though this category may, in fact, be a subcategory of paternal image, I coded it as a separate category to eliminate ambiguity.

10. For content analysis reliability information, see the online appendix, http://facstaff. uww.edu/chappc/.

11. The scores presented in figure 3.1 are the number of times a candidate used a word from the LIWC religious words default dictionary, divided by the total number of words across all that candidate's speeches (see Pennebaker, Francis, and Booth 2001).

12. Issue variables were coded for campaigns from 1980 to 2004. Overall, about 34 percent of religious passages made a reference to domestic policy matter and about 10 percent made a reference to a foreign policy matter. Qualitatively, issue appeals generally appeared to be fairly superficial, not sustained attempts to defend a policy on religious grounds. Moreover, there was no clear evidence of a modal or typical religious issue. Issues framed in religious terms ranged from a posture toward the Soviet Union to education to small business. In contrast, identity references appeared in 70 percent of the religious passages, with civil religion identity being the clear modal choice.

13. Dole, for example, frequently discussed abortion, although never in a religious context. Consider this emblematic passage: "And if you send me a partial birth abortion bill I will sign it; I will not veto it. And I don't care what your view is on abortion, pro-life or pro-choice. If you understood this procedure you would be against it. Dr. Koop said—Dr. Koop said—Dr. Koop, whom President Clinton loves to quote, says it's never necessary; in fact, it can harm the mother. This is Dr. Edward Everett Koop. So let's get it, let's pass that bill. I'll sign it" (October 23, 1996, Macon, GA, Annenberg/Pew Archive of Presidential Campaign Discourse). Consistent with Rozell and Wilcox (1996), Dole reframes the issue as a medical matter, citing the authority of a doctor and justifying his position on the grounds of maternal health, not moral or religious dictates. A further analysis of moral or cultural issues is available from author, upon request.

14. Others, particularly Domke and Coe (2010), have examined how candidates and parties discuss cultural issues in general. This is outside the scope of the present project; here I am primarily concerned with how explicitly religious language is used to frame an array of political issues.

15. Candidates vary significantly in the extent to which they invoke these religious identities. Using an ANOVA, between-candidate differences are significant in culture wars and civil religion at $p < .001$, and for subgroup religion at $p < .1$.

16. A t test indicates that, on average, civil religion appeals make modestly more God references ($p = .07$, two-tailed), whereas no such association exists for culture wars and subgroup references.

17. To test this, I regressed civil religion on passage length and references to a blessed nation. Blessed nation references significantly predict the invocation of civil religion identity ($p < .001$).

18. In an interesting speech to the National Baptist Convention in 1988, Michael Dukakis made reference to both Christian responsibility and the special status of America in the same passage.

19. Subgroup passages have an average LIWC first-person plural pronoun score of 1.8, whereas all other passages average 4.7. Difference is significant at $p < .001$ (two-tailed test).

20. Interestingly, passages making reference to a culture war tend to score modestly higher on third-person plural pronouns such as *they* and *them*, consistent with the notion that culture wars rhetoric is concerned with identifying outgroups. This difference is significant at $p < .1$ (two-tailed test).

21. To further test the relationship illustrated in figure 3.3, I used a binary logistic regression to predict shared and pluralistic rhetoric from passage length and each of the three identity variables. Consistent with figure 3.3, civil religion identity has a significant positive relationship ($p < .001$) with shared conceptions of American religiosity. Subgroup religion identity has a positive relationship with pluralistic religiosity ($p < .001$).

22. These differences are statistically significant. I used a binary logit model to regress civil religion on each of the God concept variables. Both the "paternal" and "provider" God concepts significantly predicts civil religion rhetoric ($p < .05$). For details, see the online appendix, http://facstaff.uww.edu/chappc/.

Chapter 4. Religious Rhetoric and the Politics of Emotive Appeals

1. One exception to this is Roseman, Abelson, and Ewing's (1986) examination of the relationship between emotional stimulus and emotional response in campaign materials. This innovative study combines a content analytic categorization of the promotional material of public affairs organizations with a test of which discrete emotions (anger, hope,

fear, or pity) this material induces. This study concludes that varied appeals to discrete emotions have specific and systematic effects. For example, whereas angry and pitying subjects were most persuaded by appeals to those emotions, respectively, fearful subjects were more persuaded by hopeful appeals. Brader's (2006) work also includes a focus on how message characteristics (particularly music and images) can induce different emotional states. See also Huddy and Gunnthorsdottir (2000).

2. To my knowledge, an English translation of Marty's (1908) work does not exist; I am relying on Caffi and Janney's (1994) review.

3. Similarly, using online diaries in the weeks following September 11, 2001, Cohn, Mehl, and Pennebaker (2004) document a prolonged depression following this national tragedy. This suggests that the program can be used as a good barometer of the public mood.

4. Similarly, Sigelman (2002) uses WDAL to draw inferences about Reagan's personality. Comparing pre-presidency speeches (which were generally written by Reagan himself) with presidential radio addresses (which were written with the aid of speechwriters), Sigelman finds significant differences in both the activity and the positivity of "the two Reagans." Thus, he cautions that there are significant limitations on drawing personality inferences about public speakers based on public addresses.

5. Hatfield, Calcioppo, and Rapson (1994) review an impressive array of evidence suggesting that emotional contagion is a prevalent across a variety of contexts.

6. Hatfield, Calcioppo, and Rapson outline three conditions in which individuals can "infect" others with their own emotions. First, "they must feel (or at least appear to feel) strong emotions," a process at which political candidates excel. Second, "They must be able to express (facially, vocally, and/or posturally) those strong emotions." Again, presidential candidates are expected to be well-rehearsed in this regard. Finally, "When others are experiencing emotions incompatible with their own, they must be relatively insensitive to and unresponsive to the feelings of others" (Hatfield, Calcioppo, and Rapson 1994, 146). Politicians are thus quite proficient in their ability to induce emotions without being "infected" themselves. For example, Hatfield, Calcioppo, and Rapson remark that Clinton was known for his ability to "resonate with people's feelings but resist getting caught up in their anger" (1994, 179). Likewise, they cite a study of Reagan's facial expressions in which viewers responded to the president's emotional displays. Reagan supporters and opponents had very different recollections of Reagan appearing in a televised newscast, with opponents reporting negative reactions even to positive emotional displays. Both supporters and opponents, however, tended to mimic his positive facial displays, and skin resistance levels showed that supporters and opponents alike were more relaxed when Reagan had positive facial displays (McHugo et al. 1985; see also Sullivan and Masters 1988).

7. In the case of WDAL, a large list of English words (8,742, representing about 90 percent of commonly used words) were scored along three dimensions: *Pleasantness*, *Activation*, and *Imagery*. Because it is unclear how imagery is related to emotion, I do not consider this dimension further. Each word was rated an average of eight times for *Pleasantness* and *Activation*, and five times for *Imagery*. Thus, all the measures of affect that WDAL computes are essentially composites of the judges' scoring words along up to these three dimensions. Conceptually, *Pleasantness* scores are related to the *Valence* dimension used in many two-dimensional models, whereas *Activation* scores are related to the *Arousal* dimension. WDAL thus computes scores for the percentage of high- and low-arousal words (i.e., activity and passivity) and positive- and negative-valence words (i.e., pleasant and unpleasant) in a given text. WDAL also computes composites of these

dimensions: "sad" is a composite of passivity and negativity, "nasty" is a composite of activity and negativity, "nice" is a composite of passivity and positivity, and "fun" is a composite of activity and positivity. "Nice" is not reported in this chapter, because there are no real theoretical expectations about its political ramifications. In terms of discerning expected effects, these measures have the advantage of grafting onto Russell's (2003) Core Affect model and other related two-dimensional models of emotion. LIWC, in contrast, arranges words categorically. A word, such as *angel*, might simultaneously belong to numerous categories (emotive and otherwise), such as "religion," "optimism," and "positive emotion." Numerous judges were responsible for sorting words into their respective categories. Any given word is sorted into one (or more) of seventy-two non-exclusive categories. So, the LIWC category "anxiety" includes all words that fall in the category "anxiety," and the LIWC output is a percentage of all anxiety words in a given text. Although LIWC does not parallel any particular model of emotion, its hierarchical arrangement does provide us with the ability to test numerous affective categories with precedents in the persuasion and judgment literature. For example, all the discrete emotions are arranged in the superordinate categories "negative emotion" and "positive emotion," which allows us with to examine the general valence of a given message. In addition, LIWC contains measures of discrete emotions such as anxiety and optimism, which may have important effects on judgment, as suggested by the Affective Intelligence model (Marcus, Neuman, and MacKuen 2000). So, although the WDAL *Valence-Arousal* approach cannot adequately differentiate, say, anxiety from anger, the judges who developed the LIWC dictionary ultimately had the differences between these discrete categories in mind.

8. For examples of words scored in the different affective categories of LIWC and WDAL, see the online appendix, http://facstaff.uww.edu/chappc/.

9. It is unclear precisely how to interpret the high WDAL "nasty" score. WDAL codes text along two dimensions: *Valence* and *Activation*. High "nasty" scores correspond to passages high in activity and negativity. Because anger and anxiety are also both theoretically high activity and negativity, I use the WDAL "nasty" measure only as a general indicator that culture wars rhetoric tends to have a negative valence. I rely primarily on the LIWC measures to draw conclusions about discrete emotions. See also Russell (2003).

10. For details, see the online appendix, http://facstaff.uww.edu/chappc/.

11. Specifically, using an ANOVA, I find evidence of significant between-year variation ($p < .05$) on each of these three variables.

12. Differences on the WDAL "nice" measure, not reported in this chapter, are not statistically significant. This measure is intended to capture passive positive rhetoric, which is not necessarily consistent with heuristic processing in the first place. Thus, this null finding is not surprising.

13. Obama is second only to Reagan in this respect. Obama also scored quite high on the LIWC sadness measure.

14. For this analysis, separate bivariate correlations were obtained for every candidate, looking only at observations for which the WDAL sad scores were greater than 0. Thus, the analysis speaks to the question: When candidates use sad language, what else do they pair it with? Like Obama, Dole in 1996 and Regan in 1984 also had positive significant correlations between sad and optimism; nearly every other candidate had a negative correlation between these variables.

15. Bush had a religious optimism score of 0.032, whereas Kerry had one of 0.019. In contrast, Bush's 2004 campaign registered the lowest negative emotion score in the sample, whereas Kerry's was among the highest.

Chapter 5. The Consequences of Religious Language

1. Green, Palmquist, and Schickler's (2002) argument for the stability of partisan attachments uses the stability of religious affiliation as a point of comparison.

2. This is similar to Layman's (2001) distinction among behaving, believing, and belonging and to Manza and Brook's (1999) distinction among a secular vs. unattached cleavage, a traditionalism cleavage, and a denominational membership cleavage. See also Leege and Kellstedt (1993); Mockabee, Wald, and Leege (2007).

3. Scholars use different terminology to characterize this divide. Layman (2001), for example, uses the terms *traditionalist* and *modernist*.

4. For example, in a September 2004 interview on *The Tavis Smiley Show* (on PBS), Wallis said " 'We are not single-issue voters.' So that all of Christian ethics and values can't get reduced down to one or two hot-button social issues, as if abortion and gay marriage are the only religious values, issues in this campaign. The ad says caring for the poor and vulnerable is a religious issue. How we go to war is a religious issue. Caring for the environment, God's creation, is a religious issue. Truth-telling, human rights—all these things are religious values, questions."

5. Data were collected October 15–19, 2004.

6. Specifically, I examined the extent to which abortion salience, same-sex marriage salience, and moral values salience predicted vote choice, controlling for church attendance and party identification. I modeled vote choice as a function of all these issue-salience variables at once and also ran the model with one issue variable at a time to reduce multicollinearity. In addition, I examined interactions between issue importance variables and ideology to test for the possibility that cultural issues mattered only for ideologically conservative voters. Although several of these issues were significant predictors of vote choice for Bush, in no case did the statistical controls for issues dramatically diminish the strength of the relationship between church attendance and vote choice. This suggests that issues alone were not driving the "religion gap" in 2004.

7. For a discussion of moral values issues voting in greater detail, with evidence that voters concerned with moral values are generally concerned with a candidate's representational style, not substantive issues, see chapter 6.

8. Evidence indicates that a connection between religious rhetoric and political behavior is likely. For example, Leege et al. argue that "Through the manipulation of various psychological mechanisms rooted in primary group attachments, political elites attempt to frame issues in such a way to mobilize specific portions of the electorate and demobilize other portions" (2002, 253). Leege et al., however, do not consider any measures of rhetoric such as those developed in chapters 3 and 4; instead, they urge the *direct study* of "candidates, issues, groups, and party images" as an important direction for future research. See also Guth et al. (1995) and Layman and Green (2005).

9. Scholars have made the link between religious communication and political attitudes indirectly by studying exposure to religious messages (Reese and Brown 1995; Hollander 1998; Wilcox, DeBell, and Sigelman 1999), the religious beliefs of political elites (Rozell, Wilcox, and Green 1998, Layman 1999), and the political content of worship services (Brewer, Kersh, and Peterson 2003).

10. This hypothetical example is based on Hogg's conclusion that the salience of a social identity depends on both the accessibility and fit of a particular identity. Individuals use "accessible categories" to "make sense of their social context" (Hogg 2006, 119). Depending on the context, categorizations may vary in how well they help people account for social similarities and differences.

11. For example, Smith understands *American evangelicalism* as an identity which "thrives on distinction, engagement, tension, conflict, and threat. Without these, evangelicalism would lose its identity and purpose and grow languid and useless" (1998, 89). Smith uses the term *evangelism*, as opposed to *orthodoxy*, but it is this commitment to religious distinction and exclusivity in which I am ultimately interested. Individuals who are vested in maintaining these group-based distinctions should be most persuaded by sectarian rhetoric. From a very different theoretical vantage, Iannaccone defines *fundamentalism* as "sectarianism," or "the degree to which a group demands *sacrifice* or *stigma*, or equivalently, the degree to which it *limits*, and thereby *increases the cost* of nongroup activities, such as socializing with members of other religions or pursuing secular pastimes" (1997, 104). Each of these characterizations suggests an orientation toward religious exclusivity that could potentially be activated by sectarian rhetoric.

12. The method for obtaining subgroup scores was modified slightly to obtain more precise estimates than those used in chapter 3. Specifically, because subgroup coding involves just a simple word count of religious subgroups, I was able to use the entire speech database rather than just the sample of seventy-five speeches per candidate. In addition, because the measure of orthodoxy used in this chapter is biased toward Christian orthodoxy, I limited this variable to Christian subgroups. Specifically, I coded all references to Christ, Christian, Protestant, Catholic, Presbyterian, Lutheran, Congregational, Episcopal, Methodist, Baptist, Disciples of Christ, Holiness, Assemblies of God, Nazarene, Pentecostal, Mormon, Jehovah's Witness. Of these, references to Christian, Catholic, and Baptist were by far the most common. To calculate frequency, I divided this count by the total word count for all the candidate's speeches. Aggregated by candidate, this word frequency score was significantly related to the hand-coded measure of sectarian identity presented in chapter 3 ($r = .622$, $p = .02$, $n = 14$).

13. Detailed information on the construction of these variables can be found in chapters 3 and 4, as well as in the online appendix, http://facstaff.uww.edu/chappc/. Because neither LIWC nor WDAL contains a measure of enthusiasm that directly maps to enthusiasm as it is understood by political psychologists (i.e., Marcus, Neuman, and MacKuen 2000; Brader 2006), I averaged the WDAL "fun" variable and the LIWC "positive feeling" scores. See the online appendix for details, http://facstaff.uww.edu/chappc/.

14. One potential objection to this approach is that, if candidates systematically vary their language over the course of a campaign, taking an average over several months of campaigning might lead to biased or inaccurate estimates. The data suggest, however, that the candidates were quite consistent in their rhetorical style across a campaign; for details, see the online appendix, http://facstaff.uww.edu/chappc/.

15. Data from the American National Election Study (ANES), http://www.electionstudies.org. The 2008 ANES was not included in this analysis because pre- and postelection measures of the dependent variable were not obtained.

16. Measuring attitude change using pre- and postelection measures presents complex statistical challenges (Allison 1990; Finkel 1995). For a detailed discussion of the dependent variable, see the online appendix, http://facstaff.uww.edu/chappc/.

17. Across all seven elections studied, $\alpha = 0.673$.

18. One ANES question asked respondents the extent to which the Bible should be taken literally. This single question is a relatively narrow view of orthodoxy, and more important, the response options on the ANES did not adequately distinguish respondents at the conservative end of the scale (Layman 2001, 63). In addition, the response options on this ANES item changed following the 1988 election. Thus, the ANES biblical literalism question is not the best measure for the present inquiry.

19. For a discussion of how the date of interview affects the results, see the online appendix, http://facstaff.uww.edu/chappc/.

20. Detailed information on the construction of these variables can be found in the online appendix, http://facstaff.uww.edu/chappc/.

21. Interested readers can find statistical details in the online appendix, http://facstaff.uww.edu/chappc/.

22. Interested readers can find the full multilevel regression results in the online appendix, http://facstaff.uww.edu/chappc/.

23. For full regression results, see the online appendix, http://facstaff.uww.edu/chappc/.

Chapter 6. Civil Religion Identity and the Task of Political Representation

1. One excellent example is Layman and Green's (2005) careful examination of the culture wars thesis. The authors conclude that "The orthodox-progressive religious divide is most relevant to political behaviour in the special policy, religious and political contexts in which logical, psychological, social and electoral sources of constraint are likely to be in effect" (Layman and Green 2005, 83). In particular, the orthodox-progressive divide is related to substantive issue-based voting for individuals who see abortion as a salient issue and are aware of party differences on this issue. This implies that substantive policy-based representation may be an important electoral expectation of voters, albeit a rather limited segment of the electorate.

2. Civil religion theorists disagree about the extent to which all of these factors coexist. For example, whereas some place an emphasis on the common elements of faith traditions, Bellah (1967) argues forcefully that civil religion should be understood on its own terms as a transcendent religious reality. Theorists such as Rousseau (1762) and Tocqueville (1840) tend to emphasize the connection between civil religion and the maintenance of democratic institutions.

3. Flere and Lavrič (2007) have conducted similar research examining civil religion as an identity orientation in comparative perspective.

4. Social identity theorists typically define a social identity as involving both the awareness of one's objective group membership and a sense of attachment to the group (Tajfel 1981; Conover 1984). This understanding of identity is important because it generates insights into how individuals will respond to identity-laden cues. Previous research has shown that social identities can be primed as a basis of political evaluation (Jackson 2005; Transue 2007) and that group members will display stronger conformity to group norms. For example, Huddy and Khatib's (2007) measure of national identity—which is empirically and theoretically distinct from other belief-oriented measures of patriotism—is a powerful predictor of political participation, insofar as the norm of participation is socially desirable behavior. Similarly, I expect that members of American civil religion should display a willingness to evaluate candidates on quasi-religious grounds when primed with cues suggesting that quasi-religious factors are normatively appropriate standards of political evaluation.

5. In particular, Wimberley (1980) has pointed out the critical role the presidency plays in the American civil religion.

6. The CRI scale used in the National Civil Religion Identity Study has very good reliability ($\alpha = 0.897$). An extended ten-item scale was used in the civil religion priming experiment, described later in this chapter. Although the priming experiment drew on an undergraduate population and consequently had a much lower scale mean, the ten-item scale also had good statistical properties ($\alpha = 0.874$). For additional methodological details, see the online appendix, http://facstaff.uww.edu/chappc/.

7. In addition, an exploratory factor analysis indicated that that CRI is empirically distinct from both religious fundamentalism and national identity.

8. In my sample, whites scored an average of 0.57 on the CRI scale, African Americans scored 0.56, and Latinos scored 0.49. None of these differences were significant at the $p < .05$ threshold.

9. Age is correlated with CRI at $r = .285$ ($p < .05$). At the most extreme ends of the scale, Americans ages 18–35 scored 0.47 on the CRI scale, whereas Americans over the age of 65 scored 0.73. Although this is a substantial gap, CRI is still well represented among younger Americans.

10. An ANOVA confirms that the civil religion differences between major religious traditions are statistically significant, at $p < .001$.

11. For the results, see the online appendix, http://facstaff.uww.edu/chappc/. This finding is consistent with Wimberley and Christenson's (1981) findings from the late 1970s that individuals who identified as Unitarian, Jewish, or "no preference" tended to score much lower on the CRI scale. Interestingly, self-identified Christians are a declining percentage of the U.S. population, and an increasing number of Americans do not identify with organized religion at all. Insofar as civil religion identity is linked with Christian denominational self-identification, there may be a weakening of civil religion identity underway.

12. Perhaps nowhere is this tension between civil religion as a unifying force and civil religion as an instrument of exclusion more evident than Reverend George Docherty's sermon on the Pledge of Allegiance (discussed in chap. 2). After arguing that Christians, Jews, and Muslims are all included in the "American way of life," Docherty quite remarkably takes great pains to argue that "an atheistic American is a contradiction in terms . . . . These men, and many have I known, are fine in character; and in their obligations as citizens and good neighbors, quite excellent. But they really are 'spiritual parasites.' And I mean no term of abuse in this. I'm simply classifying them. A parasite is an organism that lives upon the life force of another organism without contributing to the life of the other. These excellent ethical seculars are living on the accumulated spiritual capital of a Judeo-Christian civilization, and at the same time deny the God who revealed the divine principles upon which the ethics of this country grow" (1954). Thus, even while carving out a place for multiple denominational traditions, Docherty explicitly argues that the definition of an American implies adherence to the civil religion.

13. See also Wolfe's (1998) discussion of a "quiet faith." Wolfe's findings suggest that Americans tend not to see an "American faith" in overly divisive terms.

14. This is consistent with Hillygus and Shields's (2005) finding that moral values voters were not overwhelmingly concerned with the issues of abortion and same-sex marriage (voters were most concerned with issues such as the Iraq War, terrorism, and the economy). Nevertheless, given that civil religion voters did weigh moral character and family values when making their decision, the evidence suggests that moral values voters were still uniquely concerned with image-based dimensions of candidate evaluation.

15. Part of the reason for the difference between high- and low-CRI respondents involves question-order differences on the surveys, whereby some respondents answered a series of religiosity questions before answering the salience questions (see later discussion). On key issues, question-order bias does interact with civil religion identity to magnify differences on the dependent variable. Along these lines, readers might question the appropriateness of examining all respondents together (as I do in figures 6.2 and 6.3). To address this objection, I also ran separate analyses looking at only respondents in the control condition, in which no religious cue was present. The results support the claim that high-CRI respondents are more concerned with a representative style than substantive issues. All differences between high- and low-CRI voters on family values, moral character, and religion are sig-

nificant at $p < .01$. Differences on substantive issues—abortion and same-sex marriage—fail to reach the $p < .1$ threshold for statistical significance, and in fact, *low*-CRI respondents actually reported being *more* concerned about the same-sex marriage issue. Differences on being "proud of country" were also significant in the expected direction. Differences on "someone like me" failed to meet the threshold for statistical significance, although the difference was signed appropriately. Differences between fundamentalist respondents on abortion and same-sex marriage are also significant in the expected direction. In short, the question-order manipulation embedded in the survey does not affect the substantive thrust of the findings presented in this section.

16. To test whether these relationships are statistically significant, I examined separate bivariate regressions predicting issue or image salience from the CRI score. Consistent with the argument, CRI score significantly predicts concern with moral character, family, and candidate's religion ($p < .001$). CRI score is not significantly related to concern about same-sex marriage; however, it does have a small statistically significant relationship with abortion. To further examine these relationships, I replicated each of these regressions, controlling for party identification. The results of controlling for party identification indicate that the relationship between CRI score and concern about religious image is robust, whereas the relationship between CRI score and concern about abortion (a religious issue) is spurious, disappearing when the analysis controlled for party identification. See the online appendix, http://facstaff.uww.edu/chappc/ for regression results.

17. Church attendance and CRI score tend to have similar relationships to political issue salience. That is, when I replicated the analysis in figure 6.2 using church attendance rather than CRI score, I obtained a similar result. The gulf between symbolic criteria for high- and low-CRI individuals, however, is even larger than the church attendance difference. Moreover, the gulf between cultural issues is even smaller when we compare high- and low-CRI respondents as opposed to frequent and infrequent church attenders. CRI score and church attendance are both nondenominational measures of religious adherence, and they appear to differentiate issue salience in a similar manner. CRI score is much better, however, at gauging differences in symbolic concerns. Thus, the CRI results presented in this chapter can be seen as having a strong parallel with the religious commitment findings in chapter 5.

18. In other words, American national identity and civil religion identity appear to explain different components of the variance in "pride in country." See the online appendix, http://facstaff.uww.edu/chappc/.

19. Because I collected original survey data in this chapter, I substituted a measure of self-identified religious fundamentalism for the religious orthodoxy measure that was used in the previous chapter (Layman 2001, 85). Although the measurement strategies are different, both ultimately capture the respondent's sense of religious exclusivity.

20. For an example, see the online appendix, http://facstaff.uww.edu/chappc/.

21. Fundamentalism significantly predicts the salience of abortion and same-sex marriage at $p < .001$. See the online appendix, http://facstaff.uww.edu/chappc/.

22. Only 6.5 percent of the sample said that *fundamentalist* described them "a great deal."

23. This is a ten-item version of the CRI scale administered in the National Civil Religion Study. Although conceptually similar to the scale used in the national study, modifications were made both to accommodate survey length and to better tap identity-relevant aspects of civil religion.

24. For details, see the online appendix, http://facstaff.uww.edu/chappc/.

25. It should be noted that I actually used a 3 × 3 design, manipulating not only the religious identities but also the use of emotive language. Specifically, in addition the candi-

date web page containing rhetorical styles for control, civil religion, or subgroup religion, the web page also contained control, enthusiastic, or angry rhetoric. The analyses presented here simplify this design in two ways. First, I have excluded all three anger conditions from further analysis. These conditions were included in the survey to address specific questions about emotion and group-based thinking, but in practice angry civil religion rhetoric is quite uncommon. Second, in further analyses I have averaged together the enthusiastic and control conditions. In other words, I have considered only the identity manipulation, not the emotive differences. Extensive testing presented elsewhere (Chapp 2009) suggests that enthusiastic language primarily influences the likelihood of voter turnout, not vote choice.

26. To examine this relationship further I regressed "proud of country" on Christianity, dummy variables for the religious conditions, and an interaction between Christianity and the rhetorical condition. The results, reproduced in the online appendix, http://facstaff.uww.edu/chappc/, indicate that the interaction between the civil religion cue and Christianity is moderately significant ($p = .071$).

27. Although the current findings are generally consistent with those in chapter 5, it is interesting to note that the subgroup religion condition also appears to activate a civil religion orientation as a basis of candidate evaluation. This may be due in part to the unique student sample, which exhibited very little variance on other religious orientations of importance, such as fundamentalism.

28. It should be noted that these do not meet the $p < .05$ threshold for statistical significance, due to the difficultly of obtaining a large enough non-Christian sample. These results should be taken only as suggestive.

29. Trait assessments were measured by asking respondents, "Based on the website you just looked at, how well do you think the following words or phrases characterize Ed Mitchell?" Respondents rated the candidate on a scale of 1 to 5, ranging from "not well at all" to "extremely well."

30. This difference is significant at $p = .013$ when comparing the control to the subgroup religion condition, and at $p = .054$ when comparing the control to the civil religion condition.

31. Like the trait assessment, emotional responses were measured by asking the respondents, "Thinking back to the website you just looked at, how well do the following words or phrases characterize how the website made you feel personally?" Respondents rated the candidate on a scale from 1 to 5, ranging from "not well at all" to "extremely well."

32. For example, Domke and Coe argue that the "golden rule" of religious campaigning involves "signal[ing] to devout religious believers that they share and appreciate these citizens' faith, but do so without pushing away religious moderates and secular minded voters" (2010, 130). Likewise, Hart has written that "political rhetoric must avoid being overly religious, and religious rhetoric overly political (2000, 49).

REFERENCES

Abdelal, Rawi, Yoshiko M. Herrera, Alastair Iain Johnston, and Rose McDermott. 2006. "Identity as a Variable." *Perspectives on Politics* 4:695–711.

Abramowitz, Alan, and Kyle Saunders. 2005. "Why Can't We All Just Get Along? The Reality of a Polarized America," *Forum* 3(2): art. 1, http://www.bepress.com/forum/vol3/iss2/art1.

Ahlstrom, Sydney E. 1972. *A Religious History of the American People.* New Haven, Conn.: Yale University Press.

Aiello, Thomas. 2005. "Constructing 'Godless Communism': Religion, Politics, and Popular Culture, 1954–1960." *Americana* 4(1), http://www.americanpopularculture.com/journal/articles/spring_2005/aiello.htm.

Albanese, Catherine L. 2001. *American Spiritualities: A Reader.* Bloomington: University of Indiana Press.

Albertson, Bethany. 2005. "Religious Language and Implicit Political Cognition." Paper presented at the annual meeting of the American Political Science Association, Washington, D.C.

Allison, Paul D. 1990. "Change Scores as Dependent Variables in Regression Analysis." *Sociological Methodology* 20:93–114.

Althaus, Scott L., Peter F. Nardulli, and Daron R. Shaw. 2002. "Candidate Appearances in Presidential Elections, 1972–2000." *Political Communication* 19(1): 49–72.

American Presidency Project. 1999–2012. americanpresidency.org (http://www.presidency.ucsb.edu).

Anderson, Lisa. 2004. "Faith Takes Key Role in Political Landscape." *Chicago Tribune,* November 4.

Annenberg/Pew Archive of Presidential Campaign Discourse. 2000. CD-ROM. Annenberg School for Communication, University of Pennsylvania.

Arkin, Mark M. 2001. "The Federalist Trope: Power and Passion in Abolitionist Rhetoric." *Journal of American History* 88(1): 75–98.

Bartels, Larry M. 1993. "Messages Received: The Political Impact of Media Exposure." *American Political Science Review* 87(2): 267–85.

——. 2008. *Unequal Democracy: The Political Economy of the New Gilded Age.* New York: Russell Sage.

Bates, Stephen. 2004. "Godless Communism and Its Legacies." *Society* 41(3): 29–33.

Baum, Matthew A., and Samuel Kernell. 1999. "Has Cable Ended the Golden Age of Presidential Television?" *American Political Science Review* 93(1): 99–114.

Bellah, Robert N. 1967. "Civil Religion in America." *Daedalus* 96:1–21.

———. 1975. *The Broken Covenant: American Civil Religion in Time of Trial.* New York: Seabury Press.

Bercovitch, Sacvan. 1978. *The American Jeremiad.* Madison: University of Wisconsin Press.

Billig, Michael. 2003. "Political Rhetoric." In *Oxford Handbook of Political Psychology,* ed. David Sears, Leonie Huddy, and Robert Jervis, 222–50. Oxford: Oxford University Press.

Bodenhausan, Galen V., Lori A. Sheppard, and Geoffery P Kramer. 1994. "Negative Affect and Social Judgment: The Differential Impact of Anger and Sadness." *European Journal of Social Psychology* 24:45–62.

Bolce, Louis, and Gerald De Maio. 1999. "The Anti-Christian Fundamentalist Factor in Contemporary Politics." *Public Opinion Quarterly* 63(4): 508–42.

Bower, Gordon H. 1991. "Mood Congruity of Social Judgments." In *Emotion and Social Judgments,* ed. Joseph P. Forgas. Oxford: Pergamon.

Brader, Ted. 2006. *Campaigning for Hearts and Minds: How Emotional Appeals in Political Ads Work.* Chicago: University of Chicago Press.

Brauer, Jerald C., ed. 1976. *Religion and the American Revolution.* Philadelphia: Fortress Press.

Brewer, Marilynn. 1999. "The Psychology of Prejudice: Ingroup Love or Outgroup Hate?" *Journal of Social Issues* 55(3): 429–44.

Brewer, Mark D., Rogan Kersh, and R. Eric Petersen. 2003. "Assessing Conventional Wisdom about Religion and Politics: A Preliminary View from the Pews." *Journal for the Scientific Study of Religion* 41:125–36.

Bryan, William Jennings. 1896. "Cross of Gold." Speech delivered at the 1896 Democratic National Convention in Chicago, http://historymatters.gmu. edu/d/5354/ (accessed April 2008).

Buchanan, Patrick J. 1992. "1992 Republican National Convention Speech." Speech delivered in Houston, Texas, http://www.buchanan.org/pa-92–0817-rnc.html (accessed April 2008).

Caffi, Claudia, and Richard W. Janney. 1994. "Toward a Pragmatics of Emotive Communication." *Journal of Pragmatics* 22(3–4): 325–73.

Campbell, Angus, Phillip E. Converse, Warren E. Miller, and Donald E. Stokes. 1960. *The American Voter.* Chicago: University of Chicago Press.

Campbell, David E., John C. Green, and Geoffrey C. Layman. 2011. "The Party Faithful: Partisan Images, Candidate Religion, and the Electoral Impact of Party Identification." *American Journal of Political Science* 55(1): 42–58.

Chapp, Christopher. 2009. "Religious Political Participation: Affect, Identity, and Rhetorical Cues." Paper presented at the annual meeting of the Midwest Political Science Association, Chicago, April 2–5, 2009.

Chong, Dennis, and James N. Druckman. 2007a. "Framing Public Opinion in Competitive Democracies." *American Political Science Review* 101(4): 637–55.

——. 2007b. "Framing Theory." *Annual Review of Political Science* 10:103–26.

Cohn, Michael A., Matthias R. Mehl, and James W. Pennebaker. 2004. "Linguistic Markers of Psychological Change Surrounding September 11, 2001." *Psychological Science* 15(10): 687–93.

Conover, Pamela Johnston. 1984. "The Influence of Group Identification on Political Perception and Evaluation." *Journal of Politics* 46:760–85.

——. 1988. "The Role of Social Groups in Political Thinking." *British Journal of Political Science* 18(1): 51–76.

Crosby, Donald F. 1978. *God, Church, and Flag: Senator Joseph A. McCarthy and the Catholic Church.* Chapel Hill: University of North Carolina Press.

Cummings, Henry. [1781] 1998. "A Sermon Preached at Lexington on the 19th of April." In *Political Sermons of the American Founding Era*, ed. Ellis Sandoz, 657–82. Indianapolis: Liberty Fund.

Danforth, Samuel. [1670] 2006. "A Brief Recognition of New-Englands Errand into the Wilderness." Libraries at the University of Nebraska-Lincoln Faculty Publications, digital commons, ed. Paul Royster, http://digitalcommons.unl.edu/libraryscience/35.

Davis, James H. [1894] 1967. "A Political Revelation." In *The Populist Mind*, ed. Norman Pollack, 203–27. Indianapolis: Bobbs-Merrill.

DeSteno, David, Nilanjana Dasgupta, Monica Y. Bartlett, and Aida Cajdrie. 2004. "Prejudice from Thin Air: The Effect of Emotion on Automatic Intergroup Attitudes." *Psychological Science* 15(5): 319–24.

DeSteno, David, Richard E. Petty, Derek D. Rucker, Duane T. Wegener, and Julia Braverman. 2004. "Discrete Emotions and Persuasion: The Role of Emotion-Induced Expectancies." *Journal of Personality and Social Psychology* 86(1): 43–56.

Djupe, Paul A., and Christopher P. Gilbert. 2003. *The Prophetic Pulpit: Clergy, Churches, and Communities in American Politics.* Lanham, Md.: Rowman & Littlefield.

Docherty, George. 1954. "One Nation under God." New York Avenue Presbyterian Church sermon archive, http://www.nyapc.org/congregation/Sermon_Archives/?month=1954-02 (accessed April 2008).

Domke, David, and Kevin Coe. 2010. *The God Strategy: How Religion Became a Political Weapon in America.* Oxford: Oxford University Press.

Donnelly, Ignatius. 1892. "The Omaha Platform." History Matters, http://historymatters.gmu.edu/d/5361/ (accessed April 2008).

Druckman, James N. 2004. "Priming the Vote: Campaign Effects in a U.S. Senate Election." *Political Psychology* 25:577–94.

Druckman, James N., and Justin W. Holmes. 2004. "Does Presidential Rhetoric Matter? Priming and Presidential Approval." *Presidential Studies Quarterly* 34:755–78.

Druckman, James N., Lawrence R. Jacobs, and Eric Ostermeier. 2004. "Candidate Strategies to Prime Issues and Image." *Journal of Politics* 66:1205–27.

Druckman, James N., and Kjersten Nelson. 2003. "Framing and Deliberation: How Citizens' Conversations Limit Elite Influence." *American Journal of Political Science* 47:729–45.

Duhamel, Paul, and Cynthia Whissell 1998. *Whissell's Dictionary of Affect in Language*. Computer software. Collingwood, Canada: Human Development Consulting.

Dunbar, Samuel. [1760] 1998. "The Presence of God with His People." In *Political Sermons of the American Founding Era*, ed. Ellis Sandoz, 207–30. Indianapolis: Liberty Fund.

Edelman, Murray. 1964. *The Symbolic Uses of Politics*. Urbana: University of Illinois Press.

Edwards, Jonathan. 1739. *A History of the Work of Redemption*. Jonathan Edwards Center at Yale University, ed. John F. Wilson, http://edwards.yale.edu/research/major-works/history-of-the-work-of-redemption/.

——. [1741] 1962. "Sinners in the Hands of an Angry God." In *Jonathan Edwards: Representative Selections with Introduction, Bibliography, and Notes*, ed. Clarence H. Faust and Thomas H. Johnson, 155–72. New York: Hill and Wang.

——. [1746] 1972. "Concerning the Nature of the Affection and Their Importance in Religion." In *Puritan Rhetoric: The Issue of Emotion in Religion*, ed. Eugene E. White, 119–57. Carbondale: Southern Illinois University Press.

Ellis, Richard J. 2005. *To the Flag: The Unlikely History of the Pledge of Allegiance*. Lawrence: University of Kansas Press.

Emmons, Robert A., and Raymond F. Paloutzian. 2003. "The Psychology of Religion." *Annual Review of Psychology* 54:377–402.

Evans, John H., and Lisa M. Nunn. 2005. "The Deeper Culture Wars Questions." *Forum* 3(2): art. 3.

Feldman, Noah. 2005. *Divided by God*. New York: Farrar, Straus and Giroux.

Finke, Roger, and Rodney Stark. 1989. "How the Upstart Sects Won America, 1776–1850." *Journal for the Scientific Study of Religion* 28(1): 27–44.

Finkel, Steven E. 1995. *Causal Analysis with Panel Data*. Thousand Oaks, Calif.: Sage.

Fiorina, Morris P., Samuel J. Abrams, and Jeremy C. Pope. 2010. *Culture War? The Myth of a Polarized America*. New York: Pearson.

Fitfield, James W. 1954. "Freedom under God." *American Mercury*, June, 45–51.

Flere, Sergej, and Miran Lavri&ccaron. 2007. "Operationalizing the Civil Religion Concept at a Cross-Cultural Level." *Journal for the Scientific Study of Religion* 46(4): 595–604.

Fowler, Robert B., Laura Olson, Allen Hertzke, and Kevin den Dulk. 2004. *Religion and Politics in America: Faith, Culture, and Strategic Choices*. 3rd ed. Boulder: Westview Press.

Franklin, Benjamin. [1788] 1993. "The Antifederalists Compared with the Ancient Jews as Rejecters of Divine Constitutions." In *The Debate on the*

Constitution: Federalist and Antifederalist Speeches, Articles, and Letters during the Struggle over Ratification, ed. Bernard Bailyn, 2:401–5. New York: Library of America.

Froese, Paul, and Christopher Bader. 2010. *America's Four Gods: What We Say about God, and What That Says about Us.* Oxford: Oxford University Press.

Gaertner, Samuel, and John F. Dovidio. 2000. *Reducing Intergroup Bias: The Common Ingroup Identity Model.* Ann Arbor: Taylor and Francis.

Gangestad, Steven W., and Mark Snyder. 2002. "Self-Monitoring: Appraisal and Reappraisal." *Psychological Bulletin* 126(4): 530–55.

Garrison, William Lloyd. 1831. "To the Public." PBS Africans in America resource bank, http://www.pbs.org/wgbh/aia/part4/4h2928t.html (accessed April 2008). Originally published in *The Liberator,* January 1, 1831.

———. 1838. "An Address Delivered in Marlboro Chapel, Boston, July 4, 1838." Antislavery Literature Project, http://antislavery.eserver.org/tracts/garrison marlborochapel/garrisonmarlborochapel.html.

Genovese, Eugene. 1998. "Religion and the Collapse of the American Union." In *Religion and the American Civil War,* ed. Randall M. Miller, Harry S. Stout, and Charles Reagan Wilson, 74–88. Oxford: Oxford University Press.

Glaser, Jack, and Peter Salovey. 1998. "Affect in Electoral Politics." *Personality and Social Psychology Review* 2(3): 156–72.

Goodrich, Elizur. [1787] 1998. "The Principles of Civil Union and Happiness Considered and Recommended." In *Political Sermons of the American Founding Era,* ed. Ellis Sandoz, 909–40. Indianapolis: Liberty Fund.

Graham, Billy. 1954. "Satan's Religion." *American Mercury,* August, 41–46.

———. 1955a. "A Christian America." *American Mercury,* March, 68–72.

———. 1955b. "Our Bible." *American Mercury,* December, 99–103.

Greeley, Andrew. 1972. *The Denominational Society.* Glenview, Ill.: Scott Foresman & Co.

Green, Donald, Eric Palmquist, and Eric Schickler. 2002. *Partisan Hearts and Minds.* New Haven, Conn.: Yale University Press.

Guth, James L., John C. Green, Lyman A. Kellstedt, and Corwin E. Smidt. 1995. "Faith and the Environment: Religious Beliefs and Attitudes on Environmental Policy." *American Journal of Political Science* 39:364–82.

Gutterman, David S. 2005. *Prophetic Politics: Christian Social Movements and American Democracy.* Ithaca, N.Y.: Cornell University Press.

Hammersla, Joy Fisher, Lisa C. Andrews-Qualls, and Lynne G. Frease. 1986. "God Concepts and Religious Commitment among Christian University Students." *Journal for the Scientific Study of Religion* 25(4): 424–35.

Hart, Roderick P. 2000. *Campaign Talk: Why Elections Are Good for Us.* Princeton, N.J.: Princeton University Press.

———. 2005. *The Political Pulpit Revisited.* West Lafayette, Ind.: Purdue University Press.

Hatfield, Elaine, John T. Cacioppo, and Richard Rapson. 1994. *Emotional Contagion*. Cambridge, UK: Cambridge University Press.

Herberg, Will. 1954. *Protestant—Catholic—Jew: An Essay in American Religious Sociology*. New York: Doubleday.

Hill, Peter C., and Ralph W. Hood Jr. 1999. "Affect, Religion, and Unconscious Processes." *Journal of Personality* 67(6): 1015–46.

Hillygus, D. Sunshine, and Todd Shields. 2005. "Moral Issues and Voter Decision Making in the 2004 Presidential Election." *PS: Political Science and Politics* 38(2): 201–9.

——. 2008. *The Persuadable Voter: Wedge Issues in Presidential Campaigns*. Princeton, N.J.: Princeton University Press.

Hogg, Michael A. 2006. "Social Identity Theory." In *Contemporary Social Psychological Theories*, ed. Peter J. Burke, 111–36. Stanford, Calif.: Stanford University Press.

Hollander, Barry A. 1998. "The Priming of Religion in Political Attitudes: The Role of Religious Programming." *Journal of Communication and Religion* 21:67–83.

Hoover, J. Edgar. 1957. "The American Ideal." *American Mercury*, October, 99–103.

Huddy, Leonie. 2001. "From Social to Political Identity: A Critical Examination of Social Identity Theory." *Political Psychology* 22(1): 127–56.

Huddy, Leonie, and Anna H. Gunnthorsdottir. 2000. "The Persuasive Effects of Emotive Visual Imagery: Superficial Manipulation or the Product of Passionate Reason?" *Political Psychology* 21(4): 745–78.

Huddy, Leonie, and Nadia Khatib. 2007. "American Patriotism, National Identity, and Political Involvement." *American Journal of Political Science* 51(1): 63–77.

Hunter, James David. 1991. *Culture Wars: The Struggle to Define America*. New York: Basic Books.

Iannaccone, Lawrence R. 1997. "Toward an Economic Theory of Fundamentalism." *Journal of Institutional and Theoretical Economics* 153(1): 100–121.

Jackson, Melinda Sue. 2005. *Identity Matters: Political Identity Construction and the Process of Political Influence*. Ph.D. dissertation, University of Minnesota–Twin Cities.

Jacobs, Lawrence R., and Robert Y. Shapiro. 1994. *Politicians Don't Pander: Political Manipulation and the Loss of Democratic Responsiveness*. Chicago: University of Chicago Press.

James, William. 1902. *The Varieties of Religious Experience*. New York: Dolphin Books.

Jamieson, Kathleen Hall, and Paul Waldman. 1997. "Mapping Campaign Discourse: An Introduction." *American Behavioral Scientist* 40(8): 1133–38.

Jennings, M. Kent, and Laura Stoker. 2007. "Changing Relationships between Religion and Politics: A Longitudinal, Multigenerational Analysis." Paper presented at the annual meeting of the International Society of Political Psychology, Portland, Ore., July 4–7.

Jensen, Lene Arnett. 2009. "Conceptions of God and the Devil across the Lifespan: A Cultural-Developmental Study of Religious Liberals and Conservatives." *Journal for the Scientific Study of Religion* 48(1): 121–45.

Kaid, Lynda Lee. 2003. "Effects of Political Information in the 2000 Presidential Campaign." *American Behavioral Scientist* 46(5): 677–91.

Kennedy, John F. 1960. "Speech to the Greater Houston Ministerial Association." National Public Radio, http://www.npr.org/templates/story/story.php?storyId=16920600 (accessed April 2008).

——. 1961. "Inaugural Address." Bartleby.com, http://www.bartleby.com/124/pres56.html (accessed April 2008).

Kinder, Donald R. 1998. "Communication and Opinion." *Annual Review of Political Science* 1:167–97.

Kirkpatrick, David O. 2004. "Battle Cry of Faithful Pits Believers against the Rest." *New York Times*, October 31.

Klapper, Joseph T. 1960. *The Effects of Mass Communications.* Glencoe, Ill.: Free Press.

Kohut, Andrew, John C. Green, Scott Keeter, and Robert C. Toth. 2000. *The Diminishing Divide: Religion's Changing Role in American Politics.* Washington, D.C.: Brookings Institution Press.

Ladd, Jonathan McDonald, and Gabrial S. Lenz. 2008. "Reassessing the Role of Anxiety in Vote Choice." *Political Psychology* 29(2): 275–96.

Lakoff, George. 1996. *Moral Politics: What Conservatives Know That Liberals Don't.* Chicago: University of Chicago Press.

——. 2008. *The Political Mind: Why You Can't Understand 21st Century American Politics with an 18th Century Brain.* New York: Viking.

Lambert, Frank. 2008. *Religion in American Politics: A Short History.* Princeton, N.J.: Princeton University Press.

Langdon, Samuel. [1788] 1998. "The Republic of the Israelites as an Example to the American States." In *Political Sermons of the American Founding Era*, ed. Ellis Sandoz, 941–68. Indianapolis: Liberty Fund.

Layman, Geoffrey C. 1999. " 'Culture Wars' in the American Party System: Religious and Cultural Change among Partisan Activists since 1972." *American Politics Quarterly* 27:89–121.

——. 2001. *The Great Divide.* New York: Columbia University Press.

Layman, Geoffery C., and John C. Green. 2005. "Wars and Rumors of Wars: The Contexts of Cultural Conflict in American Political Behaviour. *British Journal of Political Science* 36:61–89.

Leege, David C., and Lyman A. Kellstedt, eds. 1993. *Rediscovering the Religious Factor in American Politics.* New York: M. E. Sharpe.

Leege, David C., Kenneth D. Wald, Brian S. Krueger, and Paul D. Mueller. 2002. *The Politics of Cultural Differences: Social Change and Voter Mobi-*

lization Strategies in the Post-New Deal Period. Princeton, N.J.: Princeton University Press.

Lerner, Jennifer S., and Dacher Keltner. 2000. "Beyond Valence: Toward a Model of Emotion-Specific Influences on Judgment and Choice." *Cognition and Emotion* 14(4): 473–93.

Lincoln, Abraham. 1854. "Speech on the Kansas-Nebraska Act." AMDOCS: Documents for the Study of American History, http://www.vlib.us/amdocs/texts/kansas.html (accessed April 2008).

——. [1865] 2002. "Second Inaugural Address." In *This Fiery Trial: The Speeches and Writings of Abraham Lincoln*, ed. William E. Gienapp, 220–21. Oxford: Oxford University Press.

Lippmann, Walter. 1922. *Public Opinion*. New York: Free Press.

Lloyd, Henry Demarest. [1894] 1967. "The Divinity of Humanity." In *The Populist Mind*, ed. Norman Pollack, 69–70. Indianapolis: Bobbs-Merrill.

Lodge, Milton, Kathleen McGraw, and Patrick Stroh. 1989. "An Impression Driven Model of Candidate Evaluation." *American Political Science Review* 83(2): 399–419.

Madison, James. [1788a] 1986a. "Federalist 37." In *The Origins of the American Constitution: A Documentary History*, ed. Michael Kammen, 174–80. New York: Penguin Book.

——. [1788b] 1986b. "Federalist 49." In *The Origins of the American Constitution: A Documentary History*, ed. Michael Kammen, 198–202. New York: Penguin Book.

Manza, Jeff, and Clem Brooks. 1999. *Social Cleavages and Political Change: Voter Alignments and U.S. Party Coalitions*. Oxford: Oxford University Press.

Marcus, George E. 2000. "Emotions in Politics." *Annual Review of Political Science* 3:221–50.

Marcus, George E., W. Russell Neuman, and Michael MacKuen. 2000. *Affective Intelligence and Political Judgment*. Chicago: Chicago University Press.

Marty, Anton. 1908. *Untersuchungen zur Grundlegung der Allgemeinen Grammatik und Sprachphilosophie*. Halle: Niemeyer.

Marty, Martin E. 1987. *Religion and Republic: The American Circumstance*. Boston: Beacon Press.

Mather, Cotton. [1690] 1965. "The People of God." In *Puritan Political Ideas*, ed. Edmund S. Morgan, 233–50. Indianapolis: Bobbs-Merrill.

Mayer, Henry. 1998. *All on Fire: William Lloyd Garrison and the Abolition of Slavery*. New York: St. Martin's Press.

Mayflower Compact. 1620. The Avalon Project at Yale Law School, http://www.yale.edu/lawweb/avalon/amerdoc/mayflower.htm (accessed April 2008).

Mayhew, David R. 1974. *Congress: The Electoral Connection*. New Haven, Conn.: Yale University Press.

McCarthy, Joseph. 1950. "Speech of Joseph McCarthy, Wheeling, West Virginia, February 9, 1950." History Matters, http://historymatters.gmu.edu/d/6456 (accessed April 2008).

McHugo, Gregory J., John T. Lanzetta, Denis G. Sullivan, Roger D. Masters, and Basil G. Englis. 1985. "Emotional Reactions to a Political Leader's Expressive Displays." *Journal of Personality and Social Psychology* 49(6): 1513–29.

Meacham, Jon. 2006. *American Gospel: God, the Founding Fathers, and the Making of a Nation.* New York: Random House.

Mead, Sidney E. 1974. "The 'Nation with the Soul of a Church.'" In *American Civil Religion,* ed. Russell E. Richey and Donald G. Jones, 45–75. New York: Harper & Row.

Meet the Press. 2004. NBC News. Television program, November 4. http://www.msnbc.msn.com/id/6430019/ns/meet_the_press/t/transcript-november/.

Mendelsohn, Matthew. 1996. "The Media and Interpersonal Communications: The Priming of Issues, Leaders, and Party Identification." *Journal of Politics* 58:112–25.

Miller, Alan S., and John P. Hoffmann. 1999. "The Growing Divisiveness: Culture Wars or a War of Words?" *Social Forces* 78(2): 721–45.

Miller, Perry. 1953. *The New England Mind: From Colony to Province.* Cambridge, Mass.: Harvard University Press.

———. 1956. *Errand into the Wilderness.* Cambridge, Mass.: Harvard University Press.

Miller, Randall M., Harry S. Stout, and Charles Reagan Wilson, eds. 1998. *Religion and the American Civil War.* New York: Oxford University Press.

Mockabee, Stephen T., Kenneth D. Wald, and David C. Leege. 2007. "Reexamining Religiosity: A Report on the New Religion Items in the 2006 ANES Pilot Study." American National Election Studies, http://www.electionstudies.org/resources/papers/Pilot2006/nes011907.pdf.

Morgan, Edmund S. 1958. *The Puritan Dilemma: The Story of John Winthrop.* Boston: Little, Brown.

———, ed. 1965. *Puritan Political Ideas.* Indianapolis: Bobbs-Merrill.

Murphy, Andrew R. 2009. *Moral Decline and Divine Punishment from New England to 9/11.* Oxford: Oxford University Press.

———. 2008. "What's Wrong with Wright's Words." Religion Dispatches. April 29, 2008. http://www.religiondispatches.org/archive/206/what's_wrong_with_wright's_words/.

Nabi, Robin L. 1999. "A Cognitive-Functional Model for the Effects of Discrete Negative Emotions on Information Processing, Attitude Change, and Recall." *Communication Theory* 9(3): 292–320.

Neuendorf, Kimberley A. 2002. *The Content Analysis Guidebook.* Thousand Oaks, Calif.: Sage.

Newman, Richard S. 2002. *The Transformation of American Abolitionism: Fighting Slavery in the Early Republic.* Chapel Hill: University of North Carolina Press.

Noffke, Jacqueline L., and Susan H. McFadden. 2001. "Denominational and Age Comparisons of God Concepts." *Journal for the Scientific Study of Religion* 40(4): 747–56.

Noll, Mark A. 2006. *The Civil War as a Theological Crisis.* Chapel Hill: University of North Carolina Press.

Olson, Laura R., and John C. Green. 2006. "The Religion Gap." *PS: Political Science and Politics* 39:455–59.

Overby, L. Martin, and Jay Barth. 2006. "Radio Advertising in American Political Campaigns: The Persistence, Importance, and Effects of Narrowcasting." *American Politics Research* 34(4): 451–78.

Paine, Thomas. [1776] 2004. *Common Sense,* ed. Edward Larkin. Toronto: Broadview.

Pennebaker, James W., Martha E. Francis, and Roger J. Booth. 2001. *Linguistic Inquiry and Word Count (LIWC): LIWC2001.* Mahwah, N.J.: Lawrence Erlbaum.

Pennebaker, James W., Matthias R. Mehl, and Kate G. Niederhoffer. 2002. "Psychological Aspects of Natural Language Use: Our Words, Our Selves." *Annual Review of Psychology* 54:547–77.

Pennebaker, James W., Richard B. Slatcher, and Cindy K. Chung. 2005. "Linguistic Markers of Psychological State through Media Interviews: John Kerry and John Edwards in 2004, Al Gore in 2000." *Analyses of Social Issues and Public Policy* 5:195–204.

Pew Research Center for the People and the Press. 2004. "Mid-October 2004 Omnibus," http://pewresearch.org/databank/datasets/.

———. 2007. "The U.S. Religious Landscape Survey." Forum on Religion and Public Life, http://religions.pewforum.org/ (accessed April 2008).

———. 2008. "How the Faithful Voted." Forum on Religion and Public Life, http://pewforum.org/Politics-and-Elections/How-the-Faithful-Voted.aspx#1 (accessed November 2011).

Pitkin, Hanna Fenichel. 1967. *The Concept of Representation.* Berkeley: University of California Press.

Pollack, Norman. 1967. *The Populist Mind.* Indianapolis: Bobbs-Merrill.

Prothero, Stephen R. 2007. *Religious Literacy: What Every American Needs to Know.* New York: Harper Collins.

———. 2008. "An Election That Is, and Isn't, about God." *USA Today.* November 3.

Putnam, Robert D. 2000. *Bowling Alone: The Collapse and Revival of American Community.* New York: Simon & Schuster.

Putnam, Robert D., and David Campbell. 2010. *American Grace: How Religion Divides and Unites Us.* New York: Simon and Shuster.

Rahn, Wendy M., Brian Kroeger, and Cynthia M. Kite. 1996. "A Framework for the Study of Public Mood." *Political Psychology* 17(1): 29–58.

Rahn, Wendy M., Jon A. Krosnick, and Marijke Breuning. 1994. "Rationalization and Derivation Processes in Survey Studies of Political Candidate Evaluation." *American Journal of Political Science* 38(3): 582–600.

Raudenbush, Stephen W., and Anthony S. Byrk. 2002. *Hierarchal Linear Analysis: Applications and Data Analysis Methods.* Thousand Oaks, Calif.: Sage.

Reese, Laura A., and Ronald E. Brown. 1995. "The Effects of Religious Messages on Racial Identity and System Blame among African Americans." *Journal of Politics* 57(1): 24–43.

Reeves, Thomas C. 2001. *America's Bishop: The Life and Times of Fulton J. Sheen.* San Francisco: Encounter Books.

Richardson, Herbert. 1974. "Civil Religion in Theological Perspective." In *American Civil Religion,* ed. Russell E. Richey and Donald G. Jones, 161–84. New York: Harper & Row.

Riker, William H. 1996. *The Strategy of Rhetoric: Campaigning for the American Constitution.* New Haven, Conn.: Yale University Press.

Roccas, Sonia, and Marilynn B. Brewer. 2002. "Social Identity Complexity." *Personality and Social Psychology Review* 6(2): 88–106.

Roof, Wade Clark, and Jennifer L. Roof. 1984. "Review of the Polls: Images of God among Americans." *Journal for the Scientific Study of Religion* 23(2): 201–5.

Roseman, Ira, Robert P. Abelson, and Michael F. Ewing. 1986. "Emotion and Political Cognition: Emotional Appeals in Political Communication." In *The 19th Annual Symposium on Cognition: Political Cognition,* ed. Richard R. Lau and David O. Sears, 279–94. Hillsdale, N.J.: Lawrence Erlbaum.

Rosselli, Francine, John J. Skelly, and Diane M. Mackie. 1995. "Processing Rational and Emotional Messages: The Cognitive and Affective Mediation of Persuasion." *Journal of Experimental Social Psychology* 31(2): 163–90.

Rossiter, Clinton. 1949. "John Wise: Colonial Democrat." *New England Quarterly* 22(1): 3–32.

Rousseau, Jean-Jacques. [1762] 1988. "On Social Contract or Principles of Political Right." In *Rousseau's Political Writings,* ed. and trans. Alan Ritter and Julia Conaway Bondanella, 84–174. New York: W. W. Norton.

Rozell, Mark J., and Clyde Wilcox. 1996. "Second Coming: The Strategies of the New Christian Right." *Political Science Quarterly* 111(2): 271–94.

Rozell, Mark J., Clyde Wilcox, and John C. Green. 1998. "Religious Constituencies and Support for the Christian Right in the 1990s." *Social Science Quarterly* 79:815–27.

Rude, Stephanie, Eva-Maria Gortner, and James Pennebaker. 2004. "Language Use of Depressed and Depression-Vulnerable College Students." *Cognition and Emotion* 18(8): 1121–33.

Russell, James A. 2003. "Core Affect and the Psychological Construction of Emotion." *Psychological Review* 110:145–72.

Salovey, Peter, and Deborah Birnbaum. 1989. "Influence of Mood on Health-Relevant Cognitions." *Journal of Personality and Social Psychology* 57(3): 539–51.

Sandoz, Ellis, ed. 1998. *Political Sermons of the American Founding Era.* Indianapolis: Liberty Fund.

Schwarz, Norbert. 2000. "Emotion, Cognition, and Decision-Making." *Cognition and Emotion* 14(4): 433–40.

Schwarz, Norbert, Herbert Bless, and Gerd Bohner. 1991. "Mood and Persuasion: Affective States Influence the Processing of Persuasive Communications." *Advances in Experimental Social Psychology* 24:161–99.

Sengupta, Jaideep, and Gita Venkataramani Johar. 2001. "Contingent Effects of Anxiety on Message Elaboration and Persuasion." *Personality and Social Psychological Bulletin* 27(2): 139–50.

Seward, William H. 1850. "Freedom in the New Territories." U.S. States Senate Art and History Collection, http://www.senate.gov/artandhistory/history/common/generic/Speeches_Seward_NewTerritories.htm (accessed April 2008). Originally published in the *Congressional Record*, 31st Congress, 1st session, app., 260–69.

Sheen, Fulton J. 1953. *Life Is Worth Living*. New York: McGraw-Hill.

Sherkat, Darren E. 2001. "Tracking the Restructuring of American Religion: Religious Affiliation and Patterns of Mobility, 1973–1998." *Social Forces* 79:1459–92.

Sigelman, Lee. 2002. "Two Reagans? Genre Imperatives, Ghostwriters, and Presidential Personality Profiling." *Political Psychology* 23(4): 839–51.

Sigelman, Lee, and Emmitt H. Buell Jr. 2003. "You Take the High Road and I'll Take the Low Road? The Interplay of Attack Strategies and Tactics in Presidential Campaigns." *Journal of Politics* 65(2): 518–31.

Smith, Christian R. 1998. *American Evangelicalism: Embattled and Thriving*. Chicago: University of Chicago Press.

Smith, Craig R. 2005. *Daniel Webster and the Oratory of Civil Religion*. Columbia: University of Missouri Press.

Smith, Daniel A., Matthew DeSantis, and Jason Kassel. 2006. "Same-Sex Marriage Ballot Measures and the 2004 Presidential Election." *State and Local Government Review* 38(2): 78–91.

Snyder, Mark. 1974. "Self-Monitoring of Expressive Behavior." *Journal of Personality and Social Psychology* 30(4): 526–37.

Stanford Political Communication Lab. 2000. *In Their Own Words: Sourcebook for the 2000 Presidential Election*. E-book. Stanford, Calif.: PCL-Stanford.

Stiles, Ezra. 1783. "The United States Elevated to Glory and Honor." Libraries at the University of Nebraska-Lincoln electronic texts in American studies, ed. Reiner Smolinski, http://digitalcommons.unl.edu/etas/41/ (accessed April 2008).

Stout, Harry S. 1977. "Religion, Communications, and the Ideological Origins of the American Revolution." *William and Mary Quarterly* 34(4): 519–41.

Stout, Harry S., and Christopher Grasso. 1998. "Civil War, Religion, Communications: The Case of Richmond." In *Religion and the American Civil War*, ed. Randall M. Miller, Harry S. Stout, and Charles Reagan Wilson, 313–59. Oxford: Oxford University Press.

Sullivan, Denis G., and Roger D. Masters. 1988. " 'Happy Warriors': Leaders' Facial Displays, Viewers' Emotions, and Political Support." *American Journal of Political Science* 32(2): 345–68.

Sumner, William Graham. 1906. *Folkways.* New York: Ginn.

Tajfel, Henri. 1981. *Human Groups and Social Categories.* Cambridge, UK: Cambridge University Press.

Thornwell, James Henley. 1862. "Our Danger and Our Duty." University of North Carolina–Chapel Hill Documenting the American South electronic collection, http://docsouth.unc.edu/imls/thornwell/thornwel.html (accessed April 2008).

Tocqueville, Alexis de. [1840] 2006. *Democracy in America.* Trans. George Lawrence. Ed. J. P. Mayer. New York: Harper Perennial.

Transue, John E. 2007. "Identity Salience, Identity Acceptance, and Racial Policy Attitudes: American National Identity as a Uniting Force." *American Journal of Political Science* 51(1): 78–91.

Valentino, Nicholas. 1999. "Crime News and the Priming of Racial Attitudes during Evaluations of the President." *Public Opinion Quarterly* 63:293–320.

Virginia Baptist Association. 1863. "Address of the Baptist General Association [of] Virginia: June 4th, 1863." University of North Carolina–Chapel Hill Documenting the American South electronic collection, http://docsouth.unc.edu/imls/baptist/baptist.html (accessed April 2008).

Wald, Kenneth, and Allison Calhoun-Brown. 2006. *Religion and Politics in the United States.* 5th ed. Lanham, Md.: Rowman and Littlefield.

Weaver, James Beard. [1892] 1967. "A Call to Action." In *The Populist Mind*, ed. Norman Pollack, 109–69. Indianapolis: Bobbs-Merrill.

Webster, Daniel. 1820. "Discourse, Delivered at Plymouth, December 22, 1820, in Commemoration of the First Settlement of New-England." University of Missouri Libraries Special Collections, http://mulibraries.missouri.edu/special collections/webster.htm (accessed April 2008).

Webster, Noah. [1787] 1993. "An Examination of the Leading Principles of the Federal Constitution." In *The Debate on the Constitution: Federalist and Antifederalist Speeches, Articles, and Letters during the Struggle over Ratification,* ed. Bernard Bailyn, 1:129–63. New York: Library of America.

Webster, Pelatiah. [1788] 1993. "Reply to the Pennsylvania Minority." In *The Debate on the Constitution: Federalist and Antifederalist Speeches, Articles, and Letters during the Struggle over Ratification,* ed. Bernard Bailyn, 1:566–69. New York: Library of America.

Welch, Michael R., and David C. Leege. 1988. "Religious Predictors of Catholic Parishioners' Sociopolitical Attitudes: Devotional Style, Closeness to God, Imagery, and Agentic/Communal Religious Identity." *Journal for the Scientific Study of Religion* 27(4): 536–52.

Westen, Drew. 2007. *The Political Brain: The Role of Emotion in Deciding the Fate of a Nation*. New York: Perseus.

Whissell, Cynthia. 1994. "A Computer Program for the Objective Analysis of Style and Emotional Connotations of Prose: Hemingway, Galsworthy, and Faulkner Compared." *Perceptual and Motor Skills* 79:815–25.

Whissell, Cynthia, and Lee Sigelman. 2001. "The Times and the Man as Predictors of Emotion and Style in the Inaugural Addresses of U.S. Presidents." *Computers and the Humanities* 35:255–72.

White, Eugene E. 1972. *Puritan Rhetoric: The Issue of Emotion in Religion*. Carbondale: Southern Illinois University Press.

Wilcox, Clyde, Matthew DeBell, and Lee Sigelman. 1999. "The Second Coming of the New Christian Right: Patterns of Popular Support in 1984 and 1996." *Social Science Quarterly* 80:181–92.

Williams, Rhys H., and Susan M. Alexander. 1994. "Religious Rhetoric in American Populism: Civil Religion as Movement Ideology." *Journal for the Scientific Study of Religion* 33(1): 1–15.

Wimberley, Ronald C. 1979. "Continuity in the Measurement of Civil Religion." *Sociological Analysis* 40(1): 59–62.

——. 1980. "Civil Religion and the Choice for President: Nixon in '72." *Social Forces* 59(1): 44–61.

Wimberley, Ronald C., and James A. Christenson. 1980. "Civil Religion and Church and State." *Sociological Quarterly* 21(1): 35–40.

——. 1981. "Civil Religion and Other Religious Identities." *Sociological Analysis* 42(2): 91–100.

Winthrop, James. [1788] 1993. "Cherish the Old Confederation like the Apple of Our Eye." In *The Debate on the Constitution: Federalist and Antifederalist Speeches, Articles, and Letters during the Struggle over Ratification*, ed. Bernard Bailyn, 1:762–73. New York: Library of America.

Winthrop, John. [1630] 1965. "Christian Charitie: A Modell Hereof." In *Puritan Political Ideas*, ed. Edmund S. Morgan, 75–93. Indianapolis: Bobbs-Merrill.

Wise, John. [1717] 1965. "Vindication of the Government of New England Churches." In *Puritan Political Ideas*, ed. Edmund S. Morgan, 251–66. Indianapolis: Bobbs-Merrill.

Wolfe, Alan. 1998. *One Nation after All*. New York: Viking.

Wuthnow, Robert. 1988. *The Restructuring of American Religion: Society and Faith since World War II*. Princeton, N.J.: Princeton University Press.

Young, Michael P. 2001. "A Revolution of the Soul: Transformative Experiences and Immediate Abolition." In *Passionate Politics: Emotions and Social Movements*, ed. Jeff Goodwin, James M. Jasper, and Francesca Polleta, 99–114. Chicago: University of Chicago Press.

Zaller, John. 1992. *The Nature and Origins of Mass Opinion*. Cambridge, UK: Cambridge University Press.

INDEX

Note: Page numbers in *italics* indicate figures; those with a *t* indicate tables.

church-state separation, 4, 127, 130, 132

civil religion, 3–4, *5*, 53–57, *55*, 106, 131–32; communication style of, 10; culture wars rhetoric and, 57, 72–75, *73*, 97–98; definition of, 7; emotive tenor of, 31–37; language of, 40–44; psychology of, 126–29, *128*, 139n4; Rousseau on, 136

civil religion identity (CRI), 12, 18–31, 47; candidate evaluation and, *92*, 92–93, 97–98, *122*, 122–23, 123t; centrality of, 50–55, *53*, 105–8; definition of, 107; family values and, *128*, 129; limits of, 58–60; political representation and, 104–30, 133–35; scale of, 108–11, *109*; subgroups and, 48; voters and, 112–17, *114*, *115*, *119*

Civil War, 23–27, 36, 142n13

Clinton, Bill, 41–43, 77; on civil religion, 57; religious appeal of, *92*, *93*

Coe, Kevin, 145n14, 153n32

cold war, 36–37, 47, 143n19; anticommunism during, 28–31, 47

Constitution, Confederate, 24

Constitution, U.S., 21–24, 28, 108; church-state separation in, 4, 127, 130, 132; Emerson on, 21; Graham on, 29; Langdon on, 141n7

contraceptives, distributed by schools, 86–87

CRI. *See* civil religion identity

Crosby, Donald, 31

culture wars rhetoric, 3–4, *5*, 8–10, 43–44, *53*, 54–56, 117, 135–36; civic religion identity and, 72–75, *73*, 97–98; polarization of, 66, 73, 139n4; tone of, 57, *58*, 79; utility of, 139n8; variables in, 47, 88–89

Cummings, Henry, 33–34

Danforth, Samuel, 32–33

Dasgupta, Nilanjana, 10

Davis, James H., 27–28

Declaration of Independence, 21, 25, 28–29, 35–36

Democratic Party: Catholics and, 82–83, 106, 131, 136–37; civil religion identity and, 110–11; religious voters in, 67, 75–78, *76*

DeSantis, Matthew, 85

DeSteno, David, 10

diversity. *See* pluralism, religious

Djupe, Paul, 83

Docherty, George, 29–30, 142n18, 151n12

Dole, Bob, 39, 52, 87, 145n13

Domke, David, 145n14, 153n32

Donnelly, Ignatius, 36

drug abuse, 3, 39, 44, 70, 87

Dunbar, Samuel, 140n5

Edelman, Murray, 134

education reform, 1, 93, 139n2; Obama on, 51, 52

Edwards, Jonathan, 20–21, 28, 33, 65, 143n23

Eisenhower, Dwight, 29, 30, 143n19

Ellison, Keith, ix–x

Emerson, Ralph Waldo, 21–22

emotion scores, 68–72, *70*, *73*

emotive appeals, 4, 6–7, 9–10, 61–80; by abolitionists, 34–35; of civil religion, 31–37; by Populists, 35–36; of Puritans, 31–33; during Revolutionary War, 33–34; role of, 65–67

Evangelicals, 48, 59, 67, 83, 85, 149n11

Evans, John H., 139n6

Ewing, Michael F., 145n1

exclusion. *See* inclusive/exclusive religious rhetoric

Falwell, Jerry, 104, 105

family values, *114*, 121, 123, 151n14; civil religion identity and, *128*, 129

favored nation variable, 47–48, 54–55, *109*, 109–10, 141n7
Federalist Papers, 23, 63
Fitfield, James, 36–37
Flere, Sergei, 107–8, 150n3
Fox News channel, 112–13
Franklin, Benjamin, 22, 141n10
Froese, Paul, 48
fundamentalists, 117, 130, 149n11. *See also* Evangelicals

Garrison, William Lloyd, 34–35
gays. *See* same-sex marriage
Gilbert, Christopher, 83
Glaser, Jack, 64
God concept variables, 48–49, 58–59
Goodrich, Elizur, 21–22
Gore, Al, 77, 94
Graham, Billy, 28, 29
Grasso, Christopher, 24
Great Awakening, 20–21, 33–34, 143n21
Green, John, 83, 130, 150n1

Hart, Roderick, 50, 143n3, 153n32
Hatfield, Elaine, 146n6
health care, 2, 78; Gore on, 77; McCain on, 71; Obama on, 51
Herberg, Will, 54
Hill, Peter, 62
Hillygus, D. Sunshine, 84–85, 139n8
Hindus, 57, 60
Hiss, Alger, 142n16
homosexuality. *See* same-sex marriage
Hood, Ralph, 62
Hoover, J. Edgar, 28–29
Huddy, Leonie, 150n4
Hurricane Katrina, 65–66

Iannaccone, Lawrence R., 149n11
identity priming, 6–8, 91, 107
inclusive/exclusive religious rhetoric, 47, 52–60, *53*, *55*, *58*; civil reli-gion identity and, 58–60, 135–36; by Clinton, 43; by Reagan, 44. *See also* subgroup identity
Iraq War, 3, 51–52, 85, 139n2, 151n14

James, William, 62
Jamieson, Kathleen Hall, 143n3
Jefferson, Thomas, 140n6
jeremiads, 31–38, 65, 140n1, 143n20; of abolitionists, 34–35; during cold war, 36–37; Obama's rhetoric and, 79; of Populists, 35–36. *See also* Puritans
Jews, 30, 57, 60, 111, 151n12
Johar, Gita Venkataramani, 139n7
journalism, 45

Kansas-Nebraska Act, 25
Kassel, Jason, 85
Keltner, Dacher, 139n7
Kennedy, John F., 41, 82; inaugural address of, 106, 107, 131, 136–37
Kerry, John, 1–3; religious appeal of, 92, 93, 117; religious rhetoric of, 49, 50, 79–80
Khatib, Nadia, 150n4
Koop, Edward Everett, 14
Kramer, Geoffrey, 9

Lakoff, George, 48
Langdon, Samuel, 141n7·
Lavrič, Miran, 107–8, 150n3
Layman, Geoffrey, 83, 91, 130, 150n1
Lease, Mary Elizabeth, 28
Leege, David C., 88, 148n8
Lerner, Jennifer, 139n7
lesbians. *See* same-sex marriage
Lexus-Nexus database, 45
Lincoln, Abraham, 25–27, 29, 30, 142n16

Linguistic Inquiry and Word Count (LIWC) software, 46, *49*, 49–50, 90–103, 147n7; emotion scores of, 68–72, *70, 73*; on Obama's religious rhetoric, 78; partisan differences and, 76

Lippmann, Walter, 63

Lloyd, Henry Demarest, 27

MacKuen, Michael, 10, 63, 101

Madison, James, 23, 63

Marcus, George, 10, 63, 72, 101

Marty, Anton, 64

Marty, Martin E., 7, 143n19

Mather, Cotton, 20

Mather, Richard, 19–20

Mayflower Compact, 19, 29

Mazzini, Giuseppe, 28

McCain, John, 61; emotive appeals by, 71; religious rhetoric of, 133; support among clergy for, 139n3

McCarthy, Joseph, 28, 29, 36, 142n16

Miller, Perry, 32

Mondale, Walter: religious rhetoric of, *49*, 50, 52, 95, 104, 105; on social safety net, 77–78

monotheism, "minimal," 53, 125

Mormons, 111, 149n12

Murphy, Andrew, 33

Muslims, 30, 57, 60, 111, 151n12

National Civil Religion Identity Study, 108–11, *109*, 113–15, 118, 120, 123; self-monitoring scale of, 127–29, *128*, 150n6

Neuman, W. Russell, 10, 63, 72, 101

Nixon, Richard M., 107

Noll, Mark A., 142n13

nuclear weapons, 37

Nunn, Lisa M., 139n6

Obama, Barack, 2, 3; on education reform, 51, 52; on health care, 51; religious affiliation of, 139n3; religious rhetoric of, 78, 79, 81, 133

Olson, Laura, 83

Omaha Platform, 36

orthodoxy, 105–6, 149n11; candidate evaluation and, 91–103, *92, 96, 99–101*; measure of, 89, 91, 150n1

Overby, L. Martin, 143n2

Paine, Thomas, 34, 140n6

Palin, Sarah, 3

partisanship, 67, 75–78, *76*; civil religion identity and, 110–11

Pennebaker, James, 68

Pew Research Center for the People and the Press, 85, 139n2

Pitkin, Hanna, 104, 134

Pledge of Allegiance, 29–30, 151n12

pluralism, religious, 7–8, 39–43, 136–37, 139n4; inclusiveness of, 47, 143n2; rhetoric of, *55*, 55–57, *58*

Populism, 27–28, 35–36

priming, identity, 6–8, 91, 107

Prothero, Stephen, 2, 62–63, 111

Puritans, 4, 8, 18–21, 140n1; emotive appeals of, 31–33; Webster on, 25. *See also* jeremiads

Putnam, Robert D., 139n4

Rabaut, Louis, 29

Rapson, Richard, 146n6

Reagan, Ronald, 17, 37, 146n4; on culture wars, 57; emotive appeals by, 70–71, 76–77; ingroup appeals by, 44

religious commitment, 90–103, *92, 96, 99–101. See also* orthodoxy

religious identity, 12, 18–31, 40–50

religious images, 123, 124t

Republican Party: civil religion identity and, 110–11; religious voters in, 67, 75–78, 76
Revolutionary War, 4, 23, 33–34
Richardson, Herbert, 8
Riker, William H., 141n11
Roosevelt, Franklin Delano, 82
Roseman, Ira, 145n1
Rossiter, Clinton, 140n6
Rousseau, Jean-Jacques, 136, 150n2
Rove, Karl, 2, 112–13
Rozell, Mark, 52, 145n13

Salovey, Peter, 64
same-sex marriage, 11, 83–85, 104, 113, 114, 123, 124t; civil religion identity and, 127–29, 128; fundamentalists and, 130; state initiatives against, 139n3
school prayer, 44, 73, 75
Schwartz, Norbert, 9
self-monitoring scale, 127–29, 128, 150n6
Sengupta, Jaideep, 139n7
September 11th attacks, 1, 146n3, 151n14
Sermon on the Mount, 21, 142n16
Seward, William H., 25
Sheen, Fulton J., 31, 37
Sheppard, Lori, 9
Shields, Todd, 84–85, 139n8
Sigelman, Lee, 68, 146n4
slavery, 24–26, 35
Smith, Al, 82
Smith, Christian R., 149n11
Smith, Craig, 25
Smith, Daniel, 85
Snyder, Mark, 127
Sotomayor, Sonya, 104

Stanford University Political Communication Lab, 45, 143n3
Stiles, Ezra, 141n8
Stout, Harry S., 34
subgroup identity, 42–44, 53, 53–55, 143n2; civil religion and, 48, 135–36; definition of, 47; shared religious rhetoric in, 55, 56–57; vote choice and, 119. See also inclusive/exclusive religious rhetoric
substance abuse, 3, 39, 44, 70, 87

terrorism, 1, 3, 85, 139n2, 146n3, 151n14
Thornwell, James Henley, 23–24
Tocqueville, Alexis de, 136, 150n2
Transue, John, 8

Wallis, Jim, 84, 148n4
Warren, Rick, 139n3
Washington, George, 21, 141n7
Weaver, James Baird, 35–36
Webster, Daniel, 25, 141n8
Weld, Theodore, 35
Whissell, Cynthia, 68
Whissell's Dictionary of Affect in Language (WDAL), 68–69, 146n4, 146n7; emotion scores of, 73; on Obama's religious rhetoric, 78; partisan differences and, 76
White, Eugene, 21, 33
Wilcox, Clyde, 52, 145n13
Williams, Rhys, 36
Williams, Roger, 57
Wimberley, Ronald, 40–41, 107
Winthrop, John, 20, 37, 141n9
Wise, John, 140n6
Wright, Jeremiah, 3